The National Trust for Historic Preservation
Economic Benefits
of Preserving
Old Buildings

Economic Benefits of Preserving Old Buildings

NATIONAL TRUST FOR HISTORIC PRESERVATION

THE PRESERVATION PRESS

THE PRESERVATION PRESS
National Trust for Historic Preservation
1785 Massachusetts Avenue, N.W.
Washington, D.C. 20036

The National Trust for Historic Preservation is the only national private, nonprofit organization chartered by Congress with the responsibility for encouraging public participation in the preservation of sites, buildings and objects significant in American history and culture. Support for the National Trust is provided by membership dues, endowment funds, contributions and matching grants from federal agencies, including the U.S. Department of the Interior, National Park Service, under provisions of the National Historic Preservation Act of 1966.

This book presents papers from the Economic Benefits of Preserving Old Buildings conference, sponsored by the National Trust for Historic Preservation in Seattle, Wash., July 31 — August 2, 1975. Cosponsors of the conference were the city of Seattle and the Historic Seattle Preservation and Development Authority. Endorsing sponsors included the American Institute of Architects, American Institute of Planners, National Association of Home Builders, National Association of Housing and Redevelopment Officials and the Urban Land Institute.

Since this book was first published, some changes have occurred in federal programs and tax incentives available for preservation. Current information, including a list of other books published by the Preservation Press, may be obtained by contacting the National Trust for Historic Preservation.

Library of Congress Cataloging in Publication Data

Economic benefits of preserving old buildings.

    Papers from the Economic Benefits of Preserving Old Buildings Conference, held in Seattle, Wash., July 31-August 2, 1975, cosponsored by the city of Seattle and the Historic Seattle Preservation and Development Authority.

    Reprint. Originally published: Washington, D.C.: Preservation Press, 1976.

    1. Historic buildings—Conservation and restoration—Economic aspects—United States—Congresses. I. National Trust for Historic Preservation in the United States. II. Economic Benefits of Preserving Old Buildings Conference (1975: Seattle, Wash.) III. Historic Seattle Preservation and Development Authority.

E159.E27 1982	338.4'336369'0973	82-3572
ISBN 0-89133-037-2		AACR2

Reprinted 1978, 1982.

Cover design by Tom Engeman.

Contents

GOVERNMENT ASSISTANCE IN PRESERVATION FINANCING

INTEGRITY: THE FOUNDATION OF THE PRESERVATION PROCESS

PRIVATE FINANCING FOR PRESERVATION

PRESERVED BUILDINGS AS PROFITABLE REAL ESTATE

CONFERENCE SUMMARY

Foreword

The concept of recycling architecturally sound and historically significant old buildings has attracted an increasing amount of attention and interest during the past several years. Originally this concept was promoted predominantly by preservationists; now it is gaining the support of architects, planners, developers, realtors, bankers and government officials. The primary factor for this growing endorsement, and indeed a central source of controversy, has been the question of financial feasibility and profitability. Although the reuse and adaptive use of old buildings has proven repeatedly to be financially and environmentally profitable, many people in the business community still hesitate to fully accept this form of development.

Preservationists have long advocated the sensitive reuse of old buildings for it demonstrates the quintessence of preservation—the integration of our architectural heritage with the present in a functioning relationship. Putting such a concept into practice is progress not only for individuals, but for cities and towns as well.

Despite the visibility of numerous financially successful preservation projects in the United States, information has not been readily available to the general business community. It was evident that a greater understanding of the financial potential in preservation development was needed. In an effort to examine this concept and its application, the National Trust for Historic Preservation sponsored a national conference entitled "Economic Benefits of Preserving Old Buildings" on July 31–August 2, 1975, in Seattle, Wash.

To achieve greater involvement in the preservation of old buildings, the validity of preservation development as a financial alternative to new construction had to be properly addressed at the conference. Therefore conference sessions were designed to focus on the various aspects of developing old buildings for reuse and to assess each of these aspects according to its economic benefits. The people who could best address this type of inquiry are not normally considered a part of the historic preservation community. The National Trust asked architects, planners, developers, realtors, representatives of banking and financial institutions, as well as members of municipal, state and federal governments to speak at the conference. The program attracted a similar type of person: professionals for whom sound economic justification is a necessary factor in determining the feasibility of a project.

The conference was considered successful because it did more than merely present a complex concept. It brought the successful performance record of preservation development into clearer focus. Equally important, the conference showed that the recycling of old buildings, as an alternative to new construction, is a business technique that offers significant profitability as well. The conference also reminded the participants that historic preservation is concerned with the challenge of energy conservation, town and city revitalization and the aesthetic ingredients that enhance the quality of life.

The lack of printed information on the economics of preserving old buildings has plagued preservationists for some time and one of the purposes of the conference was to fill this void. This book was prepared to share the benefits of the conference and to offer information on this important aspect of preservation.

JAMES BIDDLE, president
National Trust for Historic Preservation

The Seattle Experience: Making Historic Preservation Profitable

4

PIONEER SQUARE HISTORIC DISTRICT *with Pioneer Building in foreground, Seattle, Wash. (Carleton Knight, III)*

Economics Aside

WES UHLMAN

Wes Uhlman has served as mayor of Seattle, Wash., since 1969 and was instrumental in the passage of all the preservation ordinances discussed in this paper.

The subject of preserving historic buildings calls to mind a conversation that allegedly took place between two men who themselves are historic figures in American literature. F. Scott Fitzgerald supposedly said to Ernest Hemingway, "You know, the rich are really quite different from you and me." Hemingway's reported response was, "Yes, they have more money."

In a discussion of historic preservation and its value, some zealot might observe that old buildings are, in fact, quite different from the modern structures that dominate cities today. An obvious response to that might be, "Yes, they've been here longer." Moreover, they are smaller, and they have certain inherent economic benefits over new construction. The last distinction is most important, for historic preservation does make good, hard economic sense from the viewpoint of business people. It makes equally good sense from the perspective of city government, as we try to redevelop the central city and expand the tax base. When done well, preservation can mean money for business and tax dollars for government. What more could anyone ask?

But there is more to historic preservation than the bottom line on someone's ledger. I hope that those who see what historic preservation means for Seattle will understand the real value to the city of hanging on to older buildings and restoring them to usable condition. I hope that those who walk through Pioneer Square are moved in some small way by the haunting beauty and grandeur of those fine old buildings.

The point of all this is that there is a qualitative difference between old and new buildings. It is much more than a difference in age, or even in style of architecture. It is a matter of history—a historical perspective that gives us the depth of vision to better understand where we are by knowing where we have been. That kind of perspective is extremely important to Seattle and to other cities throughout the United States. In fact, the more we are overtaken by the complexities of modern urban problems, the more essential that sense of history becomes.

It is not entirely coincidental that the renaissance of Pioneer Square began just about the time the bottom dropped out of the local economy in 1969 and 1970. The rich history of Pioneer Square provided something substantive to cling to during those troubled times. When the very survival of the city seemed to be at stake, the identity of Seattle represented by those old bricks and stones seemed to give new hope and a focus of action as a united community.

At the turn of the century, Pioneer Square was the jewel in Seattle's crown, a fine place full of harmonious architecture and much activity. But that did not last long. Newer, bigger buildings were constructed to the north as the downtown grew and expanded. Gradually, over a series of decades, Pioneer Square was abandoned. By the middle of this century it had a Skid Road in the modern sense of the term—a backwater of cheap hotels, dingy taverns and unhappy people down on their luck.

Demolish or Restore?

Ultimately, the city was faced with the choice of what to do with Pioneer Square. It was essentially the same choice that every other city faces: Should we tear it down and start over or try to salvage and restore what was already there?

Seattle chose the second alternative, not only because it was economically smarter, but because there was a psychological and spiritual benefit to it as well. The resurrection of Pioneer Square reminded residents of the proud heritage of the city and proved that the same kind of spirit and commitment could live today in Seattle.

That is not to say that the job was easy. In fact, it was probably much easier to build Pioneer Square in the first place than to save it from demolition 80 years later.

After all, it was an age when new was good and old was bad, when progress meant change and the more of it the better. The arguments for demolishing Pioneer Square and replacing it with an urban renewal project, parking lots and even a freeway were the same arguments heard in cities throughout the country: Slums should not be preserved; restoring old buildings means throwing good money after bad; the crime rate in Pioneer Square demands a cleaning from the foundations up.

But we persisted. We fought the battles in the courts and in the political arenas and worked closely with private developers to show how restoration could be an economically sound investment.

City Commitment

Before the private sector could be expected to finance the preservation of Pioneer Square, the community had to make the commitment that it wanted preservation.

That commitment took two general directions. One was legislative, and the other consisted of various capital improvements in the area. Of the two, legislation has been by far the most important. Three major city ordinances have really made possible the redevelopment of Pioneer Square.

Legislation

The first ordinance, signed into law on May 1, 1970, was the real keystone of the whole operation. In a classic battle with a number of speculators and major property owners, the Pioneer Square Historic District was established and a five-member historic preservation board set up to review "all architecture and historic preservation matters within the Historic District." The board makes certain that developments there are consistent with the overall goals of the preservation ordinance. No demolition can take place until the board reviews and recommends it.

A second ordinance, passed in August of 1973, established a Special Review District in Pioneer Square. This gives additional control over the kinds of changes and developments in land use that can take place in the district. This control was considered necessary because of county construction of a huge domed stadium just a few blocks south of the district. As with any kind of development of this scope and nature, tremendous pressure to use the land in Pioneer Square for stadium activities, such as parking, hamburger joints and bars, was expected. That was not wanted and now, thanks to the Special Review District, it will not happen.

The most recent ordinance, which took effect in early 1974, is known as a "minimum maintenance ordinance." This law gives the city superintendent of buildings the authority to step in when any building in the historic district has deteriorated to the point where preservation is in danger or when it poses a safety hazard to its occupants or the general public.

The superintendent of buildings can issue an order for the work that needs to be done. If that order is not overturned by an appeal process and the owner still does not comply, the city can do the repair work and recover the cost from the owner.

These are strong measures, and they have worked. But it should be emphasized that the city did not by any means force these down the throats of the Pioneer Square landowners. After a short time, they came to the realization that preservation makes sense—and means dollars. They have worked closely with the city in developing and implementing these laws.

It should be obvious why these property owners have supported preservation efforts. After all, they have the most to gain from an upgrading of the area. But before any one landlord puts a lot of money into fixing up a building, that owner wants to be sure that the person next door and the owner across the street are going to do the same thing. These ordinances assure that everyone will be playing by the same rules and that an investment will not be wiped out later by less scrupulous developers.

The localized legislation is so successful that it inspired the passage of the citywide Landmarks Preservation Ordinance. Most textbooks will say that Seattle went about things backward. Scholars say one should start with a citywide ordinance, then move into specific neighborhoods. However, the initial successes in Pioneer Square and at the Pike Place Public Market served to inspire public confidence in preservation and to develop a constituency supportive of citywide preservation. So Seattle started small and worked its way up.

Capital Improvements

The second part of the effort has been in direct services and public improvements in Pioneer Square.

First, a district manager was appointed to work with the historic preservation board. The manager's job is to come up continually with ways for the city to be involved in Pioneer Square without spending a lot of money. There have been some good ideas. For example, when federal funding was received for three new city parks, two of them were put in Pioneer Square. These are both small, cobblestoned urban parks that fit in well with their setting and add to the residents' and visitors' enjoyment of the area. Another federal grant made it possible to make a pedestrian mall out of a street going through the heart of Pioneer Square.

Historic streetlights are going into the district. The area needed new lighting anyway, and the city arranged for a style similar to that actually used there in 1910. Period drinking fountains use the 1910 era castings, complete with base fountains for small animals.

When additional office space for some city departments was needed, we leased that space in Pioneer Square. It is within walking distance of city hall, prices are competitive and the lease money contributed to the restoration of a fine old building. City leadership has encouraged other government agencies to turn to Pioneer Square for space; other public facilities include a post office, the metropolitan transit authority, a state government office and the Puget Sound Governmental Conference. The Port of Seattle has applied for a federal grant to rehabilitate an old train station for its offices.

The Magic Carpet Ride, the free, experimental downtown bus service, runs through Pioneer Square, and many office workers from the central business district take advantage of it during the noon hour, riding down to Pioneer Square to shop or eat.

As another experiment, the city went one step further in its efforts. Using model cities money, a public corporation formed by the city actually purchased one of the buildings in Pioneer Square—appropriately named the City Loan Building—and hopes to sell it to a developer who will renovate the building compatibly. $600,000 in federal revenue sharing dollars has been committed for a permanent historic preservation revolving fund.

As a sidelight, it might be mentioned that this focus on Pioneer Square as a historic district has brought attention to the problems of the traditional inhabitants of the area, the down-and-outers and derelicts who have lived there for years. Now, primarily through the Seattle model cities program and the federal government, needed services are being provided for these people, including an Indian Center, a health station and the Skid Road Shelter.

I hope this degree of involvement by local govern-

PIONEER SQUARE HISTORIC DISTRICT *with Grand Central Hotel Building in right foreground, Seattle. (Carleton Knight, III)*

ment will not be necessary in other cities, especially when the private developer recognizes the economic advantages of preservation. But it was necessary in Seattle because the city was trying something that had not been done before: sticking its neck out to see if the restoration of an entire community could really work. There were a lot of initial skeptics in Seattle; today there are many confirmed preservationists.

BENEFITS OF PRESERVATION

Of course, there were economic advantages to undertaking and encouraging a project such as this, which began in earnest during the depression that peaked in Seattle in 1970. The reconstruction activity provided steady jobs for hundreds of construction workers over a period of several years. Many new stores, shops, restaurants and offices opened, creating jobs for Seattle residents. Pioneer Square is now one of the most popular tourist attractions in the Pacific Northwest; it is now a place you must visit, instead of a place you had better stay out of. That means more money and more jobs. And one cannot help but mention the substantial increase in tax revenues to the city government: a 450 percent increase in assessed valuation in four years.

Even more important was the psychological boost received as a result of redevelopment. Once again resi-

dents were proud to be a part of Seattle. The city was something special, something that no other city duplicated because no other city had the same history.

Pioneer Square showed an alternative kind of city life, a life that had once been the rule and then had been forgotten, only to be rediscovered beneath the dirt and grime of historic buildings. It was a life more geared to the human scale, a community oriented toward people and not cars, buildings that were architecturally interesting without being intimidating, structures on a scale that did not dwarf the individual.

It is time that these more human kinds of alternative cityscapes were rediscovered. It is time that the thread of history was unraveled and that we made use of the lessons available there.

People have the power to do that. It was done in Seattle. As much, if not more, can be accomplished in other cities and towns throughout the United States. Many of them have a history much older than Seattle's, and what better time is there than this Bicentennial period to rediscover that history and, in the process, rebuild our cities to a state of greater economic and psychological health.

As the internationally renowned British architect and planner, Graeme Shankland, observed, "A country without a past has the emptiness of a barren continent; and a city without old buildings is like a man without a memory."

The old buildings that remind us of the past are the signposts pointing toward a better, richer more stable future for us all.

8

THE PERGOLA *in Pioneer Square, Seattle. (Carleton Knight, III).*

The Growing Public Stake in Urban Conservation

BRUCE K. CHAPMAN

Bruce K. Chapman is secretary of state, Washington State. He was formerly a member of the Seattle City Council.

Physical reminders of a society's past have always been important to people's identity, and in an age when we are seeking roots as seldom before, this sense of continuity has even greater value. Consequently, government today has at least as much legitimate interest in historic preservation as in new construction.

Government also must be especially concerned with conserving natural resources, and, as a recent report by the U.S. Secretary of Housing and Urban Development pointed out, existing building stock—whether historic or not—represents a massive investment in materials, labor and time. Historic preservation, or urban conservation, is our best means of recovering the worth of past investments. By encouraging new business development within the existing city, preservation can also spare government some of the cost of duplicating utilities and services in underdeveloped areas.

Better urban design is an objective of every conscientious municipality and state. Planners are realizing that people often find greater contentment in the comfortable scale and friendly texture of restored urban districts than they do in the midst of new buildings that almost seem intended to make ordinary people feel unimportant. Moreover, local governments are noting that the public's pleasure in restored older districts is one of the few advantages afforded cities in the continuing competition with suburbs for residents.

The same is true of older small towns. How odd that people travel thousands of miles to enjoy an old-fashioned Main Street in Disneyland when small towns of authentic history and charm exist everywhere, only awaiting the quickening hand of sensitive redevelopment.

Government, then, does have a great stake in urban conservation. What it lacks nationally and in most localities are the tools for making preservation work.

For years the National Trust for Historic Preservation has defined and redefined the preservation ethic. In recent years, Seattle, among other communities, has been a testing ground for many of the practices recommended by the Trust. The results are aesthetically and sociologically satisfying; they also show that good aesthetics, good sociology and good planning make good economic sense, too.

THE SEATTLE EXPERIENCE

In the early 1970s, Seattle was in a deep recession but was willing to invest in such supposed frills as old architecture, an old market, street trees, parks and the arts. Thus the city managed to rise above its economic situation, and it began to reattract young people as residents, tourists as consumers and business people as investors.

Building on the record of a few private entrepreneurs, a local public expenditure of several hundred thousand dollars was matched by a couple of million dollars in federal, state and foundation grants. These in turn eventually catalyzed millions of dollars in expanded private redevelopment of buildings and shops and helped bring to town thousands of additional money-toting visitors.

Urban conservation is no cure for failed school levies or other ills, but it did enable Seattle to cut the crime rate around the old Skid Road, its most crime-ridden area; to create a new recreation and shopping zone; and to restore the city's pride as well as its past. *Harper's* magazine decided in 1974 that Seattle was the most "livable" city in America. Urban conservation, then, is not a government frill at all, but an important part of a strategy for urban success.

PRESERVATION TOOLS

Once government accepts its responsibility to pursue a course of urban conservation, it must choose and employ a suitable set of preservation tools. However, few governments know what these tools are.

Designation of Historic Buildings

One of the most common tools is the registration or designation of historic buildings. However, some state and local registers lack any real force, while others have strict controls that are often self-defeating. For example, of all the buildings recorded by the Historic American Buildings Survey, approximately one-third have subsequently been demolished. In Seattle, on the other hand, an overly restrictive set of controls accompanies designation. But these controls are seldom invoked in controversial cases, for the simple reason that the city council will not approve initial designation in such instances. As a result, several valued Seattle landmarks were lost last year alone.

A new, middle-road ordinance is now being drafted; it establishes a process by which city preservationists in the Office of Urban Conservation are given ample time to save a building before it can be demolished. No demolition will take place if the city can show that restoration will yield a reasonable profit to the owner. The point here is that registers must have meaningful but realistic controls built in.

Historic and Special-Use Districts

A slightly more effective tool is the designation of historic districts and creation of their close legal cousins, the special-use districts. The latter need not have historical value at all, but they usually display a distinctive character worth saving.

In addition to providing the normal designation protections, historic districts help the business community by assuring investors that a tasteful restoration at one site will not be exploited and degraded by a fast-buck development next door. Lack of controls is no boon to legitimate businesses in a historic district. Such laxity allowed the failure of attempted redevelopment in such areas as Old Town in Chicago and Gas Light Square in St. Louis, where many early investors went bankrupt.

Conversely, control puts a premium on early redevelopment, making sound, restrained restoration an inevitability and rewarding the owners who pioneer in a historic district by letting them accrue the greatest proportional increases in appreciated property values.

In many special-use and historic districts, inappropriate enterprises which might detract from the character of the areas are either restricted or prohibited. For instance, in both Pioneer Square and the Asian International District of Seattle, new parking lot construction has been sharply curtailed. Each district ordinance, incidentally, is interpreted and monitored by an elected board of neighborhood residents and business people in an attempt to reduce the redtape of bureaucracy.

Among the new controls placed on owners since the establishment of the Pioneer Square district is a minimum maintenance law requiring that the facades of all buildings be kept clean, attractive and safe. This ordinance has helped spur improvements—often interior as well as exterior—in buildings that otherwise might have continued to stagnate indefinitely, as absen-

OCCIDENTAL PARK., *Seattle, Wash. (Carleton Knight, III)*

tee owners speculated on the prospects of increased values resulting from nearby restoration efforts. Such an ordinance is within the zoning power of almost every city.

Pioneer Square is now a widely hailed success story, and confidence in the future of the Pike Place Market, now under restoration, is growing. The irony of these projects is that at first both were resisted by some business groups as infringements of free enterprise. Opponents of the Pioneer Square historic district designation favored instead the previous city plan to demolish the district for a publicly financed freeway connector and parking garages. Similarly, opposition to a historic district in the Pike Place Market was based on a preference for a federally financed urban renewal scheme to construct major new buildings there.

In both cases, the alternative of preservation fortunately was supported by a majority of the merchants and other business people actually operating in the affected districts—the true entrepreneurs. As regards Pioneer Square, it is hard to imagine any federally financed renewal plan that could have revived the area as quickly as historic preservation techniques did, and with such pleasant aesthetic results, such good economic return and the relative expenditure of so few taxpayer dollars.

Some controls, then, are necessary to orderly redevelopment; they benefit not only the public interest but the private developer and owner by rewarding restoration. But that is only the beginning of the proper government role.

Local and State Plans

Every city and state should have a historic preservation plan, especially for individual historic districts within cities. A plan establishes public priorities and lets everyone know what they are. Seattle has such a plan for Pioneer Square, the Pike Place Market and the International District. However, it is a source of some amusement to local preservationists that the Pioneer Square plan was not completed until four years after the historic district was created and well under restoration.

Financial Tools

More substantial help can be obtained through a public revolving fund for historic preservation, such as the Historic Seattle Preservation and Development Authority, which the city established in 1972. The first such public fund in the country, the $600,000 authority is chartered as an independent public corporation to keep purchase decisions out of politics. It is modeled after privately financed revolving funds pioneered in Savannah, Charleston and Annapolis.

The fund is designed to acquire endangered or stagnating buildings and to find buyers who will undertake sensitive restoration and whose purchase money can be put back into the fund to enable further acquisitions. The authority does not use its funds in actual restoration and often can obtain a building with nothing more than

an option. Indeed, just the mere expression of serious financial interest by operators of such a fund is sometimes enough to spark redevelopment.

Soon the Washington state legislature will be asked by the governor to establish a similar revolving fund for urban conservation. It will be understood that such a fund should operate to save districts as well as individual buildings and to enable compatible new construction in historic districts as well as encouraging restoration.

Regrettably, the federal government, whose urban renewal program has destroyed or blighted hundreds of square miles of historic districts in the supposed intent of saving them, has yet to establish such a fund.

Another means of placing preservation in a position more competitive with new development is a tax policy permitting taxation of historic buildings on the basis of present use rather than highest and best use. The Washington State Open Space Law of 1971 provides current-use taxation for certain forms of timberland and farmland threatened by destructive development and also includes historic sites. No owner of a historic building has yet applied for such a tax adjustment, but once in use, this adjustment will probably be a popular device for compensating building owners for the loss of real or imagined development potential because of historical designation and controls.

Other Tools

Government also can boost restoration by leasing office space in historic buildings. Often the pledge of such a lease will prove decisive in an owner's ability to secure bank financing for restoration. The city of Seattle and the Metropolitan Transit Operation embraced this policy to good effect, and the state may soon adopt this approach for filling its office needs in various communities. Unhappily, again, there is so far no such interest at the federal level, and the U.S. General Services Administration continues to demolish significant old structures to erect impersonal new bureaucratic monuments.

One of the major ways in which government can assist historic districts is by providing complimentary amenities, such as trees, small parks, good street furniture and reconstructions of historic lamp posts and drinking fountains. In Seattle, the city strategy of promoting such development gives the Pioneer Square district a feeling of constant improvement and helps inspire confidence in the future of the area.

BUILDING SUPPORT FOR HISTORIC PRESERVATION

Initial development in Pioneer Square was an act of faith by a handful of architects and small business people such as Ralph Anderson and Richard White, who, with some aid from then Deputy Mayor Edward Devine, restored one short block of Occidental Boulevard. Seattle's popular historian Bill Speidel and architectural historian Victor Steinbrueck labored to stir up wider interest; when it came—chiefly from the city—a resourceful private-public alliance was begun.

After designation of the historic district, the city commissioned Arthur Skolnik as district manager, and his office soon became the guiding force in many redevelopment projects, private as well as public. District managers can intervene with city officials and bureaucrats on behalf of local merchants and developers, whose problems often are quite different from those of other neighborhoods. They can, for example, encourage the city council, the state liquor control board and the streets department to permit certain kinds of street vending.

A district manager or a local preservation officer is the kind of government insider who can mobilize departments of engineering, water and lighting to make urban conservation improvements part of their regular activities. For example, most parks departments must have learned by now that people enjoy going to plays in a recycled bathhouse or fire station as much or more than in a new auditorium. The Seattle Parks Department has undertaken scores of such adaptive reuse projects since 1969. (In fact, almost none of the money spent by Seattle on preservation capital projects has come from the official preservation budget, which is quite small.) Good preservation officers can encourage this attitude and find ways to combine various functions, space needs and funding sources.

Preservation officers can also help enlist the cooperation of other government jurisdictions—local, state and national—and even foundations and private donors. The city investment in Pioneer Square has inspired more than $250,000 in outright private gifts, $150,000 of which went to restoration of the Pioneer Square Pergola.

One lesson learned in Seattle is that just as historic preservation is a means for achieving a wider variety of community goals, so too a wide variety of agencies, organizations and economic interests can be enlisted in preservation projects in one way or another. Clubs, banks, Jaycees, arts groups, the convention and visitors bureau, airlines, the Junior League, the post office, Western Union, political parties, the downtown development society and many other groups have become nearly as important as funding sources for historic preservation as are the National Trust, the National Endowment for the Arts and other official agencies. For example, when the city lacked $40,000 for an architectural and historical study of Fort Lawton, an Army civil affairs reserve unit there was asked to volunteer use of its substantial professional talent. The unit completed a fine, thorough study at no cost to Seattle.

By the same token, preservationists must look to a multitude of potential allies for advancing the political cause or issues side of urban conservation. For their own long-term interests, they should work with businesses seeking downtown improvements (as is well demonstrated in the city of Walla Walla and in the Seattle Westlake Mall Development); with neighborhood business people who want to enhance a shopping

area; with environmentalists trying to save a park from an incompatible encroachment; with horticultural groups desiring more urban greenery; with ethnic groups wanting to recycle an old theater or bank as a community center; with arts groups who often find the gallery they want in an abandoned church or store; with community councils, historians and historical societies, urban design groups, old people, young people and all who deserve help and, by getting it, will become more committed preservationists themselves.

Two groups deserve special attention: the poor and the racial minorities. Pioneer Square is the home of the world's original "Skid Road," down which logs were skidded to Henry Yesler's waterfront mill. The road's name was applied to the whole district, which later became a tenderloin area and then a habitat for indigents.

In some cities, historic preservation is an ally of people in slums, in others it has moved them out. In Seattle, the removal of indigents in the Skid Road district was attempted in the years preceding historical designation, chiefly because of a strict enforcement of city fire codes in hotels following a major fire. However, official city policy after establishment of the historic district has been to aid and accommodate the Skid Road population, not disperse it. At worst, the panhandlers are unsightly but certainly not dangerous.

The city and county and the Seattle Housing Authority helped the Skid Road Community Council to redevelop the old Morrison Hotel as one of the nation's first municipal shelters. The state decided to maintain operation of its Skid Road branch of the Casual Labor Office, rather than consolidate it with the main office. The city council votes annual emergency appropriations to the Skid Road Community Council for winter care of indigents and supports numerous social service programs through the municipal shelter. Special parks department contracts pay Skid Roaders for part-time maintenance work in the two neighborhood parks. The city and federal government helped the Indian community establish the Indian Health Center and the Indian Social Service Center in the old Broderick Building.

The accommodation could be better, and preservation's stimulation of higher property values is an inevitable threat to the resident poor. Granted that the alternative was the urban renewal bulldozer and that government interest in the welfare of the poor is far greater than it was before district designation. But what is needed now in Seattle is a public corporation to buy and operate on a nonprofit basis the support enterprises, especially inexpensive restaurants, that permit the poor to exist. For Skid Roaders, this need is as real as that for housing.

Preservation should not invite class antagonism. Peaceful coexistence and even pleasant and instructive cooperation between the poor and the preservationist are possible in a historic district. This is both morally and politically desirable. Pioneer Square shows that such accommodation need not damage anyone economically. As the initiator of the Seattle Underground Tour,

Bill Speidel, says, "We're not Newport, R.I.; we're an old gold rush town and the original Skid Road. If we didn't have the bums around, we'd have to hire them from central casting. When a bum panhandles me for a dime I give him a quarter instead and say, 'Now don't give me that stuff about buying a cup of coffee—go have yourself a beer.'"

You don't cure poverty by moving the poor. It is better that we learn to live together.

The same is true of preservation and racial minorities. Seattle lost its historic Broadway High School last year largely because the nearby black community was not persuaded that an old school could be made as attractive and efficient as a "modern" one. Yet other cities have seen black neighborhoods champion restoration as an alternative to urban renewal. Clearly, all races need to learn more about the merits of urban conservation.

RESPONSIBILITY OF THE PUBLIC

Despite all the tools available to it, government cannot accomplish widespread urban conservation projects alone; indeed, its chief contribution is to provide a hospitable climate and setting. It is important to have government aid for urban conservation activities, but it is also vital that preservation have available private philanthropic capital and talent for generating ideas, honest criticism and information. Private energy and capital started the preservation movement in Seattle and are even more active in development these days. But we may soon find a decrease in involvement of independent citizens. Now that preservation has been embraced by the local and state governments, and now that many former firebrands are official board members, there is a danger of wilt in the old grass roots.

The state of Washington would be extremely fortunate if it could get a branch office of the National Trust for Historic Preservation established there (the nearest is in San Francisco). The area also needs to raise money for a private historic preservation revolving fund that could act in a somewhat more adventuresome fashion than the public fund can. The area should attempt to acquire the U.S. Department of the Interior's proposed national school for historic preservation, or at least should foster more regular educational training in preservation.

More than anything, the state needs a properly funded, semiprivate group to promote the cause of historic preservation. Hundreds of conservation casualties will occur in Washington State alone if some forceful citizens group is not working with the public agencies and the private sector to find ways to prevent such losses. With few exceptions, government can be counted on to initiate a new policy or undertake a project only when there is outside, independent inspiration, support and sometimes pressure. With this in mind, a group of citizens recently established the nonprofit Washington Trust for Historic Preservation, which now has offices at Fort Warden in Port Townsend. This may be the first rallying point for a statewide citizens preservation movement.

CONCLUSION

Urban conservation, then, is one of government's legitimately expanding fields of endeavor. The value of beautiful wilderness parks and scenic rivers is vitiated if our daily environment is one of cancerous schlock. The economic benefits of spectacular corporate monuments likewise are diluted when the American economy simply discards old buildings and neighborhoods and then finds itself paying the enormous costs of resulting social problems. Urban conservation is not just a romantic indulgence in nostalgia. It is a physical restatement of the long hallowed American values of frugality, good craftsmanship and community responsibility.

14

After the Seattle fire in 1889. (Museum of History and Industry, Seattle)

A History of Pioneer Square

ARTHUR M. SKOLNIK

Arthur M. Skolnik is Washington State conservator and state historic preservation officer. He formerly was city conservator for Seattle and district manager of the Pioneer Square Historic District.

What follows is a description of Pioneer Square from a technician's viewpoint, showing what transpired during the last five years, with a very brief history of the city of Seattle in the process.

A CITY'S HISTORY

Seattle is a young city. The first white person came to this area in 1851. Seattle was founded in 1869 on a small island confronted by high bluffs on one side and developed as a traditional frontier town, with lumber as the basic industry.

The city was founded on the basis of land-scraping and urban renewal or, more correctly, urban removal. The first process was done by washing down the hillsides closest to the shore to create flat land near the deep-water port. This took place in the 1870s, and the shipping industry then developed. Seattle was building ships, as well as loading them with timber and sending them out.

It was a good time to be in Seattle. The city prospered and was an active metropolitan area until the Seattle fire in 1889, which wiped out the core of the downtown commercial area, some 16 or 18 square blocks of the finest section of the city.

Within six hours there was total destruction, but the city officials immediately said, "Let's rebuild." Within about five years, the majority of Pioneer Square had been rebuilt with the latest technology. Such architects as Elmer H. Fisher from Massachusetts were brought in, and Fisher alone eventually designed more than 60 buildings in the city.

As new technology was developed and the city need for expansion grew, growth took place farther north away from Pioneer Square, which began to go downhill. Highrises and new technology brought some handsome examples of architecture, as new commercial buildings competed for space. Meanwhile, Pioneer Square continued to fall into disrepair.

EARLY INTEREST IN RESTORING PIONEER SQUARE

In the early and mid-1960s there was an effort to demolish Pioneer Square, or the better part of it, for speculative development, a proposal that would have eliminated approximately 75 percent of the historic structures. As a result of this proposal, several community leaders showed a growing concern for the future of the area. This concern was brought to the attention of city officials and culminated in 1970 with the drafting and passage of the Pioneer Square Historic District Ordinance. The ordinance established an architectural review board of five persons (now expanded to seven), who must approve any permits that would result in a change in exterior appearance in the district.

During consideration of the ordinance, the usual cries were made by the business community that the law would preserve blight and restrict property development and the growth of the downtown area. The ensuing debate resulted in wounds that took quite a while to heal, and, in fact, some of them are still unhealed. However, the city took up the responsibility after the historical designations to make sure that there was coordination of preservation activity.

POINTS OF INTEREST IN THE PIONEER SQUARE AREA

It is important to consider where Pioneer Square is in relationship to the rest of the city. To the west is the ever-expanding port, the mainstream of economic prosperity in Seattle, which was especially important when Boeing Aircraft fell apart. Directly to the south, the Dome Stadium is under construction. To the north is the central business district, where such prominent structures as the Space Needle and the Federal Office Building are located.

It was city policy not to compete with the private sector in Pioneer Square but to look after its own concerns: streets, sidewalks, the areas that needed public improvement. Without any assessments to the property owners, the city tried to make the area more pleasant and more attractive for people. (At this time in the early 1960s, the crime rate in Pioneer Square represented about 15 percent of the city's total crime, and these were serious offenses—murders and assaults, etc.)

The Pergola and the Park

The pergola is the only piece of cast-iron architecture in Seattle, and the city decided to create a major public space here, as a symbolic beginning to show municipal support for the restoration of Pioneer Square. Architects completed elaborate models and studies of what needed to be done. The street next to the park was closed. This work was accomplished through an open space grant from the U.S. Department of Housing and Urban Development (HUD), with model cities matching local funds.

The pergola restoration, complicated by the many

parts that had to be recast, was financed by a donation of $150,000 from the United Parcel Service, which was founded in Seattle.

The comfort station below the pergola has not been in use since the 1940s. Someday the city hopes to restore and reopen this facility. In the meantime, other work has continued. This includes the addition of some street furniture that was believed necessary, though perhaps not historically correct. In addition, cobblestones were brought from streets that were to be paved.

There is much concern about landscaping within the district. Also, because the large buildings that surround Pioneer Square diminish the quality of the buildings in the foreground, there is an attempt to use landscaping to limit the views out of the district.

Lights were recast and trees and a sculptural fountain added. Fixtures were built into the park for outdoor activities; these include another pergola, which is contemporary and controversial.

The park was so successful that phase 2 was immediately begun with the removal of buildings not deemed to be significant to the district. Although these could have been conserved, the advantage of having four-and-a-half blocks for a park was too great to dismiss. This project brought into the city a new texture that is much appreciated. A National Endowment for the Arts exhibit, "More Streets for People," was displayed in the park recently, and this is consistent with the kind of activities being promoted for the area.

Development has been gradual, continuing over several years, but the efforts behind it were the result of hustling. We got out, tried to find where money was available and grabbed it. Programs were customized to meet the wishes of money sources, although we did have specific purposes of our own. In short, there was an attempt to give the district a complete identity and to inspire private development at the same time.

First Avenue

First Avenue is the main architectural corridor in Pioneer Square. This street was designed as an arterial road, but with the construction of the Dome Stadium, it was believed that the street needed to be redesigned somewhat. The mayor was presented with a proposal to put a median strip of trees down the center of the street, though the city engineer objected to the idea because the city had never changed a road from arterial to nonarterial.

The mayor agreed with the proposal, and 30 days later construction had begun. Now there are 33 sycamore trees planted down the center of that street; they limit the views out of the district and also reduce the volume of traffic. And, with community support for on-street parking, there was no need to remove the parking stalls, which relate directly to increased commercial development.

To help give the district a uniform appearance, the city requested a HUD grant to fund relighting the district in a more compatible way. A unique design scheme

resulted in a pattern that reused the existing old light-poles at a new height, along with globes adapted from the early lighting devices in Pioneer Square.

Finally, the Seattle Engineering Department took down all the center-hung traffic signals and put up the corner-mounted kind. Thus, the only overhanging wires in Pioneer Square now are trolley wires.

Harbor Station

A private donation of $50,000 resulted in the restoration of the only public landing on the Seattle waterfront. The harbor station is city-managed but was restored privately. It now serves to provide access for pleasure boats as well as public boat access between the shore and ships anchored in the harbor. The city water department provided five period-type casts of drinking fountains for the area.

Occidental Mall

The street that started it all is Occidental Avenue. Because it was a nonarterial street and the stadium was to be built on the south end, it was decided that Occidental would be converted into a pedestrian mall.

Funds to build the first phase of a four-block mall were made available through a grant. The first two blocks of "Occidental Mall" are open and the third block will be completed next year under a grant from the Economic Development Administration.

This mall has become the backdrop for activities that were never envisioned for the area. For example, artists display and sell their work. At first no one could figure out what to do with benches, because the mall was such a large area. More benches were installed, but there is a law of diminishing returns, and eventually open space begins to disappear. The question of what to do with benches and seating facilities is still being considered.

Since Pioneer Square is a flat area, it is generally accessible to the handicapped. In addition, all new construction is designed for barrier-free access. That is a major concern there, one reason being that the Handicapped Division of the Seattle Department of Human Resources is located in Pioneer Square.

HOUSING AND PUBLIC SERVICES IN THE AREA

As for housing in the district, the Old Frye Hotel, now the Frye Apartments, consists of 250 units of 221(d)(3) rent subsidy apartments. However, not everyone qualifies for that kind of housing, so there is need for other types.

One hotel recently purchased by a group of architects is still being maintained as a hotel, and long-term plans are to keep it that way. In addition, the Morrison Hotel, purchased with the cooperation of the Seattle Housing Authority and the Skid Road Community Council, is the Skid Road Shelter in Pioneer Square. It provides not only housing facilities but social services for the Skid Roaders.

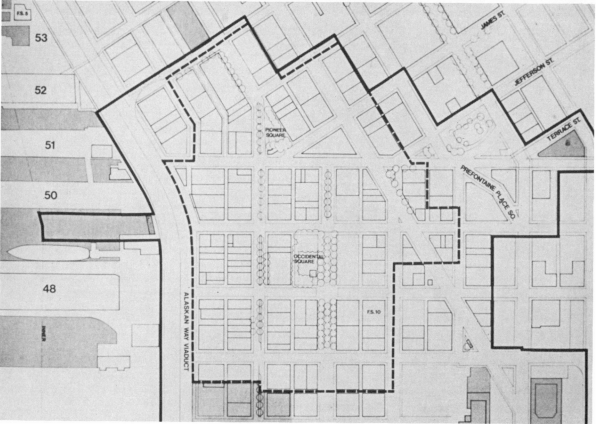

The Seattle harbor c. 1870 (top). (Museum of History and Industry, Seattle)
Map of Pioneer Square Historic District, Seattle; broken line indicates boundaries established by 1970 ordinance,
solid line shows enlargement of district in 1973. (City of Seattle, Department of Community Development)

PIONEER SQUARE PARK, *Seattle. (Arthur M. Skolnik)*

Light fixture in Pioneer Square. (Arthur M. Skolnik)

In terms of other public services, the Pioneer Square Health Station provides free or nearly free medical care for local indigents.

EXPANDING THE HISTORIC DISTRICT

The city and those persons involved in the redevelopment got so excited about Pioneer Square that they decided to go after those sites that were not in the original historic district. Thus, the district was almost doubled in size about a year-and-a-half ago. The Union Train Station with its great interior space was included and now is being investigated for use as an intermodal transportation center by the Port of Seattle. It would be used with another building in the historic district, the Kingstreet Station, which is presently used by Amtrak.

SPECIAL PROBLEMS

The Yesler Bridge over Fourth Avenue presented a unique problem. The Seattle Engineering Department first said the bridge had to be removed because there was not enough clearance for trucks to pass under it. However, the engineers have now agreed that, rather than remove the bridge, they will lower the road. So, there are many ways to solve problems!

The mayor recently announced that he will recommend to the city council use of the old Public Safety

Building as an annex to the city hall. This flat-iron structure was vacated by the city 20 or 25 years ago and was sold for $40,000 simply to get rid of it.

The Dome Stadium raised a new set of issues. More historical protection was needed, and it came in the form of a special review district ordinance. This district overlays the Pioneer Square area, though not exactly conforming with the same boundaries. An elected board concerns itself with the impact of the stadium and the possibly detrimental effects it might bring into the community.

ECONOMICS

An economic evaluation was done because of criticism of the programs. In addition, people were commenting that too much money was going into Pioneer Square. Basically, what follows is a rough breakdown done in 1974. The numbers have increased by now. Public investment totaled $2.1 million; private money was about a quarter of a million dollars; federal funds came to approximately $1 million; and about $800,000 was local money.

If the last figure is reexamined, it will be seen that only about a quarter of a million of that was specifically designated for Pioneer Square. The rest was in the city coffers in the form of funds for street lighting, paving improvements, etc. So the total investment of the city is about a quarter of a million dollars in outright expenditures. And since those monies have been spent, more than $8 million of private investment have resulted.

NEW PROVISIONS

In an area where millions of dollars are being invested, nearby deteriorating properties are major problems. To address this situation, the Pioneer Square Historic District Ordinance was amended to include a minimum-maintenance section with antineglect provisions that require property owners to repair their properties rather than demolish them. If owners do not conform within a reasonable period of time, as determined by the city superintendent of buildings, the superintendent can declare an emergency, make the repairs and put a lien on the property for the cost. This provision is being enforced: Eighty buildings have been repaired and most of the owners now are making plans for rehabilitation.

A master plan, which addresses itself to the outside pressures of the district, has been developed. However, the plan is only a guideline, not law. It is strictly a tool to help in the development and speculative assessments that are to be made during the next few years.

A capital improvement program for Pioneer Square was developed for use with the grants, proposals and donations coming in now.

Buildings continue to be restored—approximately four to six at any one time. Such changes as the closing of alleys and extension of parks are being allowed. A greenhouse built out into an alley is used as a restaurant.

A PROGRESS REPORT

The number of commercial enterprises in Pioneer Square is now more than 150. The area has become the backdrop for these activities and the revenue generated from such sources as sales and liquor taxes is huge.

There are 35 restaurants in the area, with the turnover rate at about 10 percent. Banks are coming back into the district and using local decor, although it is not a requirement. The U.S. Postal Service is there and has done a fine job of trying to maintain the area's theme by retaining a turn-of-the-century flavor in its interior decoration.

Western Union is a recent addition, and there is a little theater, too. The number of outdoor liquor licenses in Pioneer Square is probably greater than anywhere else in the country. However, the state Liquor Control Board is delighted, because there now is close control in an area where the board once had problems.

A brief look at some statistics should be interesting. Pioneer Square as planned is 25 percent completed. There are 150 buildings, and employment has gone from 1,000 persons in 1970 to approximately 6,000 today.

The market for restoration is reaching what could be called the third phase. The first phase consisted of people just looking around; the second phase was people doing initial buying; and now people are buying cumulative blocks of property, not one building but several.

The economic benefits are obvious. The tax base of Pioneer Square, which was next to nothing, is now high. We used to refer to a 450 percent increase in the tax base. Now it would be possible to cite a 1,000 percent increase. The revenue is generated in many ways and forms—property, sales and liquor taxes; increased employment; improved transit support; an untold amount of tourist dollars; and so forth. What began as a philanthropic gesture became one of the most important economic generators in Seattle's recent hard times. The impact of all this has been not only citywide but regional. In short, preservation has been an economic benefit for individuals, the city proper, the metropolitan area and the entire state of Washington.

Entrance to Grand Central in Pioneer Square, Seattle. (National Trust)

Making Historic Preservation Profitable — If You're Willing to Wait

ALAN F. BLACK

Alan F. Black is president of Black and Caldwell, Inc., a land development and construction firm that he formed in 1961.

In January 1962, a young architect named Ralph Anderson took the plunge that, in retrospect, triggered the gradual renaissance of Skid Road, which today carries the more polite name Pioneer Square. He purchased the three-story, 36-by-110-foot Jackson Building for $30,000. He sandblasted and cleaned the exterior, cleaned and refurbished the inside and moved his office to the second floor. The third floor was remodeled into a spacious skylit walkup apartment. He rented the main street level, originally the Old Tum Water Tavern, with a beautiful mosaic tile floor, to an able and established decorator. In addition to a spacious and unique office for his own architectural practice on the second floor, he had a tenant on the main floor who attracted important, so-called establishment people to that section of town.

In 1965 Ralph Anderson's close friend Richard White negotiated a long-term lease on the 60-by-110-foot Liberty Building around the corner. The following year, Ralph Anderson bought the four-story, 60-by-110-foot Union Trust Building for $75,000; it adjoined the Liberty Building. Both these buildings were gradually cleaned and refurbished as tenants were found for the space. White started an art gallery in the Liberty Building and rented space to a miscellany of other tenants for prices in the range of 80 cents to $1 a square foot per year, unserviced and with tenants responsible for finishing their own space. These three buildings began not only to carry themselves but to produce enough cash flow to allow the owners to make additional improvements to them.

In December 1968, Richard White purchased the four-story, 60-by-110-foot Globe Building for $55,000 in the same block as the other three buildings controlled by himself and Ralph Anderson. With this purchase, the available buildings in the square block bounded by South Jackson, South Main, First Avenue and Occidental were fairly well consolidated in the hands of two men who had a strong feeling for the area and were putting substantial money into improvement of their buildings. Being the first to make financial commitments to the area, they had "bought right" at figures of around $10 or less a square foot for the ground area. Except for White's leased building, they had bought on favorable low-down-payment real estate contracts. Modest additional cash outlays by the owners brought the buildings into rentable condition without the need for major improvements or financing.

During this period another architect, David Gray, bought and remodeled the 30-by-110-foot Maud Building. He converted the space to small offices and successfully leased them at $2 to $3 per square foot per year, with janitorial services included.

More and more people were coming into the area to the several newly established galleries and shops. The purchase and rehabilitation of the buildings in this block established a new identity for Skid Road. It was becoming a more vital area known by the new arrivals as Pioneer Square.

The period from January 1962 through approximately 1970 should be thought of as a somewhat separate and distinct phase in the revival of Pioneer Square. It was a period of speculative pioneering by a few visionary and venturesome souls who moved into this run-down and economically depressed area. They "bought right," buying relatively small buildings that were in fairly good shape at bargain prices before most people realized what was going on. Improvements were made to these buildings without major structural changes and with a minimum of attention to code requirements. The buildings were rehabilitated with a minimum of cost on a "seat-of-the-pants" basis and with a minimum of fuss. Existing plumbing and much of the existing electrical systems were used, a practice that made costs substantially less than later owners would incur under strict code enforcement.

As a result, these buildings could be rented for $1 to $2 a square foot per year. These were bargain prices in anyone's book and allowed a wide range of tenants to rent large square footage at minimal cost. In addition, the space was in a convenient central area that showed signs of really coming alive. All this occurred in what is termed here the phase 1 period in the redevelopment of Pioneer Square, the 1960s.

PIONEER SQUARE: PHASE 2 BEGINS

Phase 2 began in May 1970 with passage by the Seattle City Council of the ordinance establishing the Pioneer Square Historic District. This was the first legislation of its type in the state of Washington. The ordinance gave the area an identity in a legal sense. Finally there was a set of standards with the force of law to keep the area from being turned into a massive parking lot. A building of significance could no longer be torn down by a slumlord faced with a roof repair. The razing of buildings for parking lots was stopped and the concept of areawide restoration began.

GRAND CENTRAL HOTEL BUILDING *before restoration (top). Interior archways were cut through 18-inch brick bearing walls (above and right). Restored Grand Central used for shops and offices (facing page). (Ralph Anderson and Partners, Architects)*

Phase 2 is the period in which there was a commitment of substantial risk capital by private individuals to the restoration of major buildings in the district. It is also the time when the city actively began supporting restoration work and spending municipal funds—matched in some cases with federal money—on parks, malls, tree planting and other major improvements in the Pioneer Square area.

Until this time, most of the upgrading and restoration of buildings had taken place south of Main Street in one square-block area. No significant rehabilitation had been done in the two blocks north of Main Street. It seemed in 1970 that some major restoration would have to take place in the latter section. Otherwise the work done to date would be only an isolated pocket, cut off from the rest of the downtown mainstream.

The Grand Central Project

In July 1971, Ralph Anderson, Richard White and I purchased the derelict and long vacant Grand Central Hotel Building on the corner of First Avenue South and South Main Street, in the block north of the area where all the work had been done to date. It was a big, homely, four-story box of a building covering an area of 111 by 150 feet on First Avenue, with an alley and parking lot on one side. The building was bought for the same illogical and unintelligible reason the mountain climber gives for climbing: Because it's there. We did not know

what we would do with it; we had absolutely no financing for it, and certainly no prospective tenants. I suppose we felt someone had to do something, and that we might as well give it a try. Essentially, there was never a more totally emotional and unprofessional purchase of a major building.

The 66,000-square-foot building was purchased on a real estate contract for $230,000. The building had long been vacant, the roof was ruined, the windows broken and anything of value in the way of hardware or woodwork had been stolen. We signed the purchase documents, looked at the building and wondered why! The only thing going for us was a first-class pigeon rookery. We had more pigeons per square foot roosting in the building than anywhere west of the Mississippi.

With no financing and no master plan, we hired three laborers at $2 an hour to start clearing out the years of accumulated refuse and rubble. We next turned them loose beating off plaster and pulling down 85-year-old lath.

The Plan for Grand Central

During the summer of 1971 there was earnest thinking about what to do with the building. About the time of purchase there had been rumors of the possibility of the city's purchasing the half block east of the Grand Central for a park. In the fall of 1971 the city did indeed buy the parking lot property to the east, which put a new light on plans for the building. What had been the back alley side of the structure could now be considered an important visual and access point. It would also be possible to have two fronts to the building: First Avenue on the west and the proposed park on the east.

Out of this the arcade concept developed, with passage from First Avenue through the building to the park with shops opening onto an arcade. In addition to this pedestrian-oriented main floor, we planned three floors of office space above. Work was to be done in stages or phases, with the first stage being the main floor arcade area and retail shops. The three upper floors would be the second, third, and fourth stages, completed as space there was rented.

With the plan established, Ralph Anderson's office began the design and working drawings, while the three partner-owners began worrying in earnest about where the money would come from.

Financing

The building had been bought on contract for $230,000, about $15 a square foot for land area. This was about $5 a square foot more than was paid for the buildings purchased during the middle and late 1960s. Unlike those smaller buildings, this project was going to need major financing. The purchase contract did not allow subordination to future financing, so a major lender who would take out the underlying contract and supply adequate funds for the proposed project was required.

The presentation for financing was made to a nearby bank that had shown considerable interest in the area. It seemed natural that this bank would help with the financing for this first major restoration there. The local manager was enthusiastic and developed a carefully prepared presentation. A phased loan in the total amount of $650,000 was requested. Of this, $200,000 would be for the main floor and exterior, and $150,000 for each of the other three floors. This was to be an interim construction loan with permanent financing to be sought on completion when the project had proved itself. Each of the three owners would have to put in enough money to pay off the underlying contract of about $200,000 and be willing to personally guarantee the $650,000 loan.

The application for the loan was turned down January 19, 1972. This was a dark day for the three of us. We each had contributed considerable cash to keep the demolition and cleanup going through the summer and fall of 1971, and major restoration would not proceed on the building until someone was willing to commit substantial funds to the area. We felt that if anyone could get financing for a major building we should be able to, because of the buildings already owned and improved by Anderson and White and because of our overall record and reputation in respective areas of work in the community. The project was well into the working drawings and the gutting of the building was nearly completed, so the need for financing was immediate.

Each of the partners had had some contact with the Seattle Trust and Savings Bank and knew some of the

officers and principals. They were presented with the program for the building and the financing needs. Seattle Trust made a study of the area, reviewed the proposal and plans carefully and decided to help. With a projection of rents and income for the building when completed, Seattle Trust appraised the completed, fully restored building at $1 million and gave a 75 percent loan of $900,000 at 8.5 percent interest with a 15-year term. Besides the $30,000 already personally invested in the building, each partner was required to put up an additional $75,000, a total of $225,000 new equity. In addition, the loan required personal guarantees. The Seattle Trust agreement was a phased loan with disbursements tied to completion of the exterior and main floor as one stage, and each of the three upper floors as an additional stage. In mid-February 1972 we mortgaged other property and signed the papers to close the loan.

Structural Reinforcement

Meanwhile, during this period of planning for the Grand Central and searching for financing, something rather significant was happening in another area. In September 1971, some officials from the Seattle Building Department visited Los Angeles for a firsthand view of the damage caused by the severe quake of the previous spring. The Building Department people returned obviously impressed by the damage they had seen and alarmed about the risk of unreinforced brick buildings, the primary type of construction used for the buildings in Pioneer Square during the post–Seattle Fire period of 1889 to about 1910. In any major seismographic disturbance there was the chance that the brick walls might pull away from the floors and the totally unreinforced buildings would collapse.

The building code required that whenever more than 50 percent of the assessed value of a building was spent on improvements in any one year the building would have to meet current building code seismographic requirements. Because no major building had been restored to this time and because any work that had been done in the area had been spread over several years, this provision of the code had not been applied. However, the Grand Central was not going to escape some major reinforcing work.

The architects and structural engineers for the building, together with the Building Department staff, developed a compromise solution for this type of unreinforced masonry building. The walls on each floor of the building had to be tied to the floors by the installation of a properly sized steel angle around the inside perimeter of the floor, with 4-foot-on-center steel strips welded to the channel and running back along the surface of the floor. These strips were then nailed and bolted to a new plywood overlaid floor, which tied the floor together so it would act as a single diaphragm. The perimeter steel angle member was then tied to the outside of the walls by bolts drilled through the walls and fastened on the outside with escutcheon-like plates that could be decorative in design.

The Grand Central was faced with this major structural requirement, the first of many unforeseen cost overruns. It was a reasonable and proper requirement in the interest of public safety, although costly to the developers.

As soon as the building had been cleaned out, which included the removal of all plaster and wood lath, a contract was let for the structural reinforcing work, which needed to be done while the ceilings and walls were exposed and before any reconstruction work proceeded. Concurrently with this, a contract was let for the repair of all exterior masonry, including the rebuilding of the parapet. To meet the building permit requirements, the parapet was lowered and the upper section rebuilt incorporating a bond beam that would tie the parapet together.

Substantial portions of the building elevation required the removal of rotten brick and mortar and replacement while tuck pointing was being done. Finally,

neglected roof drains and downspouts had allowed water to run down the face of portions of the building and during a period of many years this process had made a soft mush of much of the brick for a depth of several courses. While the staging was in place for the tuck pointing, this rather substantial exterior brickwork repair, another unbudgeted item, was done.

The cleaning, tuck pointing and repairing of the exterior were completed in early 1972. We waited until dry weather in the late spring to do the silicone sealing of the exterior.

Interior Work

In February 1972, eight months after purchase of the building, the interior reconstruction was begun. Electrical and mechanical contracts were let for stage 1, the main floor, with runs to be installed to the top three floors for the later stages. Concurrently, workers began

UNION TRUST BUILDING, *Seattle. (Ralph Anderson and Partners, Architects)*

cutting through the 18-inch brick bearing walls for the interior archways, which formed the new entryways to the shops and opened up the arcade to other sections of the main floor.

This process of cutting large archways through the brick walls of the building was one of the large expense items in the reconstruction of the Grand Central. The work could not properly be bid, and many of the archways were located as the work proceeded—a procedure that illustrates an important phenomenon in restoration work.

The fact is that the Grand Central restoration was an evolutionary design process. We felt our way along. As the building was opened up, many things that would add significantly to its usability and improve the aesthetics became apparent.

The Grand Central was a big, ugly box of a building. Out of this box were carved entirely new spaces, putting the building, which was originally a hotel, to an entirely new use.

The Basement

One illustration of the evolutionary nature of restoration was the basement of the Grand Central. When the building was bought the basement appeared to be unusable. However, as work on the main floor arcade proceeded, it became apparent that a major stairway from the arcade to the basement might open up some usable space. A cleanup crew cleared out the mass of rotting timbers, old heating plant boilers and hydraulic water-powered elevator equipment, most of which had to be cut up with acetylene torches to be removed. The ceilings were high enough to make attractive space and the area could be dried out with drain tile to allow the pouring of concrete slab floors. Because this basement level was too low to be served by the existing sewers, sump pumps were installed to pump back up to the street sewer level.

If the basement were ever to be used, it had to be tied in with the work on the main floor. Most of the costs for the basement were unbudgeted, but we believed that eventually rental revenue from this area would justify the cost. In retrospect, this was a correct decision, but at the time it was a bit unnerving in light of the funds.

One amusing sidelight concerning the basement involved a wrought-iron pipe, 4 inches in diameter, that was uncovered. Sticking several inches up through the dirt floor of the basement, it was capped off and seemed to be there to stay. We did not want to bury an unidentified pipe under the new basement floor, so it was investigated. The job foreman drilled a small ¼-inch hole in the cap, and water spouted to the ceiling. We thought a branch of an old water main had been hit, but city records showed no line there. Water samples were taken; it was 100 percent pure, with no chlorine, which would have indicated city water. We had a high-pressure artesian well in our basement! We drove a wooden plug in the little hole we had tapped and poured the new concrete floor over it.

The Project Completed

By May 1972, the main floor arcade was ready for tenants. Since the autumn of 1971, people had been making inquiries about possible space for shops in the building. Informally people were signed up, maintaining a reasonable mix of tenants. Shop space on the main arcade was rented for approximately $2 a square foot on three to five-year leases with no percentage of escalation clauses. We were grateful just to have some tenants!

By the summer of 1972, one year after purchase of the building, the main floor was fully rented and the basement arcade shops would be ready for occupancy by fall. Attention then turned to the three upper floors. By late summer, this space was ready for partitioning and finishing off to tenant specifications.

In September a major tenant signed a five-year lease for the entire fourth floor at $4.50 a square foot. This price covered fully improved space to the tenant's specifications, except for janitorial services, for which the tenant wanted to contract separately. These services were worth about 60 cents a square foot per year. By renting the entire floor we were able to gain additional net rentable area, which put the return close to $5 a square foot, excluding janitorial.

The fourth-floor tenants moved into their space on December 31, 1972, a year and a half after our purchase of the building.

With the fourth floor occupied and looking attractive, inquiries concerning office space on the second and third floors began. Tenants for these floors signed up at $5.50 to $6.00 a square foot per year. However, we were virtually out of money from the $900,000 loan and still had two floors to complete. Some of the funds projected for the upper floors had been used on the basement instead, and the budget had been exceeded in a multitude of other areas. Faced with this dilemma, we took the actual and projected rent roll to Seattle Trust and reviewed the overall financial situation.

We now had the basement area rented (a situation never contemplated in the original appraisal), the fourth floor fully rented at a figure of approximately $5 a square foot and additional tenants signed for space at $5.50 to $6.00 a square foot on the remaining two floors. Thus the building was given a new look by the lenders. Based on the existing rent roll and signed future tenants, a reappraisal of the building produced a value of $1.6 million.

Seattle Trust was willing to loan 75 percent of this new appraised figure, which increased the take-out loan from $900,000 to $1.2 million. This revised loan commitment was based on a new schedule of proven rents for the building. These were rents that to date had not been charged in the area, but the Grand Central was the first air-conditioned, totally restored and fully serviced building in Pioneer Square. By "uptown" standards for comparable space, these rents were still a bargain. Seattle Trust could see the rental income to justify the new appraisal and gave us the means to finish the building.

By the summer of 1973 the last two floors of office space were completed and rented at $6.00 to $6.50 per square foot.

A little more than two years after the Grand Central was purchased, it was finished and rented. We had paid $230,000 for the ugly box in July 1971. Over a period of two years an additional $1,375,000 had been spent on renovation and reconstruction. Of this, $1,260,000 was for permanent capitalized reconstruction costs to the building and $115,000 for loan fees and interest.

The funds came from the $125,000 put in by each partner, (totaling $375,000 equity or "front-end" money) and $1.2 million of borrowed funds, for a total investment of $1,575,000. In addition, there was some rental income during the latter part of this period when the building was partially occupied.

The 1974 annual gross revenue, based on existing leases, was approximately $275,000 a year. This gives the owners a cash flow of about $2,000 a month or $24,000 a year after debt service and operating costs. To date, this cash flow has gone back into the building in the form of nonrecurring operating costs and additional improvements. There will be no appreciable return on the $375,000 equity investment until the original leases expire and new leases are negotiated to reflect current rental market conditions.

The three upper office floors presently rent at between $5 and $6.50 a square foot, substantially below the $7.50 to $8 a square foot that this type of air-conditioned, fully serviced space brings today in Pioneer Square. Similarly, the retail shops on the main floor and basement are on leases with no percentages and below-market rates for the area.

The Grand Central would not have been bought and restored as it is today if cold logic and feasibility studies had been the deciding factors. We did it because the building was there, because we believed in the area and its future and because, with our experience and previous record, we could act as a development team that could obtain the necessary financing to get the job done. We believe that as the area develops there will be a reasonable return on the investment, though perhaps never a return on all the personal time, work and headaches (except through some strange satisfaction in seeing it done). However, I do not regret for one moment the two years spent on this project.

The Maynard Building

When the Grand Central was finished I swore I would not do it again for a long while, but here I am, a partner with Richard White, a year into the restoration of the Maynard Building, a block north of the Grand Central. Unlike the Grand Central, the Maynard is an intrinsically beautiful building. We bought it because it was simply too handsome to ignore and offered too much potential not to be restored properly. The Maynard Building is 90 percent complete and 75 percent occupied. It is such a beautiful building I am confident it

will fill up with rents in the $7 to $8 range. These rents are now established in Pioneer Square for fully serviced, air-conditioned space in the three major buildings completed to date.

Phase 3 in Pioneer Square

With completion of these three major buildings, phase 2 is ending and the phase 3 development period lies ahead for Pioneer Square. In phase 1, from 1962 to 1970, modest but important renovation work was done on an informal and somewhat amateur basis with limited outside financing. Phase 2, beginning with passage of the Pioneer Square Historic District Ordinance in 1970, saw the complete restoration of three major buildings and important municipal recognition and support for the area. Phase 2 also established the financial feasibility of restoring major buildings. Proven rent structures were established for these buildings and financing became available. Phase 3 is beginning now, in the summer of 1975. The Pioneer Square area is an established and recognized vital part of the city, where many buildings remain to be restored. There is a market for attractive, first-class space and financing is available for the right development team.

The major stumbling blocks remaining are the few slumlords, who sit on these old buildings and will not spend penny one to fix them up, let alone to restore them. Neither will they sell their buildings at prices that will allow someone else to put together the risk capital and financing necessary to restore them. As in so many cities, the slumlords still have a negative power. I have hopes, however, that the Minimum Maintenance Ordinance passed recently by the city council will give the slumlords pause for thought. They will have to fix up or sell out. Thus many of the remaining buildings in this neglected category should gradually find their way to restoration. If the properties are realistically priced, which means a modest value put on the buildings, investor-developers will find it profitable to restore them.

The investment and restoration that took place in Pioneer Square from 1962 to 1970 during the phase 1 period certainly was the most profitable. Indeed, it should have been, because it demanded the imagination and courage that started the area going.

Phase 2 was a period of high risk and long wait for a return on investment—in short, a testing period for Pioneer Square. Expensive restoration work was done before rental rates had adjusted to reflect the true cost of the work or the fine quality of the product.

Phase 3 can be approached less emotionally and with more logic. Rents are established for top quality space in well-restored buildings. Financing is easier to obtain for projects that show economic feasibility based on the record of work recently done in the area. The period of highest risk is over, and others will now come into the area and profitably restore some of the many remaining buildings that cry out for a little love and attention.

PIONEER BUILDING *(1890, Elmer H. Fisher), Seattle. (Carleton Knight, III)*

The Pioneer Building, A Case History

EARL B. SEAMAN

Earl B. Seaman is a partner in the Theta Company and president of Heritage Group, Ltd., Development Corporation. He has been involved in the construction and development industries for 27 years.

The city of Seattle is fortunate to have within its boundaries a 15-block concentration of old buildings destined for restoration and rehabilitation, and it has prepared a comprehensive master plan for the orderly redevelopment of this historically significant and architecturally compatible district. Many cities contain similar structures, but these potential restorations are found in isolated pockets, making integrated projects impossible.

In the 1960s, people with vision saw the potential of the area as a vital, productive and living part of the urban scene. In 1970, the mayor and city council reaffirmed their dedication to the preservation and revitalization of the area by passing an ordinance establishing the Pioneer Square Historic District. This ordinance assures the orderly redevelopment of the district and the preservation of this part of Seattle's heritage.

The Pioneer Building and Restoration Feasibility

One of many buildings erected immediately after the Seattle fire of 1889, the Pioneer Building was regarded by many as the finest office building in the West. Designed by architect Elmer H. Fisher, who is credited with having produced designs for no fewer than 51 buildings in the year after the fire, it is a monument to his creative talents. Several of the Fisher designs are in evidence in the city today, but the six-story Pioneer Building, with its rust-colored brick, terra-cotta and sandstone facade, is an excellent example of the Victorian architecture of its day. The restoration of the building is an apt subject for a discussion on "Making Historic Preservation Profitable."

In assessing the merits of any real estate development, one must use the same basic premises of economics, marketability, design and location, whether dealing with new construction or the rehabilitation of old properties. However, there are additional considerations for historic buildings where a total commitment must be made to preserve the architectural and historical integrity of the structure. Working with an existing structure obviously lessens the degree of flexibility found in new construction, but developing a concept within the physical confines of a building need not limit the economic or design potential.

In considering the feasibility of restoring the Pioneer Building, the Theta Company, as developer, researched the market and determined that there was a need for quality office space in the middle price range. Although a considerable number of old office buildings on the periphery of the downtown core were available and reasonably well maintained, they lacked such safety features and conveniences as sprinklers and air-conditioning systems. The rent for these buildings was in the range of $4 to $5 a square foot. Conversely, the new highrise office towers offered prime office space at a rental rate averaging $8.50 to $9.50 a square foot.

These findings, plus the success of the recently completed Grand Central Building in Pioneer Square, led to the conclusion that additional quality office space within walking distance of the downtown core was indeed feasible and that the Pioneer Building might be suitable for such an undertaking.

Creating a Restoration Team

In selecting an architect, careful consideration was given not only to design capability, but also to experience in dealing with the various city agencies involved in the development of historic buildings. The selection of Ralph D. Anderson and Partners as architects for the project was based to a large extent on the fact that the firm had just completed the Grand Central project in Occidental Park, and because much of the motivation and leadership for the rebirth of Pioneer Square was the result of Anderson's efforts.

In any proposed venture, the developer must acquire as much knowledge as possible to make an intelligent decision about whether or not to proceed. This is even more critical in working with an existing structure. Consequently, the Anderson firm was retained to prepare a set of "as built" drawings of the building, setting forth the existing structural conditions. This was an effort to eliminate as many unknowns as possible. Fortunately, the University of Washington had in its archives the original drawings prepared by Fisher in 1889. These drawings proved invaluable in preparing the "as built" plans.

On completion of this phase, the building was deemed basically sound structurally. Earthquakes during the years had caused little or no damage. The principal structural work required was the tying of floors to walls with steel strips to meet existing seismic codes.

The selection of a contractor with restoration experience is as important as choosing the architect. Several firms were interviewed, and based on its significant expertise in the rehabilitation of old buildings, the firm of Gall and Landau Construction Company was chosen to prepare budget estimates. This completed the team of developer, architect and contractor, who jointly developed the drawings and economic projections.

It had been determined that there was a sizable market for the intended use, that the building was structurally sound and the budget estimates were practical. Thus it was concluded that the restoration of the Pioneer Building was a feasible real estate venture.

Cooperation of Banks and City Departments

The banking community of Seattle had the vision to respond to the potential of the historic district and this project in particular. While no previous marketing effort had been made or leases signed, Great Western Union Federal Savings and Loan Association granted a long-term standby commitment for the project. With this commitment in hand, Seattle Trust and Savings Bank, which has a long history of supporting the restoration efforts of the area, provided the interim financing. Seattle Trust financed the Grand Central development and the more recent Maynard Building as well as several other projects in Pioneer Square.

A strong element in the success of this restoration was the cooperation of the various city departments having jurisdiction over the effort. The commitment of the mayor and city council and their determination to assure the preservation of Seattle's heritage mirrored the prevailing attitude found throughout all levels of the city government. The working relationship between the architect and the city building and fire departments resolved many of the technical, almost daily problems normally found in planning a project of this nature. City

Interior of Pioneer Building, Seattle. (Carleton Knight, III)

Conservator Arthur Skolnik assisted in the areas of special requirements and coordination, as well as dealing with potential tenants. The support of the Historic Review Board, charged with the responsibility of administering the ordinance, showed great sensitivity to the problems of the developer. The cooperation and assistance of all of those in authority was a prime factor in minimizing potential hazards.

The Construction Phase

We employed the "fast track" method of construction, a decision made in part during negotiations to accommodate the potential tenancy. Construction began in February 1974, and despite a six-week strike during the summer, the first occupancy was in November 1974. Fast tracking was more costly but these costs were offset by the early occupancy.

With the exception of tenants on the ground floor, the building had been vacant for the previous 25 years. As determined by the research, it was basically structurally sound but deteriorating rapidly. The roof was replaced, as well as some floor members that had rotted because of leakage. The three skylights received a new structure and wire glass. The elevator penthouse was enlarged and rebuilt, and a mechanical penthouse was added. In addition, several old penthouse structures were removed, creating an access for the required additional fire stair.

The sheet metal cornice was completely rebuilt and metal detail panels were substituted to match closely the original details. (The original Fisher drawings were often referred to for dimensions, etc.)

All the parapet walls were either lowered or tied back to the main roof structure, and bond beams were added. The exterior brick, terra-cotta and sandstone were sandblasted, tuck pointed and sealed. The wooden window sash and sheet metal bays were also sandblasted, patched and repainted.

Thirty percent of the exterior window glass was broken, including most of the curved glass at the bays. This was replaced. New leaders were added and new storefronts installed at the ground floor. All floors were renailed to the joists and then tied to the exterior walls; several floors were covered with plywood diaphragms for earthquake resistance.

In several areas, walls or floors were strengthened. All interior surfaces were covered with new plasterboard and painted. A suspended acoustical ceiling was installed in the office space to conceal the new mechanical ducts and electrical systems. All the wooden detail surfaces, including the cedar doors, were recycled by stripping and restaining or repainting. A sprinkler system was installed and fire stairs and standpipes added to insure that the building would be fire safe. The finished spaces had carpet, Levolor blinds and zone-controlled air-conditioning and heating.

Construction Costs

A problem area in restorations, as with any project, is

Entrance arch to Pioneer Building, Seattle. (Arthur M. Skolnik)

the possibility of construction cost overruns. The most carefully planned budget estimates are subject to revision, in part because of the inevitability of unexpected problems or delays during the course of construction. The Pioneer Building experienced cost overruns in this area, as well as additional expenses. The latter, however, created more income-producing space. Thus, while the total project cost was in excess of the original projections, the net cash flow was also greatly increased.

The building now contains 90,500 gross square feet and a net rentable area of 68,750 square feet, producing a 76 percent efficiency.

Restored buildings do place limitations on the flexibility of design. However, there are great economic benefits in beginning with an existing structure. The gross square foot construction cost of the Pioneer Building was less than $19 a square foot, compared to more than $30 for new construction of similar quality. In addition, the Pioneer's total project cost was $2.7 million, or just under $30 a square foot, compared to an estimated $40 for a new project commanding the same rental rates.

The initial economic projections for the restoration were based on the assumption that on completion 50 percent of the space already would have been leased. In fact, on completion 85 percent of the space was leased, a demonstration that the business community is most receptive to restoration projects.

The present enthusiasm for nostalgia is but a small factor in the success of older buildings. The prime considerations are the facts that recycling has proved to cost 25 percent less than new construction, and that a sophisticated tenancy is responding to the increased interest in our heritage.

In considering the restoration of historic buildings, the developer should recognize the increased risks involved. However, with the proper disciplines, planning and the cooperation of all participants, the rewards can be most gratifying.

Conclusion

As a developer whose experience for 27 years has been mainly with new construction projects, the effort of two major restorations has only strengthened my belief that, properly done, historic preservation can be not only profitable but extremely rewarding. We are presently planning two significant restorations in Pioneer Square and we are totally committed to the continued development of the area.

And what of the future? In these days of concern over the environment and natural resources, the cities of the United States are fortunate indeed to have available great numbers of old buildings suitable for restoration. The economics have been proven, and the public has not only demonstrated its acceptance but a high degree of enthusiasm for the recycling of these properties. There is a great opportunity to contribute to the revitalization of the cities by employing these available resources. Public officials, lenders, architects and developers have not only an opportunity but an obligation to preserve the national heritage.

Municipal Action to Encourage Private Investment in Preservation

Beveled glass detail of house in Lower Munger Place, Dallas, Tex. (Bob Stump)

Public Commitment and Private Investment in Preservation

WEIMING LU

Weiming Lu is assistant director for urban design, Department of Urban Planning, Dallas, and principal staff for the city Landmark Preservation Committee. He chairs the American Institute of Planners Urban Design Department and was formerly chief of environmental design for Minneapolis.

Municipalities are now showing a greater appreciation and commitment to the preservation of local resources than in past decades. However, despite this enthusiasm, preservation still remains relatively low in municipal priorities. Cities are more preoccupied with day-to-day operations than with the long-range activities of preserving their cultural and historical heritage. Thus there is much that can and should be done to help preservation receive its proper place in the cities' lists of priorities.

What should be done and which steps should be taken first are issues that remain undefined. Many areas must be explored; preservationists must carefully think about what they wish to accomplish and how they can achieve their goals. They must ask themselves, "Why Preservation?" and "For whom?"

First, preservationists must broaden their bases of support. The preservation movement today is primarily elite-oriented and directed toward aesthetics and architecture. Could preservationists not seek common ground with environmentalists? Are there shared concerns between the two groups? And why not seek support from the local chamber of commerce and from bankers, to make them aware of the great potential for job creation, business expansion and investment in the preservation program?

Should not labor unions be included in the movement? After all, architecture is conceived by designers but carried out by bricklayers, carpenters and other builders. A landmark is a testimony not only to the genius of the designers but also to the skill of thousands of anonymous construction workers. The Minneapolis Committee on Urban Environment made a special point of recognizing this fact when drafting the Minnesota enabling legislation on preservation. Later, the cooperation that the committee received from labor leaders was vital in getting support for the proposed legislation from the Minneapolis City Council.

In Dallas, the public and private sectors show growing interest in and increasing commitment toward preservation. The Landmark Committee and the Department of Urban Planning have adopted a deliberate strategy of involving a wide cross section of the community, including bankers, real estate brokers, appraisers, lawyers, architects and planners, in preservation activities. This approach has proven to be helpful.

Second, preservationists must gain better knowledge and insight concerning the municipal decision-making processes and must help the cities find sensitive and competent administrators for preservation programs, always remembering that sensitivity to beauty and history are as important as competence in administration and community relations. Municipal decision-making processes are increasingly complex, and it is difficult for the public to fully understand them. The movement to open records and to increase citizen participation may help make a city process more understandable and, one hopes, more responsive as well. However, personalities often affect that process profoundly. Meaningful citizen participation is closely related to the attitudes of individual administrators.

The success of any municipal preservation program depends on the commitment and innovativeness of the particular municipality and also on the interest and support of the community and the sensitivity, leadership and professional competence of local administrators and planners. Recently, the city of Seattle, with strong leadership from the city administration, has shown the kind of commitment and innovativeness that other areas should emulate. Furthermore, since the interest and support of a neighborhood often determine the success or failure of a preservation program, municipal planners must be selective in choosing the times and places to launch specific neighborhood efforts.

Third, in spite of legal and financial constraints, municipalities can take a number of actions to help encourage private investment in old buildings. For example, they can:

1. Survey landmarks and educate the public to their value
2. Initiate both local and state legislation to support preservation
3. Fund capital improvements
4. Establish nonprofit corporations or preservation foundations
5. Lease or acquire landmarks, and in some cases participate in ventures with private developers
6. Use incentive zoning and tax relief to promote preservation
7. Develop design guidelines and preservation criteria
8. Prepare comprehensive preservation plans.

All these efforts can be done with volunteer help; some others merely require municipal initiative. Still others would require financial commitment by the municipality. Each of these activities will have some impact on private investment in old buildings and neighborhoods. How well the activities are orches-

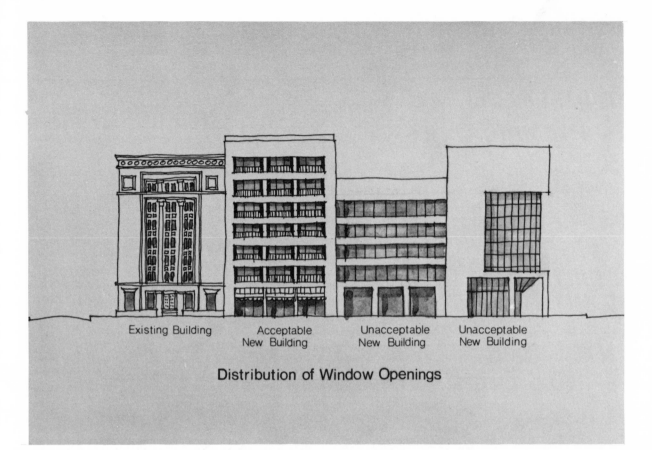

Existing Building   Acceptable New Building   Unacceptable New Building   Unacceptable New Building

Distribution of Window Openings

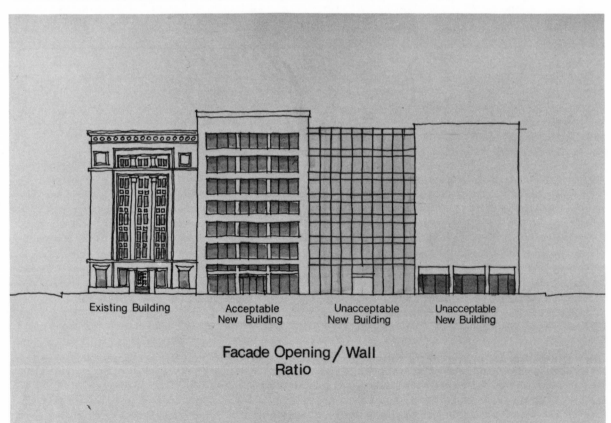

Existing Building   Acceptable New Building   Unacceptable New Building   Unacceptable New Building

Facade Opening / Wall Ratio

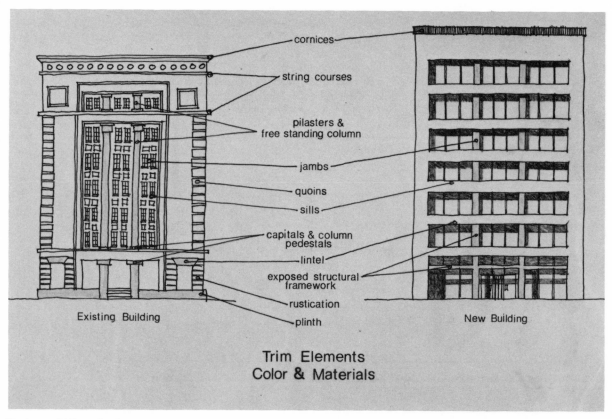

Design guidelines developed for the West End Historic District, Dallas. (Dallas Department of Urban Planning)

trated, funded and administered determines the success of the municipality.

Public Education

Municipalities can promote preservation by surveying the cultural fabric and educating the public to its value. If they succeed in projecting the importance of landmarks into the public consciousness, the chance for preserving those landmarks is greater. Unfortunately, the value of a landmark most often is not known or understood by the general public.

Survey techniques will differ with the purposes of each survey and the city being studied. The surveys themselves will vary from complex, systematic efforts, such as those done in Providence, R.I., and the Vieux Carré in New Orleans, to the simpler type done in Minneapolis and Dallas. A simple survey may include merely an architectural history of the city, a set of broadly defined selection criteria and a selected list of landmarks with concise commentary on their significance. However, there must be an understanding of the cultural and architectural history of the city, along with careful research and documentation. The survey should include not merely good but inspiring photographs done by competent photographers to bring out the beauty and significance of the landmarks.

The Minneapolis landmark survey was successfully used in work with the Minnesota Assembly to get the

Municipal Heritage Commission Bill passed in 1971. Part of the survey report has since been included in a popular guide to the Twin Cities area. In Dallas, an exhibit entitled "Options for Tomorrow's Cities" was developed in 1972 with sponsorship of the Dallas Museum of Fine Arts. The exhibit is intended to make the public more aware of preservation and to increase public sensitivity to the design that ultimately determines the quality of the environment.

At the national level, the efforts of the National Endowment for the Arts (NEA) helped identify the importance of railroad stations as a cultural resource and a part of the American architectural heritage. As a result, more municipalities are looking at their own stations and finding ways to save these endangered relics of the past. In fact, Congress amended the Amtrak Act in 1974 to provide opportunities for cities to work with NEA and the U.S. Department of Transportation to recycle and protect stations. Now funds are being sought to provide incentives for such preservation efforts. This federal activity illustrates well that when issues are injected into the stream of public consciousness, there is a better chance for positive action. Could not preservationists launch more concerted similar efforts at the local as well as the national level?

Legislation

Municipalities can initiate action for the adoption of

preservation legislation at the state level and preservation ordinances at the local level. A city with such legal authority can designate buildings or districts as landmarks and can protect them under the preservation ordinance. This can be part of a zoning ordinance or a separate provision, but it always derives from the municipal police power, in the interest of safety, health and the general welfare. When the preservation and zoning ordinances are in concert with each other, they often provide added protection to an area, and sometimes this is precisely the kind of security needed to attract private investment.

The Swiss Avenue Historic District in Dallas provides one example of municipal incentive and citizen involvement.* This area, developed between 1905 and 1925, was the home of many prominent Dallas citizens. It embodies the feeling and character of the era in a somewhat eclectic but grand architectural style unified by regular spacing and setbacks along a wide, tree-lined parkway.

The setting, still physically intact, was the victim of slow deterioration. Apartments and commercial establishments had intruded on many of the surrounding blocks. The city was particularly interested in this historic street because of the opportunity to conserve and revitalize a whole inner-city neighborhood.

The preservation concept did not receive overwhelming support from residents when the city began its efforts in the spring of 1972. There was some opposition because preservation would eliminate the chance for some owners to "capitalize their investment." Others were opposed merely because they were fearful of any new ordinance.

Fortunately, the supporters of the preservation proposal were well organized. In January 1973 they incorporated as the Historic Preservation League and continued to help the city planning staff explain the proposal to area residents. The same month, the league obtained a $500 matching grant from the National Trust Consultant Service Grant Program. The grant was used to employ an architectural historian to prepare a history of Swiss Avenue architecture, and the city staff used the study and the city land use and visual form surveys as the basis for an area ordinance.

After 18 months of work by the city planning staff and the Historic Preservation League, most residents understood the value of preservation, and support for the proposal was stronger. By early 1973 the city staff believed the area was ready to be designated.

Even before the Swiss Avenue survey, in the summer of 1971, the city launched an effort to research Texas state law and draft a preservation ordinance for Dallas. That work was fairly complete by 1972, but the planning staff waited until new preservation constituents were assured before presenting the ordinance for the city council decision. In March 1973 the council approved the ordinance with the support of many civic organizations and preservation interests.

No sooner was work fully under way on Swiss Avenue than the city received a strong challenge. A developer wanted to build a highrise apartment on the street before the designation of the area as a historic district. At the recommendation of the planning staff and the urging of neighborhood residents, the city council took a strong stand by declaring a moratorium on the issuance of all building permits on the avenue until designation could be considered. This prompted the developer to sue the city in March 1973, asking that a permit be issued. The lower court sustained the developer two months later, but the city appealed the decision. Meanwhile, Swiss Avenue was designated a landmark district in September, an action that further strengthened the city case.

The city won the appeal in February 1974. The developer then appealed to the Texas Supreme Court, which refused to hear the case. Thus, the decision of the Court of Appeals was upheld in March 1974 (see J. *Roger Crownrich* vs. *City of Dallas*, 73-2494-J.191 District Court 506 S.W. Reporter, 2nd, p. 654). The case affirmed the right of Texas cities to zone for historic preservation and to protect areas under existing zoning until permanent designation can be achieved. The strong stand taken by the city council kept the Swiss Avenue Historic District from being stillborn.

During the time that Swiss Avenue was being surveyed and the preservation ordinance was being drafted, the area received much favorable publicity. After the area was designated, it was under the protection of the landmark ordinance. A local bank committed $1 million for purchase and repair loans to residents of the area. The Historic Preservation League continued to encourage home improvements and spent $2,400 for real estate advertising, which helped continue the favorable publicity. The designation, the bank loan and the advertising effort—perhaps even the lawsuit—contributed to turning this area around dramatically. It is estimated that $750,000 has been invested in purchase and renovation in the historic district since designation. Property values have doubled and in some cases tripled during this period. In fact, the positive influence of the landmark designation has extended far beyond the district boundary, and there is a general upgrading of the adjoining areas as well.

An effective ordinance depends on good legal draftsmanship. Close collaboration between city planners and city attorneys from the beginning determines the result of such an effort. Planners also should be fully aware of the economic impacts of the proposed legislation and should be certain that the recommended ordinance is realistic. During the preparation for the West End Historic District preservation ordinance, a few property owners challenged its economic feasibility. Steps were taken to analyze the economic impacts. The planning staff attempted to approach the problem from the standpoint of the developer. Designs for selected

---

*Citizen activity is described in detail in *The Making of a Historic District: Swiss Avenue, Dallas, Texas,* by Lyn Dunsavage and Virginia Talkington (Washington, D.C.: Preservation Press, National Trust for Historic Preservation, 1975).—ed.

Dr. R. W. Baird House *in Swiss Avenue Historic District, Dallas (top). Classical porch details enrich the E. R. Brown House on Swiss Avenue. (Bob Stump)*

buildings were prepared; experienced developers were consulted; pro forma financial statements were written.

Those working on preservation ordinances must also accept the fact that the city does not own the land in the district. It can regulate under general zoning provisions but cannot mandate. For example, a developer's specific uses or design can dictate a certain kind of tenant mix in a commercial development; the city cannot and should not do the same for privately owned land. Thus there is a difference in the roles of the two. Only when the city and the private sector work closely together can preservationists hope to achieve the best results.

Capital Improvements

Legislative action alone may not be adequate. Capital improvements by the municipality often are needed to complement the preservation ordinance and make things happen. In Pioneer Square in Seattle, for example, $2.1 million of public investment has attracted $10 million in private investment. In Dallas, the program for the warehouse district includes a preservation ordinance, a $6 million development plan and an implementation program. Both the plan and the program are essential to the success of the preservation ordinance.*

The concept of capital improvement is broad. It may

*In December 1975 Dallas voters approved the first phase of funding in a special bond election.—ed.

COUNTY COURTHOUSE *in West End Historic District, Dallas. (Dallas Department of Urban Planning)*

include lighting and landscaping public areas, provision of adequate parking, extension of transit services and building of pedestrian ways. In the past, municipal bonds, benefit assessments and urban renewal grants were often used as the source for financing these improvements. Today, renewal grants are replaced by revenue sharing. In addition, an increasing number of municipalities are exploring such other means as tax increment financing to finance the needed improvements.

Leasing and Acquisition

Municipal leasing or acquisition is sometimes the only way to save a landmark. Union Terminal at the edge of downtown Dallas was built in 1916. By 1969 it had fallen into disuse. The only way to save the building was through public acquisition. Fortunately, in 1972 a major bond program was passed, and the city was able to use $5.3 million from that program to acquire the terminal.

The site later was used as the city share of a $210 million joint venture with private interests for revitalizing that section of the downtown area.

In another case, an old East Dallas library building that had been sold some years earlier to a private property owner was to be torn down to make room for a pizza parlor. While there was considerable community sentiment for saving the library, no buyer was willing to preserve the building. A group of business people formed a development corporation and purchased the library. At the urging of local preservation groups, the city leased half of the building for a neighborhood rehabilitation office and it was saved.

Joint Ventures

Municipalities can initiate joint ventures with private developers. Such partnerships can find new economic life for landmarks and revitalize downtown and inner-city areas. For example, in the acquisition of the Union

Terminal Building in Dallas, the city also acquired the 28-acre site. With the approval of the city council and the leadership of the city manager, the city was able to work out the previously mentioned joint venture with a developer. The result is a major downtown renewal project including a hotel with 1,000 rooms and a 50-story tower; a 10-acre downtown park, which provides a setting for medium-rise buildings; a sports arena or performing arts center; housing; a multimode transportation center, which will accommodate the immediate needs of buses and Amtrak as well as long-range needs for regional and local mass transit; and 2,000 parking spaces with buses connecting to the heart of downtown.

In this manner, not only will the landmark building be preserved but an undeveloped part of downtown Dallas will be revitalized. The first phase of construction will create jobs for 425 persons and an estimated payroll of $20 million. When completed, the Hyatt Regency Hotel will provide more than 500 jobs and an estimated annual payroll of $3.4 million. When all phases are completed, the project probably will have cost in excess of $210 million.

Under home rule and the council-manager form of government, Dallas has a certain flexibility in developing strategies for renewing the inner city. One program, developed under the leadership of the city manager, is designed to encourage private development of new housing in the center city. Under this program, the city will work with developers to provide an approved plan for high-risk inner-city areas and will commit itself to such actions as making capital improvements and re-routing utilities in accordance with the plan. The city council also has established a $10 million fund from which the city, at the developer's option, will buy back the property of an approved project for a specified price not exceeding a predetermined maximum. In this way, developers are assured of recovering at least part of their investment should the project run into financial difficulty. In time it is hoped that the fund will have great impact on the conservation of inner-city neighborhoods. This would help the city maintain areas that could not be protected under historical designation.

Incentive Zoning

Municipalities can also use incentive zoning as a way to promote preservation. Programs might include transfer of development rights, bonuses for certain kinds of land uses to help preserve particular districts (e.g., theaters in Time Square) or bonuses for certain kinds of public amenities (plazas, pedestrian ways, etc.). However, the effectiveness of these incentives is largely determined by the base zoning by which a particular district is being regulated. Frequently, permissive and unrealistic overzoning has nullified the possible positive effects of these incentives, leaving little chance to achieve the desired amenities (e.g., downtown Atlanta has an allowable FAR, or floor area ratio, of 20, while downtown Richmond, Va., has an FAR of 18.5).

Furthermore, there is evidence that in many cases,

incentives have been misused and have worked to the excessive advantage of developers. In such cases, even when the municipalities gain certain amenities, the burden of added traffic congestion and other problems may far outweigh the benefits. In many cities, the immediate strategy should center on finding ways to reduce the base zoning, rather than on finding a new kind of incentive zoning.

In Dallas, on the recommendation of the landmark committee and planning commission, the city council recently rezoned 55 acres of the downtown from FAR 20 to FAR 8 in conjunction with historic district designation. Thus the zoning will be more in line with the actual market situation. This action also helps protect and enhance the historical character of the district and should attract new investment into the area. By an ordinance that will be effective in two years, the Los Angeles city council recently rezoned all the downtown area within the city freeway loop from FAR 6 to FAR 11.

Tax Relief

Tax relief can also offer an incentive for preservation. However, in many cases it is difficult to obtain tax relief for landmark property owners because state laws and city charters will not allow such relief. In Texas a proposed amendment to the state constitution, if approved by voters in November 1975, will provide the basis for municipalities to act. In the last session, a bill passed by the legislature authorized state and municipal governments to enact ordinances granting tax relief to owners of landmark properties, pending passage of this amendment.*

It should be noted that in some cases tax relief should not be used to encourage development of a district. In fact, the low taxes in some downtown or inner-city areas keep the owners from doing something about their properties, and they choose to let these properties deteriorate. Low taxes, among other factors, allow the owners to wait for the big windfall, encouraging their often unrealistic dreams. In such cases, preservationists should ask for more equitable taxation, which would encourage owners to do something with their properties.

Developing Guidelines and Criteria

Municipalities can develop design guidelines and preservation criteria to insure that the character of an individual landmark or district is protected. At the same time, new buildings that complement the existing ones may be added to an area and individual landmarks can be renovated without destroying their integrity. Design guidelines must be flexible enough to permit creative designers to use their imagination. The preservation criteria should also be tailored to the specific qualities of the landmark or district. In turn, the successful design

*Unfortunately, the amendment was not approved by Texas voters.—ed.

WEST END HISTORIC DISTRICT, *Dallas. (Dallas Department of Urban Planning)*

review process can help save and, in some cases, enhance landmarks. Effectiveness of the design guidelines depends on a carefully structured process, which should foster creative dialogue between owners, architects and the landmark committee.

A few examples from the experience in Dallas are illustrative. In the case of Trinity Methodist Church, the Dallas planning staff was not interested in freezing every element of the design. Rather, the basic spirit of the architecture was described—the massing created by the sanctuary and the steeples, the Sullivanesque decoration, the stained glass windows. The staff developed a set of guidelines to protect these qualities and to make certain any renovation or addition would be compatible. It was hoped that this would discourage incompatible design, even though it could not assure excellence. The latter depends on the competence and talent of the architect commissioned to do the work.

The Swiss Avenue Historic District, developed to complement the specified land use and development standards (e.g., setback and building coverage), has 12 preservation criteria in four sensitive areas of concern: (1) qualities of the block, (2) building form, (3) building

treatment and (4) facade accentuation. For a new building to qualify, the design must meet a specified number of the 12 criteria, with minimums in each of the four areas of concern.

Knowing the pitfalls of design review, the city staff and landmarks committee use these criteria with extreme care and sensitivity. Thus far, they have worked rather well, but experience also has shown that a few of the criteria should be better defined and the staff will try to incorporate the necessary changes in future amendments to the ordinance. Furthermore, some neighborhood leaders, having experienced the success of the district, now want more stringent standards. Whether it is advisable to make any major amendment to the present ordinance remains to be determined. In any amendment, it is important that a certain degree of design flexibility be maintained while the overall character of the area is protected. The challenge here is that, through city initiatives and neighborhood cooperation, a balance must be achieved between design compatibility and diversity.

The West End Historic District Ordinance was developed to allow much greater diversity in design than that of Swiss Avenue. More than 20 design guidelines were reviewed, and out of them a simpler set was selected. These relate to materials, colors, facade openings, window setbacks, wall and opening ratios and height limits. It is believed that these guidelines can help preserve the design qualities of the area, and it is the ambience these qualities create that will determine whether the preservation and revitalization effort will be successful.*

In regard to the new civic center, the planning staff took the initiative and prepared guidelines tying the new project to the expansion of the Federal Reserve Bank, a building under landmark consideration. Here the city planning staff set up a basic framework for the design of the civic space and formulated ground rules for achieving compatibility between buildings—e.g., maintaining a common cornice height and encouraging continuity of building lines, yet allowing diversity in other elements of design and encouraging multiple uses in these public buildings. Thus far, it is encouraging to note that 90 percent of the guidelines have been adopted by the architect in preliminary design for the expansion.

Architectural Excellence

Municipalities can strive for excellence in municipal architecture, and some city buildings may become landmarks of the future. Only when each generation produces its best in architecture can one hope to build a living city, where excellence in design provides continuity through time, each generation encouraging the next. At the same time, buildings should be part of a well-thought-out urban design framework. Otherwise,

*In October 1975 the Dallas city council approved the historic district designation of 55 acres in the West End.—ed.

UNION TERMINAL BUILDING, *Dallas. (Dallas Department of Urban Planning)*

the result will be the construction of sculpture gardens rather than a cohesive design.

Change and continuity must be properly balanced in civic design. The Piazza San Marco in Venice results from 500 years of continuous civic design effort; even though there are diverse architectural expressions, together they form a cohesive whole. Kenzo Tange's Olympic Stadium in Tokyo offers a contemporary building in the traditional Japanese spirit.

Knowledge of the Neighborhood

Municipalities should learn more about their neighborhoods and the cultural and social fabric of which individual landmarks or landmark districts are a part. Cities must broaden their efforts; rather than saving a few individual landmark buildings, they should concern themselves with surrounding districts and entire neighborhoods. For example, the Dallas visual form survey, which exhibits a concern for whole neighborhoods throughout the city, was conducted at the same time as the landmark survey; each complements the other. The visual form survey gives a picture of the city buildings, spaces, roads and trees. It shows their condition and their relationship to one another—how they combine to form a neighborhood environment. This survey describes the context of a historic district or individual landmark. The landmark survey, on the other hand, gives the history of cultural and architectural development in the city.

Overall Plans and Strategies

With an understanding of landmark resources, neighborhood patterns, legal constraints and potentialities and financial feasibility, municipalities can de-velop an overall preservation plan to save landmarks as well as conserve inner-city neighborhoods. Such a plan should not only include general goals and policies, but also some achievable programs and projects that can help carry out the plan.

In conjunction with plans, municipalities must develop overall implementation strategies for neighborhood conservation, matching different facets of the program to get maximum effect. In Dallas the preservation plan is tied to the comprehensive planning program. The city staff strives to develop conservation strategies in concert with the city development process.

Minority and Ethnic Groups

Municipalities can and should work with minority groups to help understand and preserve their cultural patterns. Many ethnic neighborhoods have long since been destroyed. Little Mexicos, Little Italys and Chinatowns have been gradually wiped out by change, neglect, destruction and insensitive addition. All are endangered species. The interest here is not to perpetuate ghettos but to develop open neighborhoods where every group is free to move in or out of the area. At the same time, the unique identity and individuality of each area must be preserved.

The need of minorities to have their own identities in the city must be recognized, for through diversity a richer environment can be built. The Dallas activity in Little Mexico is a good example. After working with the community residents for a year, the city planning staff discovered the residents' strong desire for a cultural identity. One of the first things the staff did was work with the neighborhood on a focal point in the community, an ethnic-oriented park where the Cinco de Mayo festival is celebrated annually. A user design team was organized, and the city provided technical assistance to team members while they formulated their ideas for the park.

Among the many things this team suggested was a plaza with a "kiosko," or small shelter. The city staff helped them convey these ideas to the decision makers. They have been well received and the program is part of a proposed bond issue.*

Work Remaining

While the preservation movement has broadened and municipal commitment to preservation has increased during the past decade, much remains to be done:

The concept of preservation must be broadened to become a concept of conservation. This depends not merely on a new use of words but on an actual change in attitude, approach and organization for conservation activities. Preservationists must no longer take the narrow view of preservation. They must not concentrate their entire efforts on saving a few landmarks but rather on saving neighborhoods, the inner city, the downtown. They must not be elite oriented but must seek a much broader base of support. Uniting with neighborhood improvement associations, chambers of commerce, environmental groups, the labor movement, bankers, professional societies and others should be their task.

To be effective, the preservation effort should be coordinated with a comprehensive planning and urban design program. When this is achieved, preservation activities can take full advantage of the city development process. For example, parks may provide settings for distinctive landmarks, and capital improvement may be coordinated with a neighborhood conservation program. A land use plan may be better coordinated with a preservation plan, and a transportation plan would pay more attention to landmarks. Neighborhood beautification may go hand in hand with historic district preservation. With this kind of setting, there will be more incentives for private investment in old buildings and neighborhoods.

In Dallas, the preservation staff is part of the urban design staff in the city planning department. This organization permits effective coordination with other planning programs and results in an interdisciplinary staff for the preservation effort. At present, the Dallas preservation program is staffed by one full-time planner but is backed by architects, urban and graphic designers and behavioral scientists. The planning department is also constantly working with the city attorney and the building inspection and parks departments.

Attracting private investment remains the key to the success of any preservation program. Generally, 90 percent of all urban investment is from the private sector. Only when public strategy is fully in concert with private investment can preservationists hope that more landmarks will be preserved and more buildings recycled. Government simply does not have the resources to do it alone.

This paper has discussed a number of possible public actions. Just how they may be made to work with private efforts to get maximum effect is not easy to suggest. It will depend on the situation in each municipality, and sometimes different districts of a city may require different strategies. Municipal regulation, incentives, taxation and financing policies all have a profound effect on private investment. Persuasion and public education should not be left out either, for they can be powerful tools. Above all, preservationists must find ways to project the value of landmarks into the public consciousness. Only then is there a chance for greater public commitment and private investment in preservation.

*This program was included in the bond issue approved by voters in December 1975.—ed.

Zoning:
A Neglected Tool
for Preservation

ALEXANDER COOPER, AIA

Alexander Cooper, AIA, an architect and planner, is a member of the New York City Planning Commission and director of the Graduate Program for Urban Design, Columbia University Graduate School of Architecture and Planning. He has served as director of the New York City Planning Department Urban Design Group and executive director of the Mayor's Urban Design Council.

It would be less than forthright not to share an apprehension about the title "Municipal Action to Encourage Private Investment in Preservation." It would be relatively easy to achieve a consensus in many groups that the most positive municipal action to encourage private investment would be to eliminate government action. The collective wisdom, bred from aggregated and aggravated experience, would reveal that government involvement usually means more headache, more time and more expense to the private investor.

It is arguable, however, that in the arena of preservation, the proceedings between government and private investors need not be adversary. This is so for two reasons. First, the preservation of old buildings can serve a major political objective of those in government—namely, neighborhood stability. This fact, coupled with economic conditions favoring preservation over new development, augurs well for cooperation.

Second, the investor in old buildings appears to be a different breed from the typical developer. Behind the compulsory rhetoric of cost-benefit jargon (such terms as *increased payrolls, taxes* and *tourist dollars*) is a deep commitment to social and cultural values that preservationists, of necessity, are reluctant to verbalize.

The economic focus of the conference correctly places preservation in the trenches with the conventional "hard-nose" issues, with which it competes for precious government priority. Yet preservation is more than an economic issue, and within the majority of U.S. communities there is a political constituency for its values. Furthermore, even within the hallowed halls of government there are people who share those values. Thus the idea that government can encourage private investment in preservation cannot be ruled out.

Designation Standards

At the outset, this fundamental question should be raised: What is worth preserving? Because municipalities must establish "legitimate public purpose" as a precondition to action, they must answer this question. If buildings are worth preserving (and there appears to be agreement on that), what about trees, rocks, views, open spaces, streets, storefronts or marketplaces? The question is not meant to be unnecessarily philosophical or contrary, but simply to point out that there is no approved set of values to guide municipalities in prescribing legitimacy.

National legislation and subsequent local ordinances have set forth standards for the designation of individual buildings and historic districts. The procedures are conspicuously general and intentionally vague. As in most good legislation, there is considerable latitude for political activity. The designation criteria, on the other hand, are far more specific. The principal requirement is one of "significance," and the dominant categories of significance are: (1) architectural, e.g., an example of a particular type of building design; (2) historical, e.g., relating to certain people or events; and (3) group value, e.g., a major element in a historic district.

By utilizing narrow criteria, the legislation limits the attention of municipalities primarily to those areas that can comply with the findings of significance. Thus a typical city may have only one or two eligible districts, but each city has many neighborhoods that are worthy of being preserved. Although they may not be distinguished by famous residents or by a consistently high quality of architectural excellence, these areas may be unique, remarkable or otherwise vital to the proper functioning of the city. These "less-than-historic" neighborhoods meet the dual test of public purpose and significance and therefore should command the attention of municipal action.

Municipal Actions

A review of the range of municipal actions available reveals that cities can designate areas, condemn land, buy buildings, set priorities, allocate resources and provide services. In the area of financing, a municipality can provide mortgage money, mortgage insurance and tax abatement and can otherwise lend its credit for preservation purposes. It can prohibit demolition or—as all preservationists know—it can demolish.

All these measures have been taken, often in the name of preservation. However, rather than focusing on such actions, these remarks will deal with a neglected government action that dramatically affects preservation—namely, zoning.

The Range of Zoning Techniques

There are two reasons for the focus on zoning. First, New York City has been consistently innovative in the field of zoning technology, stretching to, and occasionally beyond, the courts' expanding definition of public welfare. Second, and more important, zoning confers value. Therefore, a discussion on the economics of preservation must deal with the potential value of a property, as opposed to its present value. This issue is the historic flashpoint in preservation disputes and litigation.

An intriguing definition describes "units of fantasy" as "the empty space between existing buildings and the contours of the zoning envelope." This is a rather Keatsian description of a brutal and bloody battleground. But such fantasy is the root cause of much municipal hesitation regarding preservation efforts. The unrealistic expectations of most property owners set them, often unwittingly, against the one activity that might enhance the value of their property—downzoning. Zoning down to reality is the most immediate, if slightly Draconian, measure available to municipalities.

Fortunately, downzoning is not the only strategy. New York City has more commonly zoned upward, increasing incentives to achieve preservation objectives. It also has used the device of the special zoning district, of which there are 24 in the city; this technique is adaptable to most situations. The qualifying statement here is that zoning is by and large a stepchild of development. Where there is no development, zoning is an unused tool.

The early efforts in special district zoning were not related to preservation, but rather to development. Where major activity is likely to occur, special districts can guide that development, improve circulation and assure appropriate public amenities. Prominent examples are Lincoln Center, downtown Brooklyn and the United Nations development districts. Lower Manhattan itself is blanketed by three special districts: Manhattan Landing on the East River, Greenwich Street and Battery Park City on the Hudson River.

More recently, however, special districts have been used to reinforce those less-than-historic elements of city life. New York City's effort has been directed to preservation in four categories: retail-commercial uses, physical characteristics, mixed-use areas and natural environment.

In the retail-commercial category, it was determined that the public interest was served by preserving the legitimate theater district, the quality of retail facilities on Fifth Avenue, the ethnic flavor of the shopping in the predominantly German area of Yorkville and the unique waterfront commercial fishing activity of Sheepshead Bay in Brooklyn. In all these areas, existing uses are strengthened and compatible development is encouraged.

The physical character of an area has also received attention. For instance, the Special Park Improvement District was created to preserve Fifth and Park avenues. Here the zoning stipulates that developers may build up to 20 percent additional floor areas in their projects if they contribute to an annual improvement fund for the maintenance of nearby Central Park.

Madison Avenue also is subject to a preservation district, whereby height is limited, continuous ground-floor retail activity is required and recreation areas are provided on the roofs. The Atlantic Avenue shopping strip in Brooklyn and such internationally recognized examples of planned communities as Sunnyside Gardens and Forest Hills Gardens will also be preserved through zoning.

One of the most significant and innovative districts in New York City is the South Street Seaport, an area with six blocks of 18th-century buildings. (In this case, the buildings in the area happen to be historic.) The low scale will be preserved by transferring development rights to specified neighboring sites. The city induced a consortium of banks that held mortgages within the area to release those mortgages and accept as payment the unused development rights of the low buildings—the units of fantasy referred to earlier.

Mixed-use areas, where manufacturing and housing have coexisted without intolerable friction, have also received special zoning treatment. The City Planning Commission selectively mapped the Northside and Coney Island areas of Brooklyn as Residential (Manufacturing) where residence predominates and Manufacturing (Residential) where industry predominates, to allow controlled expansion of either where such uses can grow without conflict. By this technique, buildings that previously were illegal were made legal, thereby stimulating banking interest and participation in those areas.

Finally, the natural environment is not neglected. Areas of uncommon natural beauty, such as the Staten Island Greenbelt, and scenic views, such as the lower Manhattan skyline as seen from the Brooklyn Promenade, will also be preserved.

Clearly, the range of urban experiences that are worth preserving is broad. Zoning can be a remarkably flexible tool to assist that effort—not only to prevent undesirable development but also to promote positive activity.

Successful Zoning Examples

Two illustrations will show what zoning can accomplish. The SoHo area of Manhattan is a light manufacturing district where residences were not permitted. Artists began moving into vacated loft space because of the low rents. Such illegal residency became widespread, and pressure was brought on the City Planning Commission to permit occupancy for joint living and work purposes. In an attempt to balance needs, the commission retained the underlying manufacturing zone and simply created a new permissible use, Joint Living/Work Quarters for Artists. Restrictions were applied; e.g., eligibility was limited to properties of less than 3,600 square feet.

This was done in 1970. The results are dramatic. Industrial rents have stayed the same (approximately $1.55 a square foot), and manufacturing jobs have decreased far less than the citywide average. Building sales in the area also reveal increased value. In 1970, 30 buildings were sold at an average of $6.42 a square foot. In 1974, 18 buildings changed owners at an average price of $9.78 a square foot, a 52 percent increase. In the four years since the zoning action, there have been 25 new art galleries, 20 retail stores and 5 restaurants added to the area, and not a single demolition. All this has been accomplished with a three-sentence change to the zoning resolution.

Clearly, a formerly uneconomic area has been transformed into a highly productive economic asset. Owners are staying, buildings are being rehabilitated and the banks are optimistic. The artists are now demanding an extension of the boundaries and the exclusion of nonartists (the success of their venture has attracted too much attention and too many people). To accomplish this, art was rationalized as being a light manufacturing industry.

The second illustration is the Clinton Preservation District. In this case, the government incurred an obligation to the community by placing the Convention Center there. The special district zoning that followed is the clearest example of coupling preservation with redevelopment by a redistribution of development rights.

Clinton is a predominantly low-income area and is physically undistinguished; the zoning solution is tailored to these conditions. The special district maps a preservation core surrounded by a perimeter area, where redevelopment is directed. In the preservation area, demolition for other than unsafe buildings is prohibited. New construction is limited to the scale of surrounding buildings.

In the perimeter area, a floor area bonus is offered to the developer who will rehabilitate tenement buildings, at subsidized rents, within the preservation core. The resultant savings in land cost per room that a developer achieves with a 20 percent increase in buildable floor area is applied to preserving the existing housing stock. For example, on a 25,000-square-foot lot, the size of the new building increases from 830 rooms to 1,000 rooms. This results in an equivalent savings in land cost of $385,000.

To rehabilitate a tenement where land cost is $40 per square foot and rehabilitation cost is $15,000 per apartment would cost approximately $190,000 for a building with 15 apartments. Consequently, a new building in the perimeter zone will restore two buildings in the preservation area. From the community's point of view this is a reasonable trade-off; from the city's point of view, a desirable public benefit; from the developer's point of view, a stern but equitable diminution of the additional value created by the new Convention Center.

Government Involvement

Government can create a favorable investment climate. It can do so either by directly participating in brick-and-mortar activity or by indirectly removing handicaps it has often itself created. Basically, this is a two-tiered approach by municipal government to preserving old buildings: on the one hand, historical designation for those districts and buildings that qualify; on the other hand, zoning classification for those less-than-historic districts that merit municipal attention. In exercising a zoning strategy, care must be taken that it not be applied either abstractly or uniformly. In order to be effective, the unit of zoning control must be extended from a single zoning lot to an entire area.

Finally, a policy of the New York City Planning Commission provides an appropriate conclusion. The commission does not stand behind a monolithic status quo. Rather, it supports gradual change that preserves the sanctity of buildings, of neighborhoods and of people.

LADY ADAMS' COMPANY AND HOWARD HOUSE *in Old Sacramento, Calif. (David Kahl)*.

Tax Increment Financing: A Key Preservation Tool

WILLIAM G. SELINE

William G. Seline is executive director, Housing and Redevelopment Agency, Sacramento, Calif. An architect and planner, he has worked with a variety of housing and planning agencies.

Most people working in preservation know that after all the conversation about how a building should be saved or a project restored, the most difficult question is how to finance the effort. Many municipal actions can be taken to encourage private investment in historic preservation projects, but the one above all others is tax increment or tax allocation financing. Sacramento is one of the few cities that is successfully using this tool for preserving historic areas.

Tax increment financing is a way to let the historic area pay for itself with no impact on the already strained budgets of local governments. The Sacramento Redevelopment and Housing Agency has $20 million in tax increment money ready when and where the agency would like to use it. This process does not cost the city government anything; it has in fact saved money for the city, the county and the schools.

Every state should pass state enabling legislation to use tax increment financing for preservation. A number of states already have such enabling legislation and have in fact used tax increment financing for various kinds of projects. California and Oregon are two notable examples, with Sacramento being the first city in the nation to use this financing method.

How Tax Increment Financing Works

The enabling legislation for tax increment financing is related to the redevelopment of declining areas in general, but for the purpose of this paper it will be described specifically in terms of historic preservation projects.

Historic areas may be in decline from an assessed value standpoint, so that the schools and the city and county taxing bodies receive less money each year. Buildings are crumbling, crime rates are often going up and public obligations such as lighting and police and fire protection are increasing costs.

This is how the tax increment can work in restoring such a neighborhood: The city determines the project area to be restored and freezes its tax base. From then until the project is completed, the taxing bodies continue to receive only the same low revenues as before. As investment and improvement take place in the area, there is an increased property valuation or increment above the frozen level. However, that increment is allocated to a special fund of the local redevelopment agency to be used for reinvestment back into the area.

In addition to the increment itself, the sale of bonds secured by the increment (tax allocation bonds) can pay for projects with no increase in taxes and no use of city revenue. Thus there are two ways to generate money through the tax increment process.

One caution about this process is that restoring a single structure is more difficult than improving a number of buildings in a larger area. Second, there must be some initial development in the area to start the tax increment process. In other words, a priming of the pump has to take place. This is not always a problem, however, since municipal governments can often encourage private investment or can apply for federal aid, such as community development revenue sharing money.

Most of the criticism of tax increment financing stems from a lack of understanding. This process has proven itself repeatedly in California since 1956, when Sacramento issued its first tax increment bonds.

The Old Sacramento Project

A description of how the tax increment process relates to Old Sacramento, the city's major historic preservation effort, will be illustrative. Old Sacramento is a 16-acre area of 120 buildings of the 1840 gold rush era. Stretching along the Sacramento River, it was the western terminus of the Pony Express.

The area had become a slum of the worst kind. The taxing bodies were receiving approximately $500,000 a year, with the prospect of a steady decline. Now the assessed valuation is $8 million, and the effect is money to do whatever needs to be done in Old Sacramento. In addition, this $30 million restoration project is expected to draw a minimum of 2.5 million tourists a year with a spending range of $20 million.

The Old Sacramento buildings are brick for the most part, and two or three stories tall. Upper floors are office space; lower floors and basements house retail shops, restaurants and other commercial ventures.

In another phase of this project, a parking garage is being constructed with tax allocation bonds. Parking garages are expensive and private investment groups would rather stay away from the risk. Also, in the case of Old Sacramento, the city wanted to retain management of the parking garage to insure that the public is not taken advantage of by parking prices.

Other parking facilities are being provided through tax increment financing on the periphery points of the project, since cars will not be allowed into Old Sacramento. Tax increment money will also be spent for minibuses to Old Sacramento and for historic horse-drawn street cars within the project area.

Other Aid to Private Investors

The state and the city parks departments have also

THE MORSE BUILDING *before (top) and after restoration.*
(Sacramento Housing and Redevelopment Agency)

been involved in the Old Sacramento effort. Landscape work is paid for with tax increment money, and the parks employees design and supervise the landscape work. Further, the developers are notified that after the Old Sacramento project is completed the park will be turned over to the state or city parks department. Private investors seem to feel a certain amount of security knowing that part of all of the project will eventually be operated by a parks department.

Other action has been taken in Sacramento to support private investors. This involved public restrooms, which are often neglected or put off until last in historical projects (especially when private investors are attempting to handle the total project). In Old Sacramento there were some nonprofit groups of private investors who found that historical restoration was more difficult than they first envisioned. Because of situations (not the fault of the redevelopers) involving structural collapses, these groups found themselves in financial difficulty. One of the ways that the Housing and Redevelopment Agency helped was to purchase restroom easement rights in the buildings. It was less expensive for the municipality to buy the easement than for the develop-

ers to build new facilities. This saved the day for the investors and gave them the feeling that municipal action would be taken to insure the most successful project possible.

Another aid to investors is the federal section 312 loan program of the U.S. Department of Housing and Urban Development. Old Sacramento used this program to help private entrepreneurs take on the reconstruction of some of the expensive, crumbling brick buildings. Section 312, with a $50,000 maximum at 3 percent interest for up to 20 years, is a big help to investors, especially in these times of high interest rates.

Finally, for those who do not have tax increment systems yet, there is one action that can be taken to encourage private investment that does not cost a thing. When key municipal leaders are willing to meet with lenders and private investors, this alone can often encourage private investment. When investors know that a municipality supports a project (even when it does not have money) and will do whatever is within its power to aid that project, they are more willing to make a move, and lenders are more willing to accept a financial risk.

Conclusion

The Sacramento Housing and Redevelopment Agency manages 5,000 housing units, as well as various kinds of development projects throughout the city and county with a budget totaling about $35 million a year. Thanks to tax increment financing, the agency is able to accomplish municipal action that might not be available in other cities. For instance, the agency will be providing housing in and around a historical project, and thus will support the office rental space in the project. A people-oriented service will be accomplished in Old Sacramento with the use of elderly housing tenants as receptionists, information staff and tour guides throughout the area.

In closing it should be stressed that, although historic preservation projects cost money, there is a financial mechanism available. Preservation can pay its own way in a state that has passed enabling legislation so its cities can use tax increment financing. It is the most effective tool yet devised for American local government use in redeveloping or rehabilitating historic properties and areas.

The Hidden Assets
of Old Buildings

PLACE VENDÔME *from the Rue de Castiglione, Paris, France. (French Government Tourist Office)*

Plus Factors of Old Buildings

GIORGIO CAVAGLIERI, FAIA

Giorgio Cavaglieri, FAIA, is a practicing architect in New York City specializing in restoration and adaptive use of urban public structures.

Up to the time of the skyscraper, customs, ways of living and building styles in America were influenced by the European inheritance. But Europeans and Americans have viewed in completely different ways the purposes of construction and the methods of urban growth.

In major European cities, the historic centers have throughout the centuries been the most desirable parts of the metropolitan areas and have kept local real estate values high. In the United States the highest value for land and buildings alike seems constantly to shift locations. New developments are more attractive to real estate investors than old ones, and new buildings are erected progressively higher, then presented to the public as more luxurious than the old ones whose demolition they forced.

The European Experience

In Rome, one piece of real estate has remained for 20 centuries one of the most expensive spots in the city. This is the site to which the Emperor Trajan returned in triumph after his conquest of the Danube and the Balkans at the beginning of the second century A.D. A thousand years or so after the column celebrating his victories was erected there, the ambassador of the Venetian Republic selected as a location for his palace and offices a lot about 200 yards from this monument. Some 500 years later, the largest insurance company in Europe chose a nearby lot for its main office, and just 50 years ago a shrewd profiteer named Benito Mussolini established his own office on the same square, in the palace that once belonged to the Venetian ambassador.

In Paris, King Louis XV, short of cash because of the drain on his pocketbook from providing castles for mesdames Pompadour, Du Barry and others, engaged in real estate speculation by erecting a few buildings on what is now the Place Vendôme. A century and a half later, a government that wanted to celebrate the Napoleonic epics considered it appropriate to erect in front of those buildings an imperial souvenir similar to Trajan's column in Rome. Finally, about another century later, in the same buildings we can admire the models of "haute couture" and buy $100 shirts with the label of Pierre Cardin. It stands to reason that establishments capable of selling shirts for $100 each are in a position to pay rather high rentals.

What makes square footage within historic buildings so commercially valuable in the large European cities? In Europe "prestige" is represented by a building that has housed the source of political power through the centuries. This is the main reason, even today, that large corporations seek to establish offices in ancient remodeled buildings in the historic centers of the cities. The Romanesque or Gothic cathedrals of the Italian squares are surrounded by the offices of insurance companies, banks and radio stations; the same thing occurs on French squares. The fashion industries of France and Italy seek to occupy the former residences of the nobility in the heart of town because people associate the noble class with being correctly and elegantly dressed at all times. Thus in Europe the prestige and psychological values of a particular edifice are translated into dollars and cents.

Why do Americans not use historic centers in the same fashion? Why should the Woolworth building find it difficult to rent its stores or offices in front of City Hall, while a set of cubbyholes with eight-foot ceilings in a glass and aluminum frame can rent in mid-Manhattan for half a million dollars a year? The immediate answer is, of course, that old buildings are difficult and expensive to maintain, and the high standard of living does not provide the supply of cheap labor that would permit old structures to face the competition of the new ones by being kept slick, clean and up-to-date.

Yet there are many different factors influencing trends and customs throughout the centuries. Perhaps there can be found in the urban United States factors that parallel the European experience and show the hidden possibilities, characteristics and qualities that work in favor of preserving and using old buildings.

Location as a Plus Factor

The first factor to analyze and consider is that of location or setting. The most obvious justification here for the continuous use of a building might well be the desirability of its location in the dense urban scene. An old building, particularly if originally erected for public use, is likely to be in a premium spot, and any effort to maintain it in active use will work in favor of preserving real estate values. Yet, a suicidal cycle follows. First, the interest of the public in a historic building makes a site well known and desirable. Recognition of the site as being in a prime location provokes a change in zoning laws that prompts the desire for higher buildings and larger volumes on that very site. Ironically, the desire for larger volumes suggests the demolition of the old building that had fostered the importance of the location.

It must be remembered that the building and real estate industries together represent one of the largest sources of financial activity in the country. Both are geared to new design and to the promotion and development of new values. This is the main reason that, at first consideration, an investor thinks of a building as something new to be constructed from the ground up.

JEFFERSON MARKET COURTHOUSE (1874), New York City, restored for use as a public library. The building is located in Greenwich Village (top, facing page). Interior of library (bottom, facing page). (George Cserna)

Yet the promotion of new values is valid and the goal of new design is obtainable with old buildings as well as with new ones; frequently, great advantages are to be had by combining new and old buildings as part of a common unit. Through imaginative treatments the environment can be enhanced and improved more by the preservation of an old structure than by its destruction and the erection of a new building.

Old courthouses, library buildings and luxury residences are frequently the cause of rising land values in central urban locations. In order to correct the suicidal cycle previously described, the additional volumes that zoning regulations allow owners to build should be considered as separate property to be sold by the owners to neighbors. Then the old luxury spaces could be updated for prestige purposes at reasonable construction costs, and additional profits could be obtained by new rentals because of the appreciation of land values. Such profits would be added to those of the sale of development rights. Moreover, the older building, being lower, should enhance the value of the newer, adjacent buildings and the ambience of the area by allowing sun, light and air to reach the street and building facades.

Visual Features

Another positive factor is that old historic buildings have visual characteristics that make them easily identifiable and remembered. As advertising, they are certainly the equal of neon signs or bronze plaques. These visual features present opportunities for developing projects nearby or in conjunction with buildings of historical character and importance. It is no coincidence that the late Aristotle Onassis decided to put his luxury Olympic Tower next to St. Patrick's Cathedral on New York's Fifth Avenue. The area affords open sky over the Gothic spires and a stability created by the presence of the most important house of worship for a third of New York City's population. Future benefits will include southern sunlight for the luxury apartments and many patrons for the building's offices and stores, thus assuring continuous tenancy.

Another potentially successful and profitable venture in combining the old and the new is the Villard Houses in New York City. There is currently a great deal of pressure for preservation and reuse, to the benefit of the Helmsley Hotel to be built behind them.

An example of the contribution old buildings can make to site development and of the value they add to land attractiveness is New York City's Roosevelt Island. There a new town for 20,000 people is being developed to replace hospitals and a mental institution, which were the only occupants for 100 years. The restored Blackwell House is the focus of attention in the small park by the water, and the Chapel of the Good Shepherd provides relief from the visual monotony between the skyscraper apartment houses.

On the other side of the continent, the transformation of an abandoned chocolate factory into a profitable retail shopping center has completely transformed the area of San Francisco that now boasts the Ghirardelli Square complex.

Problems: Original Use Design and Architects' Attitudes

Despite the importance of their locations in urban areas, old buildings are often abandoned because the original use for which they were designed no longer exists or has changed so that larger, more modern facilities are needed. At the same time, in recent years, the movement for preserving existing buildings has engaged the interest of growing numbers and a broad variety of people with many motivations. With the forthcoming Bicentennial celebration, the attention of civic groups, students and other citizens is focusing on visual expressions of American events. Thus the attraction of the historical past is compound interest on the advertising value of the prime location.

The basic motive for building construction has always been the satisfaction of consumer needs. That motive has conspired so effectively against using the work of the past that existing old structures in every community have been reduced to a very small number.

To answer the desires of the public, there must be a new realization that, while spaces are originally designed for specific functions, in reality buildings contain open volumes of specific sizes, which can easily be added to, changed or rearranged. Inside the basic shell, only imagination and technology are required to change the layout. Almost any space can be made to suit any function within certain volumetric limits. This is particularly true now that mechanical facilities can inject air and light into the interior and floors, and structural members can be removed or added, walls opened or closed and volumes supplemented or reduced. A patient rearranging of the existing layout can frequently provide charm and character, which can be translated into financial compensation.

One reason that speculators and investors shy away from the renovation of existing buildings for possible new use is that the skilled architect frequently has a "prima donna" attitude that repels a practical investor. The halo of the intellectual artist that architects have fondly cultivated for themselves has been one of the greatest shortcomings of the profession. It has kept architects aloof from the needs of society and away from where the economic action is.

Sound Construction

Existing buildings in urban communities of the United States are generally masonry wall-bearing buildings; if the structures were built during the 19th century, the masonry is brick or stone. In some of the early 20th-century buildings, the bearing is provided by steel skeletons. In all these cases structural capability exists, though in some instances it may have to be supplemented. Today's technology is such that the addition of steel beams to span spaces or of steel columns to be inserted within an old grid is only a matter of careful design and installation. Frequently such additions require only simple concepts and elementary calculations.

The preservation of existing masonry masses means, of course, that a large number of cubic feet of material such as brick and stone do not have to be cooked in ovens, manufactured with power tools or transported from quarries, kilns and factories to the construction site. This obviously means a savings in gas or electric power, a savings that rarely would appear in the pages of the estimate. The labor involved in repointing, realigning or adding new veneers might cost as much as the reassembling of new materials, but the nation would benefit by use of the old walls because of the savings obtained in power and fuel at a time of fuel shortages. The structure of a building represents approximately 20 percent of its cost.

Unfortunately, many investors try to reduce professional advice to a minimum and seek repeat plans and assembly-line designs. Yet in comparison with the possible savings of up to 20 percent of the cost of a building—and a consequent reduction in the cost per square foot of usable space—the hiring of skilled personnel to visualize, conceive and direct the changes in an existing structure represents a minimal additional cost. One must also consider that if a new building takes the site of the old one, the cost of the demolition (between 3 and 5 percent of the cost of new construction if the buildings have similar volumes) will be part of the budget. If the old building has a sound set of bearing walls and suitable horizontal members, a sizable part of the cost can be spared by preservation.

Consideration must also be given to the characteristics of the spaces contained inside an old building and the valuable advantages they offer to the user. Existing moldings, cornices, ceiling coffers or trim, carved or paneled doors or wainscotings can be a considerable asset for a property seeking to attract sophisticated groups or corporations as tenants. Thus these features are well worth the repair that may be needed.

Utilities and Costs

Before the advent of mechanical climate control, rooms with high ceilings were readily recognized as more comfortable in all weather conditions than those with low ceilings. In warm weather these rooms, having a larger volume and thus a higher cubic content of air, needed less replacement of outside air. In warm as well as cold climates, a lesser need for fresh air intake, if combined with thick insulating masonry walls, gives a better chance of maintaining the night freshness throughout the sunny hours or the temperate warmth throughout the cold periods.

Presently, if air-conditioning must be used, a volume of air larger in old buildings than in new ones must be controlled and regulated for temperature, humidity and movement. This requires costly equipment. However, part of the cost of checking and controlling an increased amount of air is balanced by the benefit of a better blending and the smaller percentage of air replacement required (if local codes permit such a smaller percentage). It is obvious that stale odors and smoke are frequently disturbing in spaces with low ceilings. If the ceiling is twice as high, discomfort usually will not occur at all and the need for complete replacement of air can be delayed for twice as long. Again, the engineer's skill can play a dominant part in the most important elements of the budget.

The Anspacher Theater is one of the New York Shakespeare Festival Public Theater building auditoriums. It has a 45 to 55-foot ceiling, and treatment of only the lowest level of air results in comfort for the audience. This solution was more economical than air-conditioning the Newman Theater, a contemporary auditorium in the same building complex with only a 10 to 22-foot ceiling and the same number of seats.

The most commonly accepted modern illumination system is the recessed light, either incandescent or fluorescent. Its standardization and monotony of design have made all modern interior spaces look boring, regimented and cold. Once more the variation of forms available in old buildings, when skillfully treated with designs suited to them, presents the opportunity for interesting solutions.

For example, within the structural system of brick vaults in the basement of New York City's Jefferson Market Courthouse, specially designed fluorescent fixtures diffuse the appropriate light in a successful manner. This detail, as well as troffers designed for the main

ANSPACHER THEATER, *New York City, former Astor library and hostel for immigrants. (George Cserna)*

reading rooms, contributed to the wide acceptance the building received. It is now the heart of Greenwich Village in New York City and has made the corner at Sixth Avenue and Eighth Street one of the most rentable commercial areas in town.

Hidden Assets

These, then, are the plus factors or hidden assets of old buildings. They show that opportunities for adap-

tive reuse are present in all cities. The main benefit of restoration and reconstruction will always be the increase in real estate value obtained through the indefinable element of character. As already mentioned, zoning and planning devices, such as the transfer of development rights, must be assured. All the other possible assets depend on the skill and creative imagination of the designer, who must consider the characteristics of the building as a challenge and an opportunity.

Interior of Chart House restaurant, Boston. (Anderson Notter Associates, Inc.)

Building Reuse in New England: Identifying the Hidden Assets

GEORGE M. NOTTER, JR.

George M. Notter, Jr., is a principal with Anderson Notter Associates, Inc., an architectural and preservation planning firm with experience in the design of new buildings for historic environments and the adaptation of old buildings.

The unique and intrinsic values found in old buildings—the hidden assets referred to in the title of this paper—develop in many ways. It should be stressed at the beginning that the identification of these values is only a first step. Their successful and creative integration into a viable aesthetic and economic reality requires a great deal of hard work and, perhaps, just a little magic.

Not every old building should be saved, nor should every new one be built. Rather, the essence of our cities is a fabric of buildings that generates an urban excitement reflecting the heritage of past growth while at the same time nurturing the dynamic potential of the future. This is just another way of saying that life is made up of both old and new.

Certainly there is a growing public awareness that to demolish the grand old structures and remove them from this fabric is to throw away many hours of human energy. But more meaningful to the purpose of this paper are the economic realities by which developers place a specific value on that energy. These are the assets to be illustrated here in their many different forms.

For example, one economic reality may simply be that the dollars involved in preserving buildings are less than the cost of new buildings. But more often than not, the total dollar expenditure for preservation, including the acquisition of the property involved, is about the same as for new construction. Thus the plus factor is achieved by developing the potential assets into a final project of greater amenity—one having the right location, more space in either height or volume, more area or more character, materials of a special quality or a potential for time savings in construction. Any one or more of these factors produces more marketability while also preserving a landmark and the environment.

It might be appropriate to quote the old New England proverb that introduced *Federal Architecture: Adaptive-Use Facilities*, produced in 1975 by the National Endowment for the Arts: "Use it up, wear it out, make it do, or do without."

Indeed the purpose here is to show some examples of fine structures where the potential for additional use and wear is great and the potential for continued contribution to the total fabric of our cities and lives is significant.

UNION STATION

Union Station in New London, Conn., is a current project. Its preservation was aided in 1974 by a $30,000 low-interest loan from the National Trust. In the summer of 1975, after a year and a half of negotiation, a land disposition agreement was signed with the local renewal agency.

Designed by architect H. H. Richardson and built in 1885, this is a building whose assets are not at all hidden, yet were not clearly seen. Many people in New London, town officials among them, viewed the station through "color-me-ugly" glasses. Placed there originally by railroad barons, it was underutilized and poorly maintained. In fact, it is a magnificent building, fantastically detailed and, in the jargon of the developer, it has a dynamite location.

This last and most important asset became apparent to us only after we were asked by the local citizens group to pursue the project in the role of developer as well as architect. This group had been instrumental in saving the station and originally retained Anderson Notter Associates to do a feasibility study. At this point, with the aid of a National Trust consultant service grant, a real estate and marketing consultant was retained to analyze the economic viability of the project. He dramatically presented to the renewal agency what he considered the three essential criteria of project feasibility: (1) Location, (2) Location and (3) Location.

Union Station is situated at the water end of the captain's walk, a pedestrian section of the main street. This is an urban renewal area, with a new bank and office building across the street, a new and greatly underutilized garage next door and a hotel planned immediately north. The next potential renewal area extends southward from the site. There is access to and from the new interstate I-95 in less than 3 minutes. In addition, a complete intermodal transportation complex is possible, with ferry service to Block Island, Long Island and Fischer's Island on the water side, the potential for bus service at the site and, of course, the existing Amtrak service at the station, a key asset indeed.

The real estate consultant summarized our position for the redevelopment agency when he said, "If I were to pick one spot in New London with the most potential, it would be here." And so, a fresh look was taken at this building. Recognizing the assets of mass, form and majesty, it was determined to develop a viable interior use to justify the continued existence of the exterior.

The station was unoccupied except for Amtrak, which needed much less space for normal operations but more space for peak periods. It was determined that Amtrak could function during normal periods with half of the

first floor and that a restaurant would be a compatible use for the other half.

Previous experience indicated that the average-sized restaurant of 125 seats would require more space than was available, even though the additional shed area was ideal for a kitchen. The possibility of a mezzanine was explored and found to provide just the right area. It related comfortably to the existing fenestration and added an element of drama to the major space.

For use during periods of peak operation, Amtrak can develop an overflow area in the basement by cutting through the first floor and gaining separate access to the tracks from the stair.

The second floor developed logically as office space, served by the two existing stairwells, one of which is rebuilt to allow the addition of an elevator. Three distinct areas, generally equivalent in size and potential income, have now been generated, and there is also a possibility of expanding into the attic.

The total project is about 20,000 square feet, not including the attic. Construction costs of $600,000, or approximately $30 a square foot, relate well to a total project cost of $750,000. The projected income of about $120,000 a year anticipates a minimum profit of about 10 percent on the investment.

The most significant interior space, the central waiting room, is not maintained today—it may even still have the original paint. But with the introduction of the mezzanine and access to the lower level, it will take on added drama. Creating additional viable economic uses for this underutilized interior will enhance the existing use of this building as a functioning train station and serve to maintain a significant structure in the present urban fabric.

Old City Hall

Like Union Station, Boston's Old City Hall was dependent on the use of imagination and sensitivity in its interior rearrangement. This project was started in 1971 by Roger Webb, whose imagination and insight brought the effort to fruition. His Old City Hall Landmark Corporation leased this building from the city for 99 years through the Boston Redevelopment Agency and then developed it as general office space.

The budget was about $22 a square foot, exclusive of the cost of work to complete the tenant space, such as interior walls, doors, lights, etc. It is interesting to note that just a year later Anderson Notter designed a new six-story office building with comparable finish in the Boston Government Center area for a budget of about $35 a square foot. Both buildings drew from the same general rental market.

Since its construction in 1862–65, the Old City Hall had remained almost unchanged on the exterior. The work there involved only a general cleaning and replacement of the double-hung sash with fixed glass.

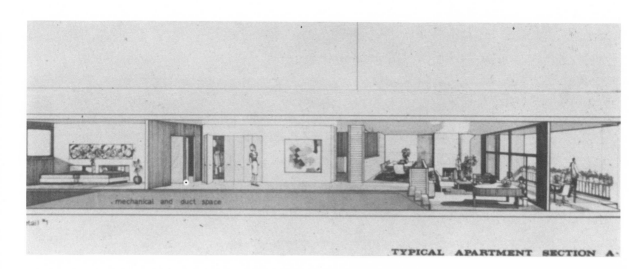

UNION STATION *(1885, H. H. Richardson), New London, Conn. (left). (Anderson Notter Associates, Inc.)*

PRINCE BUILDING *(1918), Boston. Drawings of a typical corridor floor plan (right) and a typical apartment. (Anderson Notter Associates)*

TYPICAL CORRIDOR FLOOR PLAN

mechanical and duct space

TYPICAL APARTMENT SECTION A·

The finished building stands proudly in front of a high-rise office structure and demonstrates the options cities have to maintain urban diversity.

Now to the inside: The key to development of this building lay in an understanding of its central space, which originally was filled with a monumental stairway extending through all four stories. There was no realistic way to preserve this stairway under existing codes. Although its loss was a great disappointment, the space was then available in the renovated plan for new fire stairs, elevators, toilets, mechanical risers and an interior circulation system, thus freeing the entire ring of the outer area for rentable space. This arrangement resulted in an unusually high net-to-gross ratio, comparable to that of new buildings at the time, and it allowed development of an efficient plan for either multi-tenant or single-tenant floors.

The problem of covering openings of various widths in the thick walls of the building led to the solution of using oak flooring on runners, a procedure that allowed

us to follow the curves of the arches. This detail became the central design element throughout the building; it was used first in a passageway into the building, later for entrances to the elevators and finally in the window walls of the building.

In the upper floors, this oak treatment allowed furring of the old window openings to pick up new dry-wall materials placed over the strapping and existing walls. This procedure resulted in economical wall treatment and maintenance of finished surfaces that is comparable to that possible in new office buildings. In the basement the wood theme was carried through in trim and lighting details, but the existing wall materials were stripped away to expose the richer natural materials in the restaurant space.

PRINCE BUILDING

The Prince Building is an old spaghetti warehouse on

CUSTOM HOUSE BLOCK *(top) part of Long Wharf project on Boston waterfront adapted for use as apartments (above and bottom right). Main entrance to Custom House (bottom left). (Anderson Notter Associates, bottom right photo; Paul O'Mara, ULI– The Urban Land Institute, other photos)*

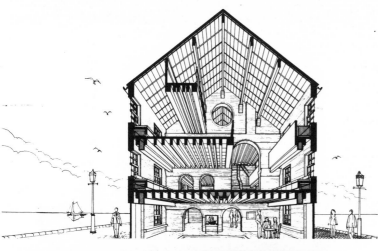

LONG WHARF *on Boston waterfront (top).*
The Gardner Building located on Long
Wharf now the Chart House restaurant (left
and bottom). (Anderson Notter Associates,
left photo; Paul O'Mara, ULI–The Urban
Land Institute, other photos)

the Boston waterfront. It was slated to be torn down but instead became the first major building in the city to be recycled.

Built in 1918 as a factory and warehouse for spaghetti waiting to be shipped overseas during World War I and beautifully located by the edge of the water, it was a natural location for apartments. A comparison of the first floor loadings allowed by the code for warehouses and apartments indicated additional capacity in the foundations for the new apartment use. After verification of this at the site, 2½ floors were added to the building—a truly hidden asset.

A two-level parking garage was fitted into the lower floor, and the corner building, a fish market, was redesigned for use as a branch of the First National Bank. A small gas station was put on the corner of the site.

A typical elevator and corridor plan seemed to waste the asset of the building's water side, so the corridor was linked to stairs that would give access to noncorridor floors above and below, with more interesting apartments extending through the entire floor from the bedroom on the city side to the living room and balcony on the water side. This floor arrangement occurs twice for each of the normal corridor floors, thereby maximizing the asset of the water.

As is typical with structures of this type, floor-to-floor heights of 12 feet were common and penetrations through the 12-inch concrete slab were difficult. To solve this problem, all of the mechanical ducts and piping were laid on top of the floor slab, punching through only for the toilets. A raised floor was built to cover these for the bedroom, kitchen and dining areas, which lead down into the living room. This technique created an inverted apartment scheme that exposes the raw concrete ceilings and mushroom columms—an economical solution that also creates an interesting space.

The final products were spectacular apartments that rented for an average of $450 a month. The cost of construction was about $12 a square foot in 1967, a good value at that time.

CUSTOM HOUSE BLOCK

The Custom House Block is located on Long Wharf on the Boston waterfront, next to the Boston aquarium, and is listed in the National Register. The initial phase of this project consisted of developing the attic area, which had remained totally unused in the early development of the building but was recognized as an asset with good

CROWNINSHIELD ESTATES, *Peabody, Mass. (Anderson Notter Associates)*

potential for water views and unique space. The interior of the building was typical of this type of structure in Boston: wooden beams and brick bearing walls.

The design approach here involved a cut into the roof at the point where low headroom made the inside unusable. An exterior balcony setback was created in the roof plane and was protected by the existing brick fire walls. This solution is compatible with the structure and still allows full development of the potential of the space, which overlooks the water.

The typical two-bedroom units rent for $650 and construction costs were about $25 a square foot, which included overall mechanical provisions for the entire building. All units have had waiting lists since completion. This was the first rehabilitation project for the developer, who is now putting his own office into the space below these units.

CHART HOUSE

Another Long Wharf project involved the Gardner Building, now the Chart House restaurant. This was the only 18th-century building on the Boston waterfront. On first view it showed signs of structural distress, but it was determined that stabilization was possible. The outside was a study in restoration: repointing and cleaning, rebuilding the windows, researching and restoring the original shutters and repairing the slate roof.

A special problem here was finding space for the mechanical equipment necessary for a restaurant operation. There was no exterior site available because all surrounding property was owned by the Boston Redevelopment Agency and was to become public space. The solution was to use louvers in the plane of the roof; establish a new roof line at the gutter in one bay; and place all cooling equipment, fans and duct work under the slate roof, ventilated totally by the louvers on each side, yet completely out of sight. Electricity was used as the energy source because gas was not available at that time and oil furnaces would have required smokestacks twice the height of the building because of adjacent highrise apartments. The use of electricity required the addition of substantial insulation, which was concealed between the existing roof joists, allowing the slate roof to be saved.

The inside of the building was treated quite differently. Instead of maintaining the small elements of the outside in a restoration, the inside was developed more as a total space. Building code requirements for the structure limited the restaurant to two levels. In this case, the mezzanine was allowable as part of one level and the interior solution expanded the volume by cutting through the bearing walls to tie the three separate areas together and make the whole read as one space.

The interior work started in a simple way. All the unnecessary elements were removed. The entire process involved penetrating the bearing walls and restructuring with the original materials. This required removing the flooring and rebuilding the new floors and stairs

out of the old beams and boards, creating the desired space and volume. Everything was then totally cleaned—wood and brick together, so that new work and old took on the same appearance.

This entire project, from start of design to completion, took six months. Work was completed in 1973, and construction costs were about $35 a square foot, exclusive of kitchen equipment and furnishings. The quality of the space and the excellent location have combined to make this the most successful restaurant of a national chain.

LINCOLN WHARF COAL BUNKER

An unusual project, the old coal bunker on Lincoln Wharf in Boston, over the harbor tunnel, was emptied when the building began to show signs of settlement. It then became available to the city for its fire boats if that use proved feasible.

The asset here is the structure itself and the fact that, with the tunnel below the piling, new piles were not practical. The reuse of the existing building reconnected to the existing piles enables the retention of a function in its current location and presents the opportunity of dealing with an interesting structure. The actual truss members inside the open storage container will be maintained to tie the building together; new floors are to be constructed inside, tied to these columns at the different levels.

Because of the low headroom, the central bay will be used for sleeping and locker areas and two levels on the outside for recreation and higher lobby space. The first floor, which was already higher to allow coal cars to come in, will work well for the fire apparatus that will drive in from both sides, using the central bay for access and storage.

The final scheme anticipates a joint ownership in condominium form with the developer-builder who will own the water half of the building and an upper floor for an office condominium. This is a bold approach by a city aware of the many facades of its heritage.

CROWNINSHIELD ESTATES

Returning to housing, the Tannery, a project for the Crowninshield Estates in Peabody, Mass., has a special asset, the site itself. The 12-acre area three blocks from the city hall was an industrial slum, having progressed through various industries until the tannery operation stopped two years ago.

The solution here was to remove all the secondary buildings, leaving only the two main brick structures, which are connected to the Federal-style mansion. The intent was to provide housing for the elderly in a downtown location, along with site development that transformed an industrial blight into a new city park.

The Federal-style building will become the community center for the project. Still connected to the other structures by the old catwalks, now glazed, it will house

laundry and community rooms while the other buildings will consist of housing units. When cleaned and
finished, these buildings become elegant in their
simplicity.

When the shed buildings are demolished, low brick
walls will shield parking and the old brick floor of the
sheds will provide paving on the site. When the pond is
cleaned up, it will become an attractive open space and,
with landscaping added, a spectacular sight. An unusual asset is the old smoke tower, which will become
the community's identifying marker. Finally, the site
plan actually incorporates old vats, cut in half and used
as planters, and leaves some of the machinery in place
as outside sculpture.

A total of 280 units will be constructed at a cost of
about $16,000 per unit, which is $3,000 to $4,000 less
than new construction and which made possible the
acquisition of the site and its considerable assets. The
total time from start to first occupancy was just one year,
and the project was 80 percent rented before completion. Financed by the Massachusetts Housing Finance
Agency, this effort represents the agency's largest venture to date into the area of adaptive reuse.

NEWBURYPORT

North of Boston near the New Hampshire line, Newburyport, Mass., was a town typical of the area. It had
experienced urban renewal in the 1960s but, unlike
other towns, had stopped this process. In 1970, with a
new redevelopment agency director, the town decided
to reevaluate existing plans, particularly regarding the
potential for integrating the remaining historic structures into a comprehensive plan for the recently created
open spaces and waterfront development.

In 1971 Housing and Urban Development money was
available to restore the buildings before they were sold
to a block developer who would do interior
renovation—not unlike the arrangement for the Quincy
Markets project in Boston. But a different approach was
chosen. It was decided that an attempt would be made
to interest the small developer in the existing individual
unit, providing guidance in its repair and rehabilitation.
The developer could then achieve the end result wanted
at less cost, often with "sweat equity" and a greater
personal commitment. The money available could then
be applied to high quality public improvements, such as
street and sidewalk repairs, multi-level access, planting
and underground utilities. These improvements could
spread beyond the renewal area to motivate an entire
town.

Today, with reclaimed space, contained traffic and
restored buildings, Newburyport has made contact
with its past and has also taken a giant step toward its
future.

OTHER PROJECTS

On Stoneholm Street in the Fenway area of Boston, an
old parking garage was developed into housing for the
singles market in 1968. The first two floors were kept as
parking and two floors were added to the top. The plan,
reflecting some of the economies of the raised floor
developed for the Prince Building, also developed for
the first time a solution for the extra-depth units. In this
case, a small stub corridor off the main corridor gave
access between the living and bedroom areas.

An interesting aspect of this project resulted from the
fact that with a budget of about $13 a square foot, it was
not feasible to remove the two intersecting circular parking ramps from the structure. Apartments were designed to fit between these, using a model that was
delivered to the contractor. The results in some cases
were one-bedroom apartments on five levels; they were
the first to rent in the project.

A school in Gloucester, just north of Boston, is under
adaptation now as housing for the elderly, financed by
the Massachusetts Housing Finance Agency. This is a
magnificent building across the street from a historic
city hall. The project provides apartments for the elderly
at comparable market rents. Units have been designed
within the standard classroom module—30 by 30, or 900
square feet. The market average is 600 to 700 square feet.
Extremely marketable in location and amenities, this
project is especially noteworthy as a revitalized and
essential element of the city's heritage.

In Worcester, Mass., a building belonging to the
Mechanics Association remains intact behind the recent
attack of first-floor commercialism. Most significant is a
third-floor concert hall with the acoustic characteristics
of Symphony Hall in Boston and of some European
halls. Currently it is being used as a roller rink but has
the potential, with proper egress and safety considerations, to be restored to its original purpose.

A convent in Marlboro, Mass., varied in space and
configuration and on a magnificent site, is to be adapted
to housing for the elderly, again with the backing of the
Massachusetts Housing Finance Agency.

There is a brewery in Albany, N.Y., that could be used
for an office or housing. There is housing in Albany
waiting for a neighborhood to be born again.

A factory in Lynn, Mass., eight blocks from the ocean
stands empty, ready for housing, with financing by the
Massachusetts Housing Finance Agency. Left over
when renewal clearance stopped, a city block in
Hartford, Conn., has the potential to be once again the
heartbeat of the city's inner core. A town in western
Massachusetts, Royalston, was studied through a National Trust consultant service grant in conjunction with
the Society for the Preservation of New England An-
tiquities. Now it stands unchanged from 100 years ago,
waiting for the use that says it belongs and can stay.

In summary, the unique and intrinsic values to be
found in adaptive reuse—the hidden assets—require
both identification and creative integration into a viable
aesthetic and economic reality. That's what preservation and adaptive reuse are about.

Continuing and Adaptive Use: Avenues to Profits

Aerial view of Trolley Square, Salt Lake City. (Trolley Square Associates)

Trolley Square: A Preservation Adventure in Salt Lake City

WALLACE A. WRIGHT, JR.

Wallace A. Wright, Jr., is managing partner of Trolley Square, Salt Lake City, and an officer in a variety of other real estate partnerships and projects.

A lot of people have asked, "How did you come up with the idea for Trolley Square?" Well, this dream hitchhiked on the back of another one. When I was a teenager, I decided to become a jet pilot, so I ran off to the Air Force. On a trip to California on a training mission in the mid-1960s I happened into Ghirardelli Square, and I thought, "Every city ought to have a project like this. I'm going back to my town and build one, and I'm going to buy those old trolley car barns to do it."

The dream was not fulfilled right away, but with perseverance I established a record in real estate and development activities (mostly offices, motels, apartments and houses). Finally, in 1969, the opportunity presented itself and I was able to acquire the property that became Trolley Square.

Location and Background

Trolley Square is situated about nine blocks from the central business district of Salt Lake City and about halfway between the downtown area and the university. It is located on a busy thoroughfare near entrance and exit ramps, so it satisfied the first requirement for a successful real estate venture—location.

The original trolley company was started in 1908 by Averill Harriman's father. He decided to get into the trolley business, selected Salt Lake City and merged several of the competing trolley companies under one ownership. This was done during the years 1908 through 1912.

Trolley Square before and during Development

When I acquired the property in 1969, it was owned by the National City Lines Company and the Utah Power and Light Company. Eight acres of the 10-acre block and about 100,000 square feet of building space were acquired at a price of $630,000 and whatever construction was possible began immediately.

Actual possession was delayed for a year, but we were allowed to proceed with sandblasting of the building exteriors. Everything outside was painted yellow, and everything inside was green. It took almost a year of constant sandblasting to get through that, but underneath that grimy yellow was beautiful warm red brick. Incidentally, although sandblasting can weaken the mortar in some cases, the mortar here was stronger than the brick.

The building had a depressing industrial character, including a six-foot-high chain-link fence topped with three strands of barbed wire, abandoned buses and above-ground fuel-storage tanks. People said to me, "Why are you going to go into that slummy area?" and I responded, "The area is a slum because of this property. When I restore it, watch what happens to the area."

The inside was divided into bays that were 57 feet wide and 420 feet long, with no openings in between, except a small passageway. These bays were opened and connected with a central mall. Miles of rusted pipe had to be removed in the process.

The building also had no windows. The bricks that were removed to create windows are now used elsewhere, in the floors, for instance.

Finding and Using the Trolley Cars

No trolley cars remained at Trolley Square when it was purchased, and we were wondering where we might find them. Ironically, my associate and I were driving down the street one day discussing that subject when he saw, emerging out of the rubble of a motel that was being torn down, the frames of two trolley cars that had been converted into motel units. Since the trolleys were steel, they survived the wrecking ball, and the demolition people did not know what to do with them. So, we acquired our first trolleys by paying $200 to have them delivered five blocks away to Trolley Square. One of these cars is now the cashier's stand for a gas station. The other is a flower shop.

Two more cars were found together as Jack's Diner. After a little restoration work, one serves as a branch for a savings and loan company and the other as a record shop.

Five interurban trolleys came from the Utah Pickle Company, which was using them to house migratory workers. These cars were bought for a couple of hundred dollars and now house small shops. A 1919 car that once traveled the streets of Ogden, Utah, was being used as a chicken coop when it was bought for $100. Some $15,000 later, the car runs again on an International Harvester Mobile home chassis and provides one answer to the mass transit problem between Trolley Square and downtown Salt Lake. It runs hourly, trading off with a double-decker English bus.

Recycling Old Parts and Structures

Another thing that a visitor sees in Trolley Square is found objects everywhere. I have scrounged the junk yards and antique stores of Utah and surrounding states. For example, the old street lights of downtown Salt Lake City were found in the salvage yard of the company that had removed them many years before;

now they are relamped with modern lighting and provide the motif for all the exterior lighting in Trolley Square. As for the gooseneck light fixtures at Trolley Square, they were the first type of electric street light used in Utah. They were at Fort Douglas originally; when they were replaced, someone gave me the poles.

The upstairs part of the old trolley blacksmith shop was refurbished with the assistance of an architectural firm that traded advice for rent and also took the space. This was the first area to show the essential character of a building that could be brought out and marketed.

The inside of the "rip shop," where major work on trolleys was done, now houses the theaters of Trolley Square. There are four of them, with 300 seats each; one projectionist can handle all four.

Ornamental iron has been copied from some of the old downtown buildings erected around the turn of the century. An old safe is in use in the jewelry store.

One problem was what to do with an ugly tower that once stored water for a fire sprinkler system. The first thought was to tear it down, but the second was that it was too ugly to tear down and had been around too long. On a visit to Vacation Island in the San Diego Harbor, I saw a decorative tower made out of telephone poles and concrete reinforcing bars. Combining that idea with thoughts of the bird cage that I used to house a magpie, plus Christmas tree lights, the tower eventually evolved into a spiral stairway, a kind of Victorian-style observation tower. The design for the balcony railing, a typical turn-of-the-century railing treatment in Salt Lake City, was copied. The light fixtures are made out of scrap pipe and round lights.

Salvaging Building Interiors

As many old buildings around Salt Lake City were torn down, I acquired the salvage rights and tried to get the "architectural goodies" out of them. The cupola from an 1880s mansion now is in Trolley Square on a new foundation and serves as a gift shop. A bay window removed with a forklift is now part of a shop. Small elements, such as shingles, are reused too.

In demolishing part of one house, I uncovered five oil paintings on the walls that had been wallpapered over. Several months later, they were identified as the work of H.L.A. Culmer, the foremost Utah artist of the 19th century. The paintings now are on permanent display in the bank at Trolley Square.

The cupola from another mansion now is a gazebo in the plaza at Trolley Square. The stained glass and front doors from the entrance to the mansion are now in a shop entrance, and a magnificent hand-carved oak stairway gives access to the mezzanine of the shop, which literally was built around elements of the house.

A glass dome came from a cathedral in Los Angeles, where it had been stored for many years; the rest of the cathedral glass was used for the interior of a restaurant. Even the doors to the cathedral were utilized.

A pulpit from a church built in the 1850s now serves as a balcony in a bridal boutique. An old arch that spanned

OBSERVATION TOWER *in Trolley Square. (Trolley Square Associates)*

a street in downtown Salt Lake City was condemned as a result of a sign ordinance change, so it was bought and moved to Trolley Square.

When my old high school burned, one of the things saved was the elevator, which I bought for $100. The space it provided now rents for $150 a month as a handbag shop—probably the world's smallest store.

Borrowing Preservation Ideas

I did a lot of traveling around, looking at different projects. That is why I do not mind anybody coming to see mine. Take any ideas I have because I have borrowed a lot myself. For instance, the concept for the multilevels came from a development named Heritage Village, in Connecticut, and the notion of the villages within the bays is from La Place, in Beechwood, Ohio. The idea for the glass structure used as a plant shop came from a Victorian greenhouse in Atlanta.

Trolley Square Tenants

Trolley Square is now Salt Lake City's second largest tourist attraction. More than 90,000 people a week come through it. However, it was not built for tourists, but for the people of Salt Lake City.

There are more than 90 stores in Trolley Square, plus the four theaters. Plans call for a total of 6 theaters, 15 restaurants and about 100 shops. The space breaks down by use as follows: Theaters take up 12 percent, restaurants 22 percent, offices 10 percent and retail about 56 percent.

Logo for Trolley Square (top). A stained glass dome from a Los Angeles cathedral adorns a cafe in the open market area of Trolley Square. (Trolley Square Associates)

Restored antique trolleys used as shops. (Trolley Square Associates)

The major tenant is a theater with 20,000 square feet, and the next major tenants are restaurants. Each is a local firm; there has never been an application from a large national tenant, and I doubt if there ever will be. There is one franchise, a Hallmark card shop, but it is locally owned.

Most of the tenants were new businesses, though some had one other store in town. Most are doing well now; 57 percent of the tenants are paying percentage rentals over the minimum rent.

Zoning and Codes

There often are questions about zoning and code requirements for safety, especially for earthquakes, and how these requirements affect a development such as Trolley Square. I believe Salt Lake City is in the same seismic zone as San Francisco, so everything possible in terms of safety had to be done. However, two city ordinances helped.

One of these ordinances allows a use variance in zoning requirements when a place has been designated a historic site. Commercial use of such sites may be allowed with special permission, and this provision allows some mansions to be preserved with new economic uses.

The second ordinance allows developers special considerations in building code variances for sites listed in the state or national register of historic property. The life safety requirements must be maintained, but as long as the restored structure is safer than the original, the city can make building code trade-offs, such as permitting fire sprinklers in lieu of noncombustible construction.

The Economics of Trolley Square

The economics of a project such as Trolley Square should also be discussed. First, the cost has been about $24 a square foot for restoration of the gross building area of 316,000 square feet. Of that, there eventually will be about 270,000 square feet in what is called GLA or gross leasable area. Recently, $8 million has been borrowed to finish the project, and it now has a value of $11 million.

This project was done entirely backwards. Normally, a developer takes an option on the area, gets some tenants and then obtains a loan. But because no one would believe in what we were trying to do, we had to start with the money we could get on our own and get tenants later. As we would get a tenant, the First Security Bank would give us enough money to complete that space. That is why work has taken so long. Some 200,000 square feet are now completed, 70,000 still remain and there are plans for the construction of a 240-room hotel, which will be built in a compatible but contemporary style that integrates the two eras by use of similar materials.

The average rent is $6 a square foot, but goes as high as $12.50. The percentages of gross receipts over minimum rents run from 4 percent for food items to 20 percent for entertainment, with an average of 6 percent.

On sales in 1974, the clothing stores brought in about $92 a square foot, the restaurants about $72, the specialty shops around $95 and the theaters approximately $50.

The area was initially purchased on a uniform real estate contract for $630,000—$30,000 down, 5.75 percent interest and a five-year balloon note. About $350,000 in personal loans got the project through the first year, before a bank would even consider it. Then, when the bank was willing, the contract was paid off and the bank loan made on an incremental basis. The loan was about half a million dollars at the time; later there was more, a little bit at a time over a five-year period. Recently we placed an $8 million long-term loan

Rendering for use in Trolley Square of parts of a house. (Trolley Square Associates)

at 9⅞ percent with a 27-year payoff; this came from a savings and loan association.

As for return on the investment, so far we have had tax losses and nothing else, with a total equity investment at this point of more than $1 million. However, we anticipate being in the black this year and within three years expect to exceed a half million-dollar-a-year cash flow profit from the project.

The tax laws are structured to favor real estate as an investment to encourage people to go into it. Those laws currently allow developers to deduct depreciation, interest and taxes from other income during loss years. Trolley Square has been able to show about a half million-dollar-a-year tax loss, while coming close to breaking even on actual cash flow.

Tax incentives are definitely the name of the game in real estate. If there were none, hardly anyone would be investing, considering the risks and long waiting period for a profit usually associated with this type of investment.

Conclusion

Trolley Square has been designated as a Utah historic site and has received wide publicity, including articles in *Time, U.S. News and World Report, Fortune* and *Nation's Business*. That publicity is part of the reason so many come to see Trolley Square. It is a working example of how our architectural heritage can be preserved by imaginative adaptive use of existing structures. This is being done at a cost less than that of new construction, while at the same time precious resources are being conserved in these times of energy and material scarcity.

One Winthrop Square, *Boston. (Childs Bertman Tseckares Associates, Inc.)*

Adaptive Office Space in Old Buildings

CHARLES N. TSECKARES, AIA

Charles N. Tseckares, AIA, an architect and planner, is a principal in the firm Childs Bertman Tseckares Associates, Inc., in Boston. He has had wide involvement in the recycling of old buildings.

In the past many buildings and spaces, historic or otherwise, were preserved or reused largely through the extraordinary efforts of preservation groups, historical societies and other individuals and organizations inspired by the spirit of philanthropy. A new era started, it seems, when federal funds were made available through urban renewal legislation aimed at the inner city. In the case of preservation, this proved to be a double-edged sword; many great spaces were destroyed but many areas were preserved. In those cities where preserving the local heritage was an important planning criterion, many buildings and neighborhoods were revitalized; parts of Society Hill in Philadelphia and the Faneuil Hall area in Boston are but two examples of this. There also are cases in which a historic building was given a new lease on life after being given to a nonprofit developer by an inspired citizenry. The Old City Hall in Boston is an example of this.

In short, the preservation of historic environments largely has come from such techniques as federal funds used to write down land cost, gifts to nonprofit groups and the like. Thus, restored buildings have received certain advantages and have not been forced to stand up to true competition in the marketplace. However, preservationists cannot hope for or expect this situation to continue. The drying up of federal renewal dollars and city and state funding sources is clear evidence that we can no longer depend on this method of preservation.

Private Development in Preservation

In 1966 the thoughtful report *With Heritage So Rich* was issued by the Special Committee on Historic Preservation under the auspices of the U.S. Conference of Mayors, with a grant from the Ford Foundation and assistance from the National Trust. The committee made these comments in its Findings and Recommendations:

> Our traditions differ from those of European countries, but we have much to learn from European experience. The weight which European governments

give to historic preservation has resulted in successful programs for saving, restoring and reconstructing many different types of buildings for viable uses. There is an excellent object lesson in the European achievement in maintaining historic buildings and areas as living parts of communities and as successful economic ventures . . . the United States, with a short history and an emphasis on its economic growth, has left historic preservation primarily to private interests and efforts. In the older, history-conscious countries of Europe, preservation leadership has been provided primarily by government . . . to carry out the goals of historic preservation, a comprehensive national plan of action is imperative . . . to meet the current crises and to accelerate the pace of historic preservation we need to increase the amount of government support and joint public and private efforts.

Rarely does this report mention the private development market and the encouragement of developers to take an aggressive role in preservation development. Perhaps the efforts of European governments in historic preservation work for them, but this does not mean that a similar role in the U.S. system is adequate to meet the challenge. It is also true that European expertise in private real estate development has not reached the same levels of aggressiveness and sophistication as in the United States, primarily because of the established land values of these older countries. Because of the American emphasis on economic growth, American real estate development skills are well developed and compose a tremendous resource that has not been wooed into preservation development.

One way to accelerate the continuing and adaptive use of old buildings is through profits and the competitive market. Preservationists must draw on the skills and techniques of real estate developers, harness their development potential and help direct their aggressiveness toward preservation efforts. They must be shown that there is a profit to be gained from reasonable risks and must be equipped with the new skills they will need in this form of development. Once this aggressiveness is channeled into a profit-making business, society will inherit the fruit of this labor in the form of a historical continuity that truly enriches people's lives.

No longer can preservationists depend or rely on philanthropy or advantaged funding sources. They must be more aggressive, learn about the problems of revitalizing old environments and identify viable alternative uses. The skills of architects, preservationists, lenders and real estate brokers must be combined with a high degree of imagination to create a healthy climate for preservation developers to work in.

Developers must learn new techniques to gain confidence in preservation work. Preservation information and experience should be pooled and disseminated to the development community through such means as the Seattle conference on preservation economics. Discussed here is one aspect of real estate development and the potential profitability of continuing use or adaptive office space in old buildings.

REHABILITATION PAST AND PRESENT

In the past, rehabilitation was an unpopular aspect of the real estate development field. Consequently, most development energies were dedicated to demolition and new construction. One of the reasons for this was the fact that there were too many unknowns and consequently too many risks in rehabilitation. In new construction there were no physical unknowns other than subsoil conditions. Construction costs were identifiable and soft costs (salaries and overhead) were moderate because the time required to move a project from conception to actual building permits was reasonable according to today's standards. Also, the market of the past 20 years reflected the beliefs that anything new was better by the sole virtue of its novelty, that time brings progress and that all change is for the better.

Today much of this thinking has changed. Developers must cope with the following facts:

1. Construction costs for both labor and material have skyrocketed and continue to escalate during the development process, causing large cost overruns.

2. The supply of materials has been limited and long delays are more and more prevalent, causing an increased construction time period and delaying cash flow.

3. Resistance to new zoning, environmental impact statements and reviews, increased building code requirements, local neighborhood opposition to new development and the "no growth" movement have caused delays and have consequently increased soft costs for developers.

4. Neighborhood reaction to the destruction of its environment has become almost militant, and many community groups have been organized with the express purpose of preserving their built environments.

5. Interest rates are more unpredictable and the cost of money is high, causing many conventional projects to be nonviable.

6. The market for office buildings has veered off in a new direction—for how long no one knows—but the impact of the standardized impersonal buildings has caused a reaction in the market, where newness itself is no longer a virtue.

7. The real estate market is more and more aware of the values inherent in many old structures and this reaction is increasing at a dramatic rate.

It seems that preservation development, which once was an unpredictable and uncontrollable form of real estate activity, should be reexamined. The myths that have kept experienced developers from preservation work should be brought into the light and put in their proper perspective. Preservation development could take on a prime role because it may significantly reduce the impact of, or better accommodate, some of today's conditions, thus becoming the development path of least resistance. A variety of these conditions can be examined in relation to preservation development.

1. Because of increases in construction costs, existing buildings are becoming better buys when analyzed on a cost performance basis. For example, a cost comparison of a newly constructed structural frame to the purchase of an existing one in an old building increasingly reveals a great value in older buildings. This is equally true of the roof, foundation, exterior skin, interior finishes, plumbing stacks, glazing and the like.

2. Because of the reduced amount of construction labor and material in rehabilitation, the length of time of a construction loan can be shortened and a developer's need for costly labor and materials is reduced. The reduced construction time can be especially beneficial in geographic areas where a building must be "buttoned up" for winter construction.

3. A lengthy development review process, environmental impact reports, local neighborhood opposition and zoning delays can often be bypassed. This leads to a shorter, smoother development process, resulting in lower soft costs to the developer and less fear of alienating the community. In fact, one result can be excellent public relations in the developer's favor, a factor that helps develop marketing momentum.

It is important for developers to realize that when one buys a building one also buys an image and immediately arouses public interest. Used in combination with the building's history, this can be the beginning of an early marketing program. This image has great value, especially in view of the change in the real estate market, which has become more aware of the values inherent in old structures. Developers should also realize that extreme neighborhood reaction to demolition is probably symptomatic of that change in the market. However, this force is easily converted into assistance for the preservation developer, and preservation groups will or should offer their active support, too.

4. With experienced architects and construction supervisors, the unknown construction risks can be minimized by excellent evaluation and feasibility work and by knowledge of how to delineate work tasks to subcontractors so that bids are competitive with new construction.

5. If developers wisely plan their projects, the more highly marketable areas, such as the lobby and models, can be given priority for design and construction. Marketing can then proceed much sooner than in new construction.

6. The energy crises and current interest in recycling resources have brought a new awakening and concern about the use of old buildings. Conservation groups have thus become an ally of the preservation movement and would support efforts to put derelict structures back on the tax rolls.

These factors form the backdrop of the current development climate and many of them will continue to wield influence for some time to come. They affect all forms of development—residential, commercial and industrial. The alliance of preservationists, historians, conservationists and environmentalists could become a formidable force to assist the preservation developer

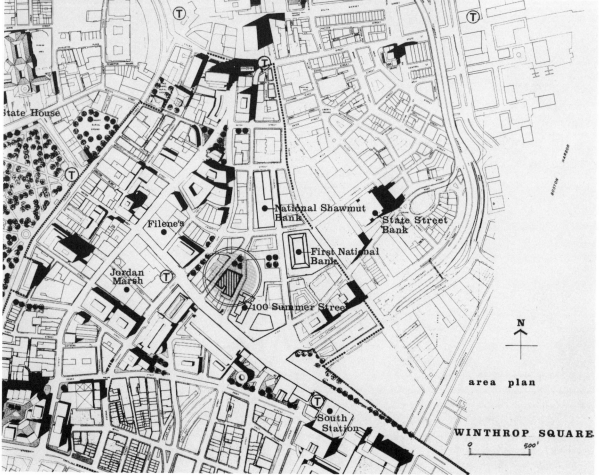

ONE WINTHROP SQUARE *(top) and area map showing its location in Boston. (Childs Bertman Tseckares Associates, Inc.)*

FIGURE 1. PROJECT VALUE CHART

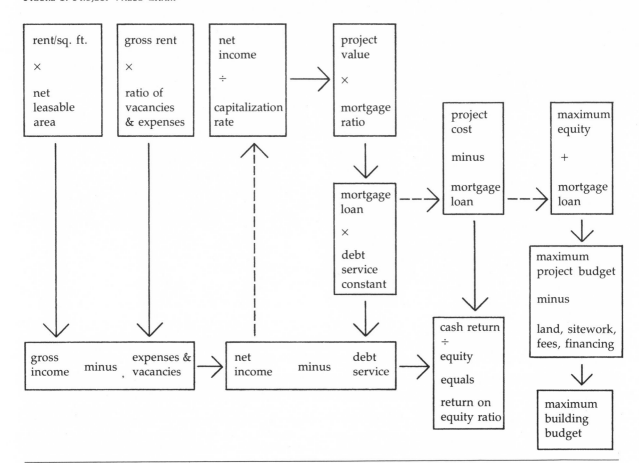

FIGURE 2. DEVELOPMENT LOAN GRAPH

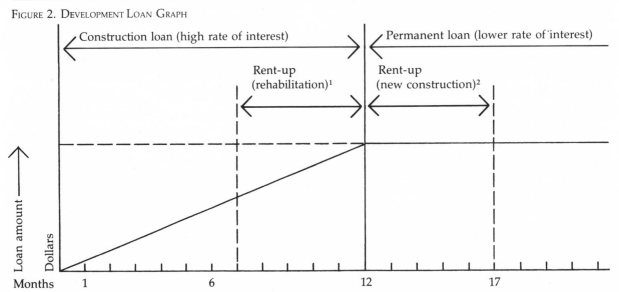

[1]With rehabilitation, because it is possible to make parts of the building marketable during construction, renting can take place coincidental with construction. The construction loan does not run the same length of time as the construction period, because these are the funds used to pay the general contractor. However, with an early rent-up, the developer receives rent receipts (cash flow) earlier, while construction continues. This rent offsets the expense of the loan and the developer can often obtain a permanent loan (which carries a lower interest rate) sooner because marketability of the building has been proven.

[2]Under normal new construction, renting takes place when the building is complete and the developer continues to pay a high interest rate on the construction loan during the renting period.

and create the atmosphere that is required to perform this kind of work. This alliance could lend support at the local level where it is so vitally needed.

PROFITABLE PRESERVATION

It is possible to be specific about the profitability of preservation development. In any kind of business venture, there are usually a few key elements that prove a venture successful or not.

Project Value

First, what are the factors generally considered by mortgage bankers in establishing project value? As seen in figure 1, the key ingredients in this formula are those that create an increase in project value to generate as high a mortgage loan as possible, thus reducing equity. This will, one hopes, lead to financing out (borrowing enough money to pay for the entire project). The key to generating a high value is keeping the capitalization rate favorable. This can be considered a constant, with the only variable being net income (a higher net income will generate a higher value). Looking at the net income for a moment, it can be assumed that for a given location the rent will stay the same and the only variable is net rentable area. The key, then, is to *increase the net rentable area as much as possible without diminishing the rental figure.*

So far, this sounds like an analysis of a new development. After all, this is one reason why the New York City method of area calculation for new office buildings came about. (Through this technique the tenant pays for a proportional share of public and mechanical equipment areas.) Because of the extraordinary floor areas required for elevators, stairs and duct space in highrise buildings, the New York method was a way of increasing the net rentable area. It was thus an answer to a unique problem. Similarly, preservation is a new development problem that requires new thinking in testing its feasibility. The real question is: For a given square-foot cost of acquiring a building and land, how many potential rentable square feet that do not immediately meet the eye have also been acquired? What is involved here is the recapture of underutilized spaces. This involves identifying existing areas, such as attics or basements, that with imagination or a minimum of expense could become desirable spaces.

An excellent example is One Winthrop Square in Boston, a building with approximately 16,200 rentable square feet per floor. At the outset, the whole building, including a basement and five floors, had 99,420 square feet of rentable space. When the building was analyzed thoroughly, there were opportunities to build new space inexpensively and there were also unused spaces that could be recaptured. For example, three towers used only as attics represented 3,000 square feet of space—about 900 for the two small ones and 1,200 for the third. Furthermore, an area in the back of the building could easily be used for a loading dock and for mechanical equipment. The area was U-shaped with three sides defined by bearing walls. A fourth wall was added to enclose the spaces, and five floors (wood frame) and a roof were installed. The cost per square foot was very low, and all that space—an addition of 2,500 square feet—is now used for mechanical equipment.

On the first floor, two mezzanines were added in areas with high ceilings. They amounted to 1,820 square feet each, totaling 3,640 square feet. That makes 9,140 square feet in addition to the original 99,420 square feet, a total of 108,560, and an increase of 9.2 percent. Now, assume 10,000 square feet added, for quick arithmetic. So, 10,000 square feet times $10 a square foot is $100,000 potential income. Now, capitalize the $100,000; that represents $1 million. So, another $750,000 could be borrowed on this building, just because of the "found" space.

Development Time

The length of time required for the development process also affects the financial feasibility of a project. Inflation in construction and financing costs has placed a premium on speed. Once a developer decides to build, each month's delay is a month's loss of rent. But this is only part of the story; the financial penalities for delay are much greater than mere loss of income. Most important is the effect of delays on the developer's equity cash requirements. By cutting development time substantially, and thereby generating early cash flow receipts and reducing interest charges, developers may cut their equity cash participation significantly. This increases the financial leverage for which they strive.

In preservation development, it is definitely possible to take advantage of this time saving because the building is generally made marketable more quickly than in new construction. Thus the developer receives a faster cash flow and can switch more quickly from a high interest construction loan to a lower interest long-term mortgage.

Figure 2 suggests that if the "rent-up" time can be moved back to be simultaneous with the later part of construction, the developer will have the opportunity of more quickly negotiating a long-term mortgage at lower interest, and the project will not have to carry a high-interest construction loan any longer.

With One Winthrop Square, for example, a purchase and sale agreement was made in October 1972. In January 1973, the former owner of the building moved out and demolition of interior partitions was begun. In August 1973, the model office, the elevator and the lobby were complete. (It takes six months to get an elevator.) In March 1974, the first major tenant, a law office that rented one full floor, moved in.

The brokers in Boston agreed that the process happened so quickly only because the owner represented the real product. That is, there was a model office exactly like the one the tenant would be getting, the lobby was complete and the image of the building established.

Gross to Net Ratio

The two elements of recapture and faster marketing time are of extreme importance; they are meaningful when testing the economic viability of old buildings and can be distinct advantages over new construction. But the gross-to-net ratio is also an important consideration regarding office space. That is, for a given number of gross square feet, how much of it is useful as rental area and how much of it is support area, such as mechanical equipment rooms, shafts and the like? In old buildings that have high ceiling heights, mechanical equipment can usually be stacked, thus reducing the amount of lost rental area. Any other method of increasing the percentage of rental area should be investigated. In a typical highrise building of new construction, an 80 percent efficiency factor is considered good. One Winthrop Square is 87 percent efficient.

Potential Layouts

The final critical element concerns the efficiency of potential layouts. With a new building the shape and proportion of the space are the principal considerations, but with old buildings, especially those whose exterior walls are load bearing, the openings in the exterior walls are also important. The more variety in potential layout a building offers, the fewer square feet tenants must rent. This makes the building highly competitive.

New buildings are erected in modules. The outside walls typically are made up of glass with horizontal modules of a standard width, say five feet. As a result, interior partitions perpendicular to the exterior walls can be erected only in the same increments. That means that if a space 10 feet wide is needed, that is fine. But if it needs to be 12 feet, it must take in the full 15. If 17 feet are needed, the room must be the full 20.

In a building with exterior bearing walls, the interior partitions can be placed anywhere; there are almost an infinite number of possibilities for space planning. For example, the firm that is a full-floor tenant at One Winthrop Square rents 16,200 square feet. The firm looked at several new Boston buildings before selecting One Winthrop Square. In the Hancock Building they would have been forced to take 17,900 square feet, which is 1,700 extra square feet or 9 percent more. At One Beacon Street, that figure would have been 18,300 square feet, an additional 2,100 square feet or 11 percent more, and at the State Street Bank Building 18,900 square feet, a 2,700-square-foot difference, or 14 percent.

The cost excess was $21,000 a year in the case of One Beacon Street, $27,000 at State Street and $17,000 at Hancock.

CONCLUSION

This discussion has been limited to office space so that certain points could be made. However, with residen-

tial, recreational and a variety of commercial uses, the same factors of maximum utilization of space, shortened construction time, quick marketing momentum and local political support effect successful adaptive use projects.

There seems to be an endless variety of uses demanded by contemporary society, and an endless variety of buildings to put them in. The communication of ideas offered by this conference will help the real estate development community, with its skills and imagination, to reexamine the potential of preservation development. It is to be hoped that preservationists will commit themselves to lending support to generate a healthy climate sympathetic to this kind of development.

The Costs
of Preservation:
Getting the Most
for Your Money

Interior of Bancroft Building, San Francisco. (Jeremiah O. Bragstad)

Preservation Costs and Commercial Buildings

HERBERT MCLAUGHLIN, AIA

Herbert McLaughlin, AIA, an architect and planner, is a partner in the San Francisco firm Kaplan/McLaughlin, Architects, Planners. He is also a partner in Conner/ McLaughlin, a development firm specializing in the rehabilitation of old buildings.

Perhaps the most threatened group of architecturally significant buildings in the United States today are downtown commercial and industrial structures. They vanish steadily, to be replaced by a melange of parking lots and new office buildings. In the main, this occurs because old buildings theoretically are not economical or efficient for contemporary office use.

That theory simply is not true. For ten years as an architect and five as a developer, I have been involved in preserving and renovating old commercial structures. This has not been an exercise in romance. Conner/ McLaughlin has held all its properties for investment and all of them are making money. The tenants, most of whom rent more than 20,000 square feet each, include the second and third largest banks in California, Security Pacific and Crocker National, plus the 3M Company, the U.S. General Services Administration and Standard Oil. The buildings involved are not small, averaging 80,000 square feet in size. These figures and experiences are not unusual.

The Development Scene Today

How does one accomplish this feat? One must start with a developer. There are a number of different kinds, and those who generally dominate rehabilitation today have acute limitations.

Rehabilitation or renovation development is characterized by romantics who will buy a building with no tenants—as was done in parts of Pioneer Square in Seattle—go in and renovate it, then rent space, usually to smaller, noncorporate tenants. The results are generally beautiful, not particularly profitable and thus not widely emulated. The resulting, smaller spaces usually are not attractive to the larger corporate tenant, who must be brought into the renovation market if larger buildings are to be saved.

The institutional developer must also be brought into rehabilitation. These include the insurance company or the large bank that wants the biggest, most impressive building in the area. In the past, these institutions have put up expensive skyscrapers whose cost is not justified by local rents, at least not from the point of view of someone who is interested in substantial profits.

These institutional developers usually put a fairly substantial amount of cash into a new building and may expect to make as little as 2–3 percent on their outlay, believing that the low return is compensated for by civic pride, public relations and inflation. Such developers should be persuaded to underwrite old buildings the way they currently underwrite new ones. To my knowledge, very few developers specialize in rehabilitation for the larger, corporate tenant.

New and Renovated Project Cost Comparisons

Office space rentals are rising rapidly, as both construction and operating costs escalate. Present low rates are generally the result of suburban competition and high vacancy rates. Consider new construction on a developer basis: The typical cost per gross square foot for a new downtown building of 15 to 20 stories is seen in Table 1. A similar developer's look at large-scale rehabilitation is seen in Table 2. Table 3 shows a comparison of operating costs for new and renovated projects.

Rehabilitation or renovation is obviously advantageous in many areas, especially in terms of the "soft" costs. These are roughly 18–20 percent of hard costs and aggregate to less than one-third of the comparable costs in new construction.

Cutting Costs

What special cost-cutting techniques apply to rehabilitation? Marketing rapidly, and thus reducing the length of time the basic structure is in interim financing, is productive. A second technique is to phase construction to conform with the marketing program, thereby reducing interim financing.

Do not improve unless it is necessary. Work on the lobbies and elevators first, then try to market from the existing space. If necessary, put in a sample suite. This is one of the great advantages of renovation. In new construction, all the improvements must go in to meet a marketing and space delivery schedule set two years before project completion. Renovations can be marketed faster from the existing building and, if tenant work is properly managed, space can be delivered from shell to occupancy very quickly.

The problem with this approach is that the renovator is marketing a dream, a vision. But a developer experienced in renovation can overcome this because tenants can visualize effects completed in other buildings and feel secure that the developer will deliver them again. When working in a town that has little or no renovation, budget some money for trips by prospective tenants to cities where examples exist.

It is also important to execute improvements as rapidly as possible. Conner/McLaughlin normally does major renovation in packages of up to 30,000 square feet in four months or less. The best effort has been 22,000

Interior of Bancroft Building before restoration. (Dan Chu)

square feet in 60 days for a complete job, excluding elevators.

Real estate fees are difficult to reduce, unless one develops for a tenant who has been approached directly, or vice versa. Any developer who hopes to continue in one town must stay in the good graces of the real estate community and pay fees accordingly.

Architects' fees can be reduced by about $1 a square foot by limiting their work to the basic building improvements and letting the tenants provide their own architectural and engineering services, as is common in new construction. However, this approach can have serious liabilities.

It should be remembered that the architect is critical, and these fees are often less in rehabilitation than in new efforts, despite popular conceptions. Also, an architect is a vital member of the marketing team, who can help inexperienced tenants visualize effects and become excited about the project. If the architect drops out after that first contact, there is a hiatus. The tenant's own architect may be in conflict with the previous advice (for reasons of logic or, often, ego) and can exert a negative influence on the conclusion of an agreement.

The architect is also a vital part of cost control at all points. Renovation marketing emphasizes the peculiarity of the building, down to the fine points of tenant improvements. Seldom is "standard" office space delivered, and the architect plays a vital role in this area. Usually, tenants can be persuaded to pay extra for nonstandard components of the improvement work, and the architect's fee can be regarded as a nonstandard improvement.

The control of construction costs is dependent on a number of factors. Most people who are experienced in renovation will note that the costs shown here are low. This came only through relentless discipline. I have the significant advantage of being both a developer and an architect with a firm that specializes in renovation and construction management. These two roles are often uncomfortable, but they do result in a consistent push for design and management economy.

The acquisition phase is critical. The first information required is a description of the potential tenant market: Is the building for the small user—1,000 square feet to 5,000 square feet—or for those who can take full floors? Buildings suitable for one are generally not for the other.

Exterior and interior of Christiana offices, Santa Monica, Calif. (Joshua Freiwald)

The full-floor tenant is infinitely preferable. Building Owner and Manager Association formulas that allow charging this type of tenant for bathrooms, lobbies and corridors and operating costs favor the developer who can capture these tenants. Even in areas where the full-floor user traditionally pays less per square foot than the partial-floor tenant, the usual differential is less than the savings to the developer.

Obviously, the acquisition decision has other cost implications. Because of code or access problems, certain floor-plan types are much more amenable to remodeling than others are. Also, changes in occupancy can give rise to serious code costs, while retention of existing use does not. The building should also be evaluated in terms of the retroactive "towering inferno" codes that are bound to be coming. An experienced architect is invaluable in this area, where code impacts have a make-or-break effect.

Good Management

Construction costs can be controlled areas in design and construction management.

So often renovation has been an intensely romantic venture, and designs have reflected that romanticism. Unfortunately, artistic successes can be financial disasters. Tenants in renovated buildings generally want romance, but their views of what constitutes romance and good design and those of the architects may vary considerably.

Corporate tenants generally want buildings that have a few overt romantic touches, such as exposed brick walls or paneled lobbies. They are not particularly concerned with details such as the height or detailing of doors or hung ceilings. Architects frequently are, and the architect's vision is an expensive one. Doors as high as nine-foot ceilings add $1 a square foot to improvement costs, for instance. The tenant should pay for such amenities but few are willing to do so. If they are provided, it is often at the cost of profits.

Aggressive construction management is also critical. It means reduced construction costs and time, hastening income. Conner/McLaughlin often acts as a limited general contractor, subbing out the electrical, mechanical and elevator work itself in advance of the normal general contractor work. It is possible to do the same with the exterior and the finish work of carpets, cabinets and draperies.

Aggressive management invariably means fast-track construction. Major work will be begun well before all general building drawings are complete, and long before many of the tenant improvement drawings are done.

Yet in today's construction market, bidding is desirable. Conner/McLaughlin uses a version of the English quantity survey method: Subcontractors are notified of the site conditions (e.g., the floor in the building and access to it, the dates of installation and the approximate quantities involved). They then bid on a unit cost. This hastens the work and gives invaluable protection in negotiation for extra work.

Conclusion

Renovation is enjoyable and can be profitable when carefully undertaken. The time is right for other architects and developers to take advantage of the savings involved in well-conceived preservation efforts.

TABLE 1

COSTS OF NEW CONSTRUCTION FOR 15 to 20-STORY DOWNTOWN BUILDING

	cost per gross square foot
Property acquisition	$ 3.00
Demolition	.15
Basic building	38.00
Tenant improvements	8.00
Subtotal (hard costs)	$49.15
Interim operation (3 years)	2.70
Architectural and legal fees	2.60
Interim cash flow	
Marketing and financing real estate fees	2.70
Developer overhead	1.00
Interim financing	6.60
Developer profit	6.00
Subtotal (soft costs)	$21.60
Total	$70.75

NOTE: An average $70.75 cost per gross square foot converts to $77.80 per net square foot. An 11 percent loan and/or profit factor yields a base rent of $8.56 before operating expenses.

TABLE 2

TYPICAL PATTERNS OF RENOVATION COSTS

	Major renovation gross cost/ sq. ft.	Minor renovation gross cost/ sq. ft.
Acquisition	$ 9.00	$14.00
Front-end renovation	2.50	1.50
Basic building renovation	10.00	7.00
Tenant finishes	8.50	8.05
Subtotal (hard costs)	$30.00	$30.55
Vacant buildings cost (interim operating costs, taxes, insurance, etc., for 1.6 years)	$ .80	$ 1.30
Architectural, engineering and legal fees	1.60	1.20
Net interim income	(1.00)	(2.00)
Marketing costs, leasing and financing fees	2.50	2.80
Developer's overhead	.50	.50
Interim financing	2.50	3.00
Developer's profit	3.00	3.00
Subtotal (soft costs)	$10.90	$ 9.80
Total	$39.90	$40.35

NOTES: Figures for major renovation cover project with no significant stair or structural work.

An average $40.35 cost per gross square foot converts to $44.40 per net square foot. An 11 percent loan and/or profit factor yields a base rent of $4.90.

Rehabilitation operating costs tend to be low, principally because of taxes, but also frequently because of energy costs. An operating cost of $3.90 was used for new construction; a comparable rehabilitation figure would be $2.85, yielding rents at the $7.55 level for a straightforward job and full-floor tenants.

TABLE 3

OPERATING COSTS COMPARISONS FOR NEW AND RENOVATED SPACE

Range for single-tenant floors, in net costs/sq. ft.	Renovated space	New space
Energy (air-conditioned)	$ .70	$ .90
Janitorial costs	.55	.55
Building operating costs, reserve, maintenance	.75	.95
Vacancy allowance	.25	.40
Taxes	.60	1.10
Total	$2.85	$3.90

Example of the "typical building" featured in paper. (Preservation/Urban Design/Incorporated)

Getting the Most for Your Money: Preservation Costs in 19th-Century Commercial Buildings

RICHARD C. FRANK, FAIA

Richard C. Frank, FAIA, is president of Preservation/Urban Design/Incorporated, an Ann Arbor, Mich., firm specializing in preservation, architecture, planning, landscape architecture, and urban design. He is a member of the National Trust Board of Trustees, a former member and chairman of the American Institute of Architects Historic Resources Committee and the former Michigan AIA state preservation coordinator.

There are three alternatives for preserving an urban building with commercial potential:

1. *Restoration.* Bringing back or refurbishing the building's architectural qualities in a precise and correct way
2. *Renovation.* Retaining the building in its original use and upgrading the fabric and systems so that it is salable, leasable or rentable
3. *Adaptation.* Finding new and economically viable uses when retaining the original function of a structure is not feasible. Museum-quality restoration is not the subject here; this kind of preservation is not practical for a commercial venture. As for renovation, Herbert McLaughlin has expertly reviewed that subject elsewhere in this book. The third alternative—preservation through changing use—will be the subject here.

In considering construction details, it seems appropriate to use as an example a familiar building type. Fairly typical throughout the country, particularly in medium and small-sized midwestern cities, this building usually is 20 to 25 feet wide and 50 to 100 feet deep, has adjacent buildings on one or both sides and is two to four (usually three) stories in height. It was probably built between 1865 and 1885 and is basically Italianate in detail.

There is a wide disparity in the cost of preserving this kind of building. Preservation/Urban Design has found that costs are ranging from $15 to $40 or more per square foot. Basically, this variation is a function of the investment in such requirements as new exits, stairs, elevators and restrooms. A large building does not require many more of these basics than a smaller one, and distributing these high fixed costs over a larger gross square footage reduces the cost per square foot.

EXTERIOR PRESERVATION COSTS

Assume that the prototype originally had considerable architectural character and that vestiges of that character remain. No matter what use is intended for the building, the exterior should be handled so as to enhance the original design. This type of preservation simply retains the character of the structure as a part of the changing urban scene.

The condition of the original exterior fabric will generally fall into one of three categories: (1) virtually unchanged, (2) altered on the ground floor only or (3) extensively altered from top to bottom. The first situation is the simplest to deal with, although sometimes expensive, depending on the condition of exterior components. Generally, one needs only to replace deteriorated and unsafe material, make the building watertight and repaint (or remove paint, as the case may be).

For the building that has been altered on the street level only, there is little question as to the proper approach. Through research and physical inspection one should be able to return to the original storefront, matching in quality and detail the unchanged upper stories of the building.

With those buildings that have been extensively altered, the common situation, there are several options. With good photographic documentation the original building front can be *replicated*. This term is used rather than *restored* because the precise details required in museum-quality restoration cannot be discerned from a photograph. However, in the community there undoubtedly are other buildings with similar characteristics that can be used as prototypes. Then, with the historic photographs as a guide, a satisfactory reproduction of the original should be possible. That it is impossible to achieve museum-quality restoration is undoubtedly an advantage in getting the most for your money.

A second option is contemporary adaptation. Wall surfaces where decorative details once existed could be used as canvas, to achieve a contemporary representation of the lost details. This would be an inexpensive approach, however, the result might not be very satisfying.

A third option is to take the building as it is, retaining and emphasizing those original elements that still exist and choosing a contemporary design approach to areas where such detail is missing. This type of treatment will probably result in an intermediate cost. Depending on how much is done to the building, there is some question as to when this method ceases to be good preservation.

Building "Zones" and Costs

Our typical building can be considered to have four

Downtown Ann Arbor, Mich., prior to preservation efforts.
(Preservation/Urban Design/Incorporated)

horizontal zones of exterior detail. From the ground up, the first zone would be the storefront; the second, an ornamental frieze; the third would be one, two or three stories of masonry punctuated with narrow rectangular windows; and the fourth, a cornice, usually with a frieze and brackets on the roof line.

ZONE 1. The original storefront was most likely composed of one or two doors (depending on the building width and upper functions) and fixed glass show windows, either plain or divided into smaller panes of varying designs. The storefront might also have had several cast-iron columns supporting the upper floors. No matter what the contemplated use of the building—commercial or office—this composition works nicely. Although the cast-iron columns might be difficult and costly to obtain, there were usually not many of them in a building. (If a building has a complete cast-iron front, the situation is completely different.)

If the columns are gone, structural support work has probably been done and, if so, replicas of cast-iron columns could be fashioned in wood. Construction in this zone should cost between $15 and $20 per square foot of exterior building surface.

ZONE 2. The lower frieze was usually constructed of wood, sheet metal or cast iron and was probably a simplified version of the upper cornice. This detail has most often been removed, not because of danger of its

falling off, but because it got in the way of storefront remodeling and modern signs. To recreate a missing cast-iron or sheet-metal frieze in this zone could be very costly—between $100 and $200 per linear foot, depending on the extent of detail. Often this zone can be successfully replicated in wood for a lower cost.

ZONE 3. Rehabilitation of this zone is usually the least expensive because it has been changed the least. The components are windows and masonry.

Unless the building has received excellent maintenance during the years (a situation that usually is not the case), wood windows need to be rebuilt or replaced. (Replacement is often less expensive.) It may be possible to replace the original double-hung wood windows with fixed insulating glass in aluminum frames; whether or not this is visually good preservation depends on the degree of other changes. If aluminum is used, color anodized aluminum is a must (although it costs 30 percent more), to make the windows blend better with the tone of the older building materials. Fixed aluminum windows, which should be used only if air-conditioning is planned, are comparable in cost with replacement wood windows, if one is considering the use of insulating glass with both. The cost should be between $100 and $150 per window opening.

The masonry undoubtedly will need to be cleaned, and if it has been painted a decision must be made about repainting or removing the paint to expose the original masonry. Paint removal is usually preferred because the building most likely was not originally painted. Removal can be successfully done with a chemical process; do not sandblast! Paint removal is slightly more expensive than repainting (40 cents per square foot compared with 25 cents) but is a surprisingly small part of the total budget. Cleaning should cost about 10 cents per square foot. When considering this zone as a whole, with windows and masonry together, treatment should cost between $2.00 and $2.50 per square foot of exterior building surface.

ZONE 4. The upper cornice is the most expensive part of the work on the exterior building front but is well worth the cost. The procedure for cast iron and sheet metal described for the lower frieze applies to the upper cornice, usually with the addition of massive brackets. The cost of restoring this zone should be between $30 and $35 per square foot of the building surface it covers.

Total Cost

Taking all four zones into consideration, the total cost of restoration or replication should be in the neighborhood of $10 to $15 per square foot of exterior building surface. For comparison, a current project in which contemporary adaptation is being considered is estimated at $5.35 per square foot of exterior building surface.

Exterior work is not mandatory in adapting a building. However, inherent in what is considered to be quality preservation is concern for the appearance of the building. Therefore, the cost of exterior rehabilitation should be considered an expenditure that is as manda-

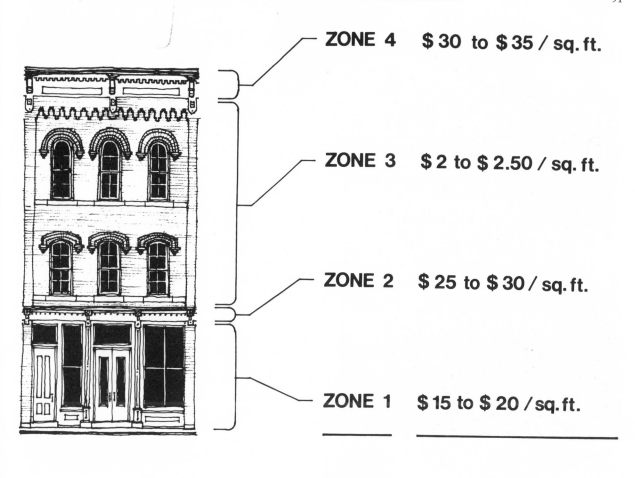

ZONE 4 $30 to $35 / sq. ft.

ZONE 3 $2 to $2.50 / sq. ft.

ZONE 2 $25 to $30 / sq. ft.

ZONE 1 $15 to $20 / sq. ft.

ENTIRE
FACADE $10 to $15 / sq. ft.

tory as code work. Again, the size of the building will determine how this exterior work affects the total cost per square foot.

INTERIOR PRESERVATION

Interior adaptation is infinitely more complex than exterior preservation. To get some idea of the alternatives, multiply the number of possible uses by the number of code requirements. Nevertheless, there are certain aspects that have a dominant effect on overall project feasibility.

The first concern, of course, is what the new use or uses will be. Typically considered are office, retail, residential and special use (e.g., entertainment). Each one of these uses has its own dollar-per-square-foot income rate, which does not vary much throughout the country. The special-use rate is probably among the higher rates per square foot ($9 to $12, plus a percentage of the gross), but the potential market must be considered. One can afford the higher cost of adaptation if the income will also be high.

The philosophy of adaptive use and the design character of interior space should be discussed from a preservation standpoint. It is generally accepted that, if a building can be saved and made economically viable, the exterior must be treated in a way sympathetic to its original design. However, the interior is "fair game." In other words, interior construction should be done in the most expedient and exciting way possible.

If the building has a great deal of original detail in good condition and if that detail fits the intended use, restoration of the interior is in order. But if little interior fabric remains, as is usually the case, or the building never had any interior detail (a warehouse, for instance), then an exciting contemporary treatment is considered to be good preservation. In other words, if the preservation impetus results from architectural or visual significance or importance to the cityscape, whatever is necessary to make the building economically viable is acceptable to the preservationist. If this approach is taken, however, a high quality of contemporary design is mandatory.

Restored "typical building" showing four zones. (Preservation/Urban Design/Incorporated)

Problems with Interiors

One of the problems in any construction, preservation or new, is the ever-increasing cost of labor and materials. This bodes well for preservation because the more existing fabric of the building that can be reused, the fewer new materials will have to be purchased. Material costs can be kept down, helping make preservation projects more competitive with new ones. Naturally, labor costs still must be reckoned with. However, with less to build, construction time is correspondingly shorter, reducing overall labor costs.

Working in interior space still poses some problems. Being confined to existing spaces, particularly if they are small, can make construction difficult. Storing materials in the place where the work is in progress is a problem. In work on a multistory building, old or new, height is always a consideration. With an old building the height problem is aggravated by the fact that materials must be lifted and passed through existing openings that are usually constricted in size.

In adaptation of an old building, new life support systems (plumbing, heating, air-conditioning and electrical) will undoubtedly be a major concern. Mechanical and electrical contractors shudder when they must start snaking their distribution systems through unknown spaces. Substantial savings can be realized by exposing these systems.

The possibility of hidden cost is probably the biggest problem. No matter how thorough the surveillance before completion of contract documents, there will always be some unknown quantities that do not turn up until construction begins. Contractors know this and try to cover these costs accordingly.

Benefits in Interiors

Still, these problems are minor compared to the economic benefits. Walls are usually exposed masonry, masonry plastered or wood stud, also usually plastered. If a masonry wall has never been painted or plastered, it can be steam-cleaned to make an acceptable interior wall surface. If a masonry wall has been plastered and has deteriorated, it is usually less expensive to completely remove the plaster and clean the wall with steam or by sandblasting (the latter is acceptable on the interior). Other plaster surfaces to be retained may require replastering. This work is not much different in cost from that of a new wall in a new building.

Floors are relatively simple. Where use permits, wood floors simply can be sanded and refinished. If this is not appropriate, carpeting can be installed easily, again at a cost no different from new construction.

Ceilings can be suspended, as is typical in new buildings, or the existing construction above can be exposed. While some sound-transmission problems are apparent, the resulting aesthetic character often outweighs the noise problem. Existing construction generally needs to be steam-cleaned and spray-painted. This should cost around 60 cents per square foot, a substantial savings over newly installed ceilings.

Code Problems

A number of cities have recently revised their zoning downtown to allow multiple uses, permitting, for example, residential, commercial and special uses all in the same building. While highly desirable in helping rejuvenate a downtown area, such zoning does present certain code problems. For instance, the residential use area must be separated from the commercial use area by a three-hour fire-rated assembly. This can be accomplished with the use of lightweight concrete on the floor above and a rated ceiling on the underside of the floor structure itself, with sprinklers for the desired fire separation.

Codes can be a significant problem, but with a sympathetic city building department and the new building code amendments being considered for historic buildings, the problems are easing. One of the best ways to resolve many code problems is to simply ''bite the bullet'' and install a complete sprinkler system in the building, surprisingly inexpensive at $1.25 per square foot. This installation greatly aids insurance costs as well.

The state of Michigan recently passed a stringent barrier-free access code to benefit physically handicapped people. Those states that do not have such codes now probably will soon. It appears that the code will have an effect on projects of the type discussed here. In all categories except single family and duplex, all levels of a building must be accessible to the physically handicapped. This means that all upper stories used by the public must be served by an elevator or other lift device. Installation of such devices has a dramatic influence on costs, pushing per-square-foot figures beyond the practical limit, especially for smaller projects. As a result, preservation of the typical building discussed earlier probably would not be feasible. Thus, if revisions of this code on behalf of historic preservation are not considered, it may spell the death knell for many worthwhile preservation and adaptive use projects.

Continuing with the subject of codes, the typical building, which most likely had only one stair, now needs two. Both usually must be constructed in a more fire-safe way than was the original. Building a fire stair in an existing building can be expensive. It is true that steel stairs are relatively inexpensive if they can be prefabricated and installed in large sections. However, because of the limitations on material delivery in an old building, this option may be impossible and stair cost therefore increased.

A four-foot-wide fire stair and a fire-rated enclosure for a floor-to-floor height of approximately 13 feet will probably cost $40 to $50 a square foot. Two vertical exits will satisfy code requirements for considerably more square footage than in this typical building before a third stair is necessary. This is a clear example in which cost affects a small building much more seriously than a large one.

Other Interior Details

If the project needs or can afford an elevator, installing one in an existing building can be difficult. For a building of three or four levels, a hydraulic elevator is usually the best solution. However installation in an existing building is difficult because of the equipment needed to construct the hydraulic lift mechanism. In many buildings such installation is impossible. The alternative is an electric elevator, which may cost from 40 to 60 percent more.

Restrooms are expensive to build anywhere and are particularly so in preservation projects. Unless the building has recently been remodeled, old plumbing is virtually worthless. Because it must be torn out and replaced within the confines of existing floors and walls, one can expect that restroom facilities will be more expensive in an old building than a new one. Again, the larger the building, the more this cost can be spread out.

More often than not, an existing heating system will have to be replaced. This is especially true if air-conditioning is to be provided in the adapted facility. However, in a project with exposed structural systems, all the tentacles that reach out from the life-support system do not have to be hidden. They can simply be run where they are needed, exposed and painted the same color as the ceiling. Or one can honestly admit their presence by painting them orange or another bright color. Heating and air-conditioning can cost in the vicinity of $5 to $8 per square foot.

Wiring may be more difficult, but it also can be exposed. Usually the building will need a complete new electrical system, and for most uses wiring will have to be placed in conduit. But this is not obtrusive even if it must be exposed. Depending on the type of uses anticipated, electrical costs can be $2 to $3 per square foot.

There are many more interior details that could be discussed, but these seem to be the most important for consideration. A reasonable solution to the high cost of preservation for small buildings is to join together several that are adjacent to one another. Stair, exit and restroom requirements will probably be the same and one can greatly expand the usable square footage to share these costs.

Ann Arbor Example

The fascination and frustration of this type of preservation can be illustrated by a project in Ann Arbor, Mich. There were problems, but through close attention to construction details and costs (among other considerations), the project is now on the verge of becoming a success.

Ann Arbor, like many cities, has recently become preservation conscious about its downtown. Preservation is being actively promoted by various groups: city officials, a business organization called Ann Arbor Tomorrow and an organization of business people dedicated to revitalizing a deteriorating section in the heart of downtown. The activity, life and health of this area has already taken a positive turn, with some establishments doing two to six times the amount of business done in the past several years. The buildings in this area are old and most are of preservation quality.

At the core of this area is a four-story hotel built in the 1880s. The adaptation of the building for residential, commercial and special uses is the dream of four men—a doctor of social psychology, a bookstore owner, a natural foods wholesaler and a jazz musician. Initially, they did not even realize that they were dealing with preservation.

This project has been a catalyst for the visual improvement of downtown Ann Arbor, and its founders have received the encouragement and backing of the citizens, Ann Arbor Tomorrow, the city, the Liquor Control Commission and even financial institutions. As a matter of fact, this strong support has probably pushed them beyond the scope of involvement they had originally envisioned. They have learned the problems, sustained the fears, skirted failure, searched out the solutions and now are close to success.

Initially the four men considered establishing a jazz club in the basement of the building and opening the ground floor for commercial shops. They knew that the rest of the building should be useful, but all they had were ideas. A schematic plan was devised, cost estimates were calculated and financial feasibility looked like this:

building value	$120,000
construction costs	605,000
soft costs	75,000
	$800,000
75% mortgage	600,000
equity needed	$200,000

They believed that they could handle the $200,000 equity.

On the basis of an encouraging response to their original schematic idea, the developers added to and refined this plan during design development and found at the completion that their financial feasibility looked like this:

building value	$120,000
construction costs	950,000
soft costs	130,000
	$1,200,000
60% mortgage	720,000
equity needed	$480,000
low appraisal, requiring additional equity	250,000
total equity needed	$730,000

Because of a low appraisal and Ann Arbor's traditional lending conservatism, the four men found to their dismay that they now needed an equity more than three times that originally envisioned. Undaunted, they reviewed all decisions and the design in detail, to discover potential cost reductions. They concluded that the project was too big and that if they could phase the work, opening the largest revenue-generating facility first, their equity capability would be increased. They would establish a successful record at this location, and the risk to the lender would be minimized because of a smaller loan. The resulting financial picture looked like this:

building value	$120,000
construction costs	268,000
soft costs	122,000
	$510,000
70% mortgage	350,000
equity needed	$160,000

After considerable help from the city, Ann Arbor Tomorrow and a prominent lawyer interested in the downtown area, the lending institutions agreed to form a consortium and provide $350,000 for financing, with each instituting a $70,000 loan. The project is now under way.

CONCLUSION

Preservation is alive in Ann Arbor and cities all over the United States. The retention, adaptation and enhancement of older existing buildings is now considered the thread that will hold a downtown together in spite of pressures to the contrary. Our preservation movement has just begun to gain momentum and I know it will be successful.

Government Assistance in Preservation Financing

Grants-in-Aid for Historic Preservation

RICHARD C. MEHRING

Richard C. Mehring is chief, Preservation Projects, Office of Archeology and Historic Preservation, National Park Service.

In the National Historic Preservation Act of 1966, Congress declared that the federal government should give maximum encouragement to agencies and individuals undertaking the preservation of historic properties. The act also called for federal assistance to state governments and to the National Trust for Historic Preservation for expansion and acceleration of their historic preservation programs and activities.

Before 1966, with the exception of certain archaeological research and protection activities, federal historic preservation programs had been limited to the acquisition or recognition of nationally significant properties and to the recording of historic properties for archival purposes. While these early programs preserved a few hundred of the most important historic properties, the task of saving thousands of others remained with state and local governments and the private sector. Lack of recognition and financial support left a vast number of significant resources in serious danger of loss through deterioration or demolition.

The 1966 act was intended to resolve this problem. Among other things, it established matching grants-in-aid of up to 50 percent for the 50 states, the District of Columbia, Puerto Rico, the Virgin Islands, Guam, American Samoa, the Trust Territory of the Pacific Islands and the National Trust for Historic Preservation. Grants may be used for preparation of comprehensive statewide historic preservation surveys and plans, and for acquisition and development of properties listed in the National Register of Historic Places.

HOW THE GRANTS-IN-AID PROGRAM WORKS

Authority for the grants program was delegated to the National Park Service, which assigned administrative responsibilities to the Division of Grants, Office of Archeology and Historic Preservation. In the past five years, $50 million has been apportioned for grants-in-aid. Besides supporting survey and planning activities, this money has assisted approximately 1,500 projects to date.

Obtaining and Using Funds

A brief chronological sequence of the granting process will help provide an understanding of how to acquire these funds.

Each state must prepare an annual apportionment warrant containing all the allowable projects listed in the National Register of Historic Places for which matching funds are available. This is submitted to the National Park Service before the beginning of the federal fiscal year. When Congress provides the annual appropriation for the program, the proposed distribution of this money is sent to the U.S. Secretary of the Interior. The Secretary apportions a lump sum grant to each state, territory and the National Trust, based on the need expressed in their apportionment warrants. The state historic preservation officer and the state review board then decide how to distribute the grant.

Under the category of survey and planning projects, funds may be used for the following: professional staff, preparation and updating of the state historic preservation plan, drafting of project plans and specifications, compilation of information for publication, support for the states' continuing activities to identify historic properties and nominate them to the National Register, research and other expenses related to the historic preservation program.

The remaining portion of the annual program grant is assigned to acquisition and development projects. This amount may be matched by cash, the appraisal value of donated property or acceptable donated services. If the state chooses, its funds may be transferred to local governments, private organizations or individuals.

Funds may be used for the acquisition of fee-simple or less-than-fee-simple title. The former involves absolute ownership; the latter may include acquisition of development rights through easements or acquisition of title subject to a life estate. When an acquisition project results in ownership resting with a private organization or individual, the public interest must be protected for a specified number of years, as determined by the amount of federal grant assistance received. In addition, deed covenants must assure continued maintenance and administration, benefit to the public and first right of refusal on behalf of the state.

Funds may be used for the protection, rehabilitation, restoration or reconstruction of historic properties, following professional standards established by the U.S. Secretary of the Interior. Conformance to these standards must be shown by plans, specifications, shop drawings or other materials submitted by the state to the National Park Service or through on-site inspections made by Division of Grants personnel.

The Park Service provides or helps locate technical assistance whenever possible for problems encountered prior to or during work on projects. All acquisition and development projects require completion reports indicating work accomplished, material used and difficulties encountered. Useful technical information is gleaned from these reports and made available to all the states. Triennial maintenance reports further assist in evaluating preservation work. In addition, the Park Service is currently reproducing and distributing archaeological reports to assist in the study of prehistoric cultures and to promulgate the most recent techniques in the field.

Grants to the National Trust

The National Trust for Historic Preservation is a private, nonprofit corporation chartered by Congress to facilitate public participation in the preservation of historic properties. The Trust owns and maintains historic properties of national significance and assists public and private agencies and individuals involved in historic preservation. Through its ability to act quickly and effectively in the private sector, the Trust provides a vital service complementary to the federal and state historic preservation programs. Grants to the Trust support the acquisition, restoration, maintenance and administration of its historic properties. In addition, a wide variety of educational and technical assistance activities are supported by grant funds, including publications, professional and technical seminars and conferences, matching consultant service grants, legal services, feasibility studies, acceptance of preservation easements and the purchase of options on endangered historic properties.

OTHER NATIONAL PARK SERVICE ACTIVITIES

The Park Service Office of Archeology and Historic Preservation has several other divisions in addition to the Division of Grants:

National Register

This is the official inventory of the nation's properties that merit preservation because of significance in American history, architecture, archaeology and culture. The National Register automatically includes all historic areas in the National Park System and all properties designated by the U.S. Secretary of the Interior as National Historic Landmarks, plus many other properties of national, state and local significance.

Districts, sites, buildings, structures and objects may be nominated by the appropriate state historic preservation officer following the recommendations of the state review board. Upon approval by the National Park Service they are listed in the National Register. In addition, federal agencies are required to identify and nominate to the National Register all eligible properties under their jurisdiction or control.

Historic American Buildings Survey

Initiated in 1933, HABS is an archival program documenting historic American architecture with measured drawings, photographs and written records. It is carried out through a cooperative agreement involving the National Park Service, the Library of Congress and the American Institute of Architects.

The basic criteria for recording are architectural merit and historical association. The archives are intended to represent a complete collection of the building arts in the United States by including examples of building types, styles, dates and geographic locations.

Through this program, professional recording advice and technical assistance are given to federal agencies, which are required under Executive Order 11593 to provide for the recording of historic properties to be demolished or substantially altered.

Historic American Engineering Record

Established in 1969, HAER is an archival effort to document American engineering achievements. The program attempts to record a complete summary of engineering technology by including significant examples of engineering solutions that demonstrate the accomplishments of all branches of the profession. It is conducted by the National Park Service in conjunction with the Library of Congress and the American Society of Civil Engineers. The program stimulates increased public interest in the emerging field of industrial archaeology through a cooperative effort with the state historic preservation officers in the preparation of National Register forms.

Interagency Programs

The Archeological and Historic Preservation Act of 1974 directs the U.S. Secretary of the Interior to administer a nationwide program for recovery of archaeological and historical materials threatened by federal construction or by federally licensed and assisted land modification activities. Administered through liaison with other federal agencies, this program—involving the Inter-Agency Archeological Services and Inter-Agency Historic Architectural Services—contracts with qualified educational and scientific institutions to perform necessary investigations.

In addition, Executive Order 11593 requires that the Secretary of the Interior advise other federal agencies on the identification and evaluation of historic properties. The National Park Service has three regional consultants who provide this advice and assistance. The Secretary also is charged with developing and publishing information methods and techniques of preservation, restoration and maintenance of historic properties. Such information is shared with federal agencies and with state and local governments. This effort currently includes the preparation of technical briefs that are intended for publication eventually in a technical handbook for historic preservation.

Surplus Property

Finally, Executive Order 11593 requires the Secretary of the Interior to review and evaluate plans to transfer surplus federal properties for historic monument purposes, to assure that the historical character of such properties is preserved through rehabilitation, restoration, improvement, repair and maintenance. The Surplus Property Act of 1944 and the Federal Property and Administrative Services Act of 1949 permit the transfer of surplus historic properties from the federal government to state or local governments without charge if they will be preserved in perpetuity. A 1972 amendment now permits historic properties to be used for compatible revenue-producing purposes.

CONCLUSION

These are the major historic preservation activities of the National Park Service. We look forward to our continuing partnership with federal, state, local and other agencies pursuing the vital goal of maintaining our national heritage.

Government Assistance in Preservation Financing: The State Sector

TRUETT LATIMER

Truett Latimer is executive director, Texas Historical Commission, state historic preservation officer for Texas and president, Conference of State Historic Preservation Officers.

As preparation for this paper, an independent survey of the 55 states and territories was conducted with the objective of gathering original research material. Much of that material was received only days before writing began.

In all candor, most of the information gathered from various groups and organizations does not isolate or pinpoint the assigned subject of this paper: What are individual states doing to assist in preservation financing for private concerns and individuals?

Of the 27 states answering the questionnaire, not a single one has any type of state-guaranteed loan program. From this, one can probably assume that no state has such a program and can therefore leave the subject to some ardent preservationist or ambitious legislator. The field is obviously wide open, and some state or territory has the opportunity of being the first in the nation to approve this innovative approach to preservation financing.

A more fertile source of information was found in the state grant-in-aid programs. Of the 27 states answering the questionnaire, only nine stated that they had some type of grant-in-aid program, the proceeds of which are primarily for the use of nonprofit organizations and government subdivisions. At this point it should be mentioned that most of the states, including Texas, have constitutional prohibitions against appropriating state funds for private purposes. Thus it will be necessary for numerous state constitutions to be amended before grant-in-aid programs can be used by private concerns and individuals for historic preservation purposes.

STATE GRANT-IN-AID PROGRAMS

Alaska has a state grant-in-aid program, but it has never been used. Connecticut appropriated $750,000 in 1967, providing up to 50 percent matching grants-in-aid to nonprofit organizations and municipalities. The statute was amended this year to allow funding to go to private individuals, but the current appropriation of $95,000 for this program has been frozen by the governor.

Colorado this year appropriated $50,000 for a grant-in-aid program with a maximum grant of $4,000, but it has not been funded by the legislature.

In 1974, Florida appropriated $534,000 for grants-in-aid for the historic preservation projects of nonprofit organizations and municipalities, with an exclusion for private individuals and concerns. No money was appropriated for the program this year.

The Georgia legislature created the Georgia Heritage Trust program and has appropriated $100,000 to provide up to 50 percent matching grants-in-aid to local government subdivisions.

Kentucky currently has an appropriation of $80,000 and can provide up to 100 percent of needed funds. Grants can go to private individuals as well as government subdivisions and nonprofit organizations.

The state of Massachusetts has appropriated $2.5 million for its Bicentennial commission; approximately 25 percent of this is to be used for historic preservation projects. The maximum project grant is $5,000, with up to 50 percent matched by the state. This program will obviously self-destruct.

Since 1974, Michigan has had an appropriation of $100,000 for a grant-in-aid program, with the maximum amount of a grant being $60,000. In the same year, Vermont appropriated $25,000 for such a program, but nothing was appropriated this year.

In Texas, the current governor twice recommended an appropriation of $250,000 per year for up to 50 percent matching grants-in-aid. In 1973 and again this year the legislature failed to appropriate the money, which could have gone to local political subdivisions and nonprofit organizations.

In almost every instance mentioned, the funding for state grant-in-aid programs was either cut drastically or completely eliminated during this tight budget year. This is a further indication that historic preservation does not enjoy the high priority it should have in the state legislatures.

Tax Incentives

Perhaps the greatest possible salvation for continuing assistance to private preservation efforts lies in the area of tax incentives. For example, in Alaska municipalities may provide for tax exemptions for designated historic properties, though none has done so.

In Connecticut the law provides as follows:

Any municipality may by ordinance provide for the abatement in whole or in part of real property taxes on structures of historical or architectural merit. Such municipality shall determine which structures within its locality shall be availal' 'e for classification as historically or architecturally meritorious, or it may delegate such determination to local private preservation or

architectural bodies. Such tax abatement shall be available to the owners of real property which is so classified, if it can be shown to the satisfaction of the municipality that the current level of taxation is a material factor which threatens the continued existence of the structure, necessitating either its demolition or remodeling in a manner which destroys the historical or architectural value.

Under this provision, it would be necessary for the Connecticut legislature to appropriate monies to each municipality that adopted the ordinance in an amount equal to the taxes that would have been paid by the designated properties. Unfortunately, even though this law has been on the statute books of Connecticut since 1967, it has never been used. However, it is an idea that offers possibilities for other states.

This year the Idaho legislature passed a new statute, effective this month, providing that local political subdivisions may exempt designated historic properties from certain taxation.

In 1973, New Hampshire adopted legislation providing for assessment of open land at current use values. Although buildings, yards and grounds are specifically excluded from current use assessment, the underdeveloped portions of land tracts having historical significance and/or listed in the National Register of Historic Places are eligible for current use taxation as "recreation land." Again, this is an innovative approach, which would offer great possibilities if states would adopt legislation providing for assessment of historical properties based on their current use. In most instances, this could preclude exorbitant property taxes on historic properties located in urban areas. At the present time such properties pay taxes at an assessed valuation based on their potential rather than current use.

In 1969, the New Mexico legislature passed a statute designed to aid private preservation efforts. This statute provides as follows:

To encourage the restoration and preservation of cultural properties listed on the official register with the written consent of the owner and which are available for educational purposes . . . shall be exempt from that portion of local city, county and school property taxes which is offset by a properly documented showing of . . . approved restoration, preservation and maintenance expenses.

The New Mexico statute could well be the one that all states should emulate in attempting to provide appropriate assistance to private preservation efforts.

On November 4, Texans will vote on a new constitution submitted by the legislature. The new finance article makes provision for ad valorem tax relief as follows:

(B) The legislature by law may provide for the preservation of cultural, historical or natural history resources by:

(1) Granting relief from state ad valorem taxes on appropriate property so designated in the manner prescribed by law; or

(2) Authorizing political subdivisions to grant relief from ad valorem taxes on appropriate property so designated by the political subdivision in the manner prescribed by general law.

In addition, the Texas legislature has passed the following, which will be effective if the proposed constitution is adopted by the voters:

Article 715Gi. Exemption of historic sites.
Section 1. The governing body of any political subdivision of this state that levies property taxes may exempt from property taxation part or all of the value of a structure, and the land necessary for access and use thereof, if the structure is:
(1) Designated as a recorded historic landmark by the Texas Historical Commission and by the governing body of the taxing unit; or
(2) Designated as a historically significant site that is in need of tax relief to encourage its preservation under an ordinance adopted by the governing body of the taxing unit.

The state of Oregon perhaps should receive the award for enacting 1975 landmark legislation in the historic preservation battle. The Oregon legislature has passed an act that gives tax benefits to historic properties listed in the National Register. The specific language is as follows:

"Historic property" means real property that is currently listed in the National Register of Historic Places, established and maintained under the National Historic Preservation Act of 1966 (P.L. 89-665); that is open to the public for site-seeing at least one day in each calendar year in accordance with rules adopted by the State Historic Preservation Officer; and that meets the minimum standards of maintenance established by rule of the State Historic Preservation Officer.

The act provides that an owner of historic property desiring classification and assessment as such shall make application to the county assessor on forms approved by the Department of Revenue. The owner shall also consent in writing to the viewing of the property by the state historic preservation officer and any state advisory committee on historic preservation. The act also delineates the review process to be developed by the state historic preservation officer and provides an appeal of that officer's decision.

The Oregon approach of exempting National Register properties from ad valorem taxation provides an entirely new concept to this form of tax relief. It would obviously place increased importance on the National Register program by substituting the evaluation criteria for acceptance to the Register for any the state might have. At least it would provide some measure of standardization to exempt properties.

PRESERVATION PROBLEMS AND PROPOSED SOLUTIONS

The problems being experienced by preservationists in the various states are as varied as the states themselves. However, they can be categorized as follows: (1) lack of interest at the executive level of government, (2) lack of preservation legislation, (3) the need to incorporate preservation legislation into the state land use programs, (4) establishment of a stable base for the existing grant-in-aid program and (5) financial problems.

In the questionnaire on which this paper is based the state historic preservation officers were asked, "What could and should your state do to help in preservation financing?" The most frequent answers were: (1) provide tax advantages to private individuals who restore and maintain approved structures; (2) establish state grant-in-aid programs similar to that of the National Park Service program; and (3) establish revolving funds on a state level to private low-interest loans for historic preservation purposes.

From the information submitted, it is obvious that state assistance to private preservation efforts is fragmented, isolated and inconsistent. With the economics of preservation becoming increasingly favorable, it is imperative for preservationists to increase their efforts in the statehouses of the nation to effect tax incentive programs for the private sector. Such incentives obviously would make up an infinitesimal percentage of the state tax dollars, yet they would provide a method by which historic properties could be preserved without the expensive process of state ownership.

CONCLUSION

Today, the value of preservation is widely recognized and has taken on an entirely new meaning. Preservationists have finally reached the point where preservation is no longer synonymous with museums or with someone's trying to reproduce the past. Preservation has come to mean the continuation of the best architectural and human qualities of both rural and urban life.

When we lose an important landmark, we lose more than an old building. We lose the memory of what has been. We lose our sense of the past, the most visible evidence of our heritage.

I would not want to believe that succeeding generations will be able to say that we tore down the structures it took our forebears 200 years to build or that we devoted our expertise to the recycling of tin cans but were not able to recycle our landmarks.

Selected Federal and National Trust Activities

JOHN L. FRISBEE, III

John L. Frisbee, III, is director of the Western Regional Office of the National Trust, located in San Francisco.

During the past several years, the National Trust has systematically accumulated information on programs that relate to historic preservation. In 1974, the Trust published *A Guide to Federal Programs*, a 400-page book that identifies more than 200 programs in some way relevant to historic preservation. In 1972, the Trust published *A Guide to State Programs*, which is currently being revised for publication early in 1976.

Many programs, only a few of which will be described here, have some application to historic preservation activities, but few, if any, are a panacea for preservation financing. Generally, they relate indirectly, in that they might serve as stimuli for private investment, largely in the form of capital improvements.

Business Development Loans

The U.S. Department of Commerce Economic Development Administration (EDA) provides for Business Development Loans. These are long-term, low-interest loans to individuals, state and local governments and local development groups to support the establishment of new firms or expansion of existing ones. These loans may cover up to 65 percent of capital costs and must be used in undertakings that result in new sources of employment. The maximum loan for a project is 50 percent of total project costs.

In the early 1960s, the Shakertown historic restoration project, located at Pleasant Hill, Ky., received a $2 million, 40-year, 3 percent loan to undertake restoration of buildings. The loan was largely predicated on the fact that it would provide new employment opportunities for residents of the depressed area of Mercer County, Ky.

CETA Funds

The programs of the Comprehensive Employment and Training Act (CETA) also can provide preservation funding. Title 6 of the act provides for the use of federal funds for public service employment under federal, state and local public employers and some nonprofit organizations.

Ninety percent of each CETA grant must be used for salaries. The maximum annual salary for any person is $10,000 from CETA funds, but the CETA dollars can be supplemented with other funds to allow payment of higher salaries.

It is possible to use CETA-funded employees to do rehabilitation work but not for new construction. Thus this program could relate indirectly to long-term, profit-oriented preservation ventures.

CETA employees have been used by the Pioneer Square Association in Seattle and by the Foundation for San Francisco's Architectural Heritage. The latter, for example, has an architect hired through CETA.

National Endowment for the Arts

The Architectural and Environmental Arts Program of the National Endowment for the Arts is applicable to planning: For example, the National Theme Awards Program supports activity in architecture and urban design. In 1973, the theme was City Edges; in 1974, City Options; and in 1975, City Scale.

Under this program, grants of up to 50 percent, usually for $10,000 to $50,000, are available for financing planning studies largely designed to promote alternative solutions to community design problems. During the past several years, a substantial number of these grants have been made for historic preservation purposes. Seattle, for example, developed the master plan for Pioneer Square in part with a City Edges grant. Having that plan has of course enabled Seattle to provide more direction for new development in the district.

Under the City Options program, the Western Regional Office of the National Trust received a grant to support a team consisting of an architect, a city planner, a lawyer and a development specialist to travel to small communities in the West to help them try to develop rehabilitation plans for old downtown commercial areas. This has been done in several communities, and it is hoped that this kind of planning activity will stimulate preservation and restoration work in these old commercial districts.

General Services Administration Provisions

Richard Mehring briefly mentioned the amendment to the Federal Surplus Property and Administrative Services Act of 1949. Title to properties received under this act must be held by local governmental entities. A property can be transferred to the locality at no cost. The local governmental entity can then work out a lease arrangement with a local developer who would develop the property for commercial purposes. In such cases, revenues over and above the cost of restoration and maintenance must be used for specified public purposes in the community.

Several examples of federal buildings that have been transferred under this particular piece of legislation come to mind. One is the Old Federal Courts Building in St. Paul, Minn., which was transferred without charge to the city and now will house a variety of facilities, including a cultural center and county offices. It also will offer restaurants and shops in leased space and will be redeveloped for about $500,000 less than the cost of comparable new construction.

Small Business Administration Programs

The Small Business Administration (SBA) may also have programs that could be used for historic preservation projects. Generally, the SBA has little money, if any, to lend directly, and mostly serves as a guarantor for conventional loans. However, SBA backing has been used in San Francisco by San Francisco Victorianna, a small company that makes replacement parts for wooden Victorian buildings. The founders of this company initially obtained an SBA-guaranteed $20,000 loan from the United Bank of California.

National Trust Programs

There are also two National Trust programs of interest. Of course, the Trust is not a federal agency, but it does have two programs that could provide stimuli to investments in preservation.

One of these is the Consultant Service Grant Program, which makes small matching grants for up to 50 percent of the costs of obtaining consultation on preservation problems. These grants are made only to member organizations, which are generally government or nonprofit groups. The largest grant made to date is for $9,000. However, since 1969, more than 100 grants have totaled in excess of $200,000.

One grant, for example, enabled the Foundation for San Francisco's Architectural Heritage to undertake a rehabilitation feasibility study of the Pacific Gas and Electric Company substation on Jessie Street in San Francisco. Current plans call for the demolition of this building as a part of the Yerba Buena Redevelopment Project, should that go through. The foundation contends that this building would make a marvelous entrance to the redevelopment area and that it has many potential commercial uses.

Another grant was to the Chillicothe, Ohio, Restoration Foundation, to help finance a rehabilitation plan for Water Street, a one-block area of significant 19th-century commercial architecture. Partly as a result of the study that was made, 56 downtown property owners have agreed to rehabilitate their commercial buildings.

Another Trust program is the National Historic Preservation Fund, a revolving fund through which the Trust makes low-interest loans, usually at 3–4 percent, to member organizations establishing local revolving funds.

A loan of $85,000 was made several years ago to the Pittsburgh History & Landmarks Foundation. The loan was used in part to encourage other community dollars. The Pittsburgh people have thus been able to raise another $700,000 locally for a preservation revolving fund.

The objective of the National Trust revolving fund is to provide seed money to help develop local funds. That local money should then be used for buying or selling historic properties to generate additional preservation projects in the community.

Historic Structures Tax Act

Currently there is a bill before Congress that could have a considerable impact on the preservation of historic structures. It is known as the Historic Structures Tax Act of 1975. The Senate bill is S. 667 and the accompanying House bill is H.R. 6373. This bill attempts to change the current situation in which there are tax incentives to put up new buildings and disincentives to restore old ones.

Richard Mehring has already mentioned the National Register of Historic Places. If enacted, the Historic Structures Tax Act would specifically affect buildings listed in the National Register.

One provision of the bill would permit a five-year writeoff of the cost of rehabilitating National Register buildings used in the taxpayer's trade or business and held for the production of income. A developer who constructed a new building on the former site of a National Register building would have depreciation limited to the straight-line method, whereas it can now be accelerated. Developers would no longer be able to deduct the cost of demolishing National Register properties or the undepreciated costs of such structures when they are demolished.

These three aspects of this act could provide additional incentives for preservation work. Again, this bill is not a panacea, but it is one additional economic tool that might be useful, along with the others described here.

Conclusion

The government programs outlined in these papers can help to catalyze community historic preservation programs. Because they can be used to stabilize a neighborhood or a potential historic district, public financial assistance programs can help to establish a climate conducive to private investment. Public officials and private investors should consider carefully how federal and state grant and loan programs can be used most effectively to stimulate private responses to public actions.

HUD Programs to Support Preservation

GEORGE A. KARAS

George A. Karas is deputy director of environmental planning, Office of Environmental Quality, U.S. Department of Housing and Urban Development. He has served on the Advisory Council on Historic Preservation as the alternate or designee of the Secretary of Housing and Urban Development for most of the years since its inception.

A solid, realistic preservation program can result in profit, both monetary and social. A sound, well-preserved neighborhood assures stable property values, opportunities for low-risk investment and long-term cash return, continuity with the past, a harmonious present and a secure future.

The federal government, and the U.S. Department of Housing and Urban Development (HUD) in particular, can make both preservation and profit making easier. Most HUD-assisted programs can be used for preservation, and they do not ignore the private profit motive. As a matter of fact, many are grounded in that motive and rely on it to be the propellant for conservation efforts. Neighborhoods cannot be preserved and made stable with a few single-shot grants; instead they must continue to attract private investment. HUD has programs that encourage such investment, and some of the obvious ones plus a few that are not so obvious will be briefly described here.

Community Development Block Grants

HUD's newest program was enacted as Title I of the Housing and Community Development Act of 1974. It is a program of community development block grants and became effective on January 1, 1975, with an initial appropriation of $2.5 billion. A slightly larger appropriation is expected this fiscal year, which began on July 1.

Enactment of the Housing and Community Development Act of 1974 marked the beginning of a new era in relations between the federal government and units of general-purpose local government. The community development block grant program replaces a number of categorical grants-in-aid programs: (1) urban renewal, (2) water and sewer, (3) model cities, (4) neighborhood facilities, (5) rehabilitation loans, (6) public facilities loans and (7) the open space program (including historic preservation).

The act was the culmination of lengthy debate on the allocation of federal community development funds and a response to the growing dissatisfaction with many features of the categorical programs. Under the new block grant program, funds go directly to the general-purpose local government, the body that is most responsive to the electorate and has the broadest authority to deal with community development. All cities of more than 50,000 population are entitled to fund amounts based on a formula that takes into account population, poverty and housing needs. In addition, many cities that have participated in urban renewal and model cities, regardless of size, are entitled to move ahead on the programs already started. Cities with population of less than 50,000 can apply for funds to be distributed on a competitive basis.

Almost all activities eligible under the categorical programs being replaced can also be carried out with community development block grant funds. To further increase local flexibility in carrying out community development, these funds may be used anywhere within a local government's jurisdiction to serve the needs of low and moderate-income residents or to meet urgent community development needs. In the area of historic preservation, the monies need not be used only for National Register structures and districts but can be applied to other local preservation purposes. No local share is required in the program, and the funds can be used as the local share to match any other federal grant, such as U.S. Department of the Interior funds for historic preservation. (Generally, one federal grant cannot be used as the required match for another.)

Neighborhood preservation activities under the new program include: (1) purchase, rehabilitation and resale (not necessarily for fair market value), (2) acquisition and disposition in whole or in part, (3) revolving funds, (4) clearance, (5) street work and sewers, (6) neighborhood facilities, and (7) historical surveys.

Section 8 Existing Housing Program

The major federal operating program for helping people with lower incomes secure decent, safe and sanitary housing is the new section 8 Existing Housing Program. Section 8 can be a powerful force for neighborhood preservation. It emphasizes the competitive forces of the private market while leaving to public housing agencies the responsibility for providing lower-income people the necessary financial and other assistance. The public housing authority provides eligible applicants with certificates enabling them to seek suitable housing, and it contracts with landlords to offer assistance on behalf of the participants. The landlord provides appropriate housing at a reasonable rent and must also provide the services and facilities customary in that locality.

This program encourages people to seek housing that meets their needs, and it provides for payment of fair market rents to owners. Thus the private economic mechanism is put in motion, and needed upkeep and maintenance are assured. When this results in increased investment in individual properties, the overall result can be the upgrading and preservation of the neighborhood and the community.

Title I Home Improvement Loan Program

In reading through historic preservation-related speeches given by HUD speakers over the years, one finds little about a division of HUD that comprises almost one-third of the department—the Federal Housing Administration, or FHA. The FHA-insured Title I Home Improvement Loan Program can be a powerful force in neighborhood preservation.

Under Title I, FHA insures loans made at market rates by private financing institutions for improvements of many different types of properties. The Emergency Home Purchase Act of 1974 expanded the program to grant additional benefits to residential properties in the National Register of Historic Places or those certified by the U.S. Secretary of the Interior to be eligible for the National Register. Persons improving such properties may receive insured loans of up to $15,000 *per dwelling unit* for a term of 15 years. There is no maximum amount for total loan coverage.

Revised procedures for administering the FHA Title I program, as modified by the 1974 act, are currently being developed. These procedures will provide for a review of the proposed improvement by the state historic preservation officer, so that no financed work on a National Register property will damage its historical value.

Under this program HUD insures lenders against losses on loans, which may be used to finance alterations, repairs and improvements that substantially protect or improve the basic livability and/or utility of existing structures. The maximum loan amount is $10,000 per dwelling unit; as indicated previously, this can go up to $15,000 per unit for National Register properties. All families are eligible to apply. Eligible borrowers include the owner of the property to be improved or a lessee having a lease extending at least six months beyond the maturity of the loan. The responsibility for credit approvals of borrowers lies with the insured lenders.

The application procedure requires the borrower to apply directly to the insured lender. There are no deadlines, and HUD does not ordinarily participate in the approval or disapproval of the loan. Reapplication in case of a refusal is also submitted to an approved lender, who decides on renewals as well.

HUD insures private lenders against losses of up to 90 percent of single loans. The maximum interest rate now is 12 percent per year, and the insurance charge is 50 cents per $100 per year, which is included in the finance charge. Loans mature in 12 years and 32 days or earlier. They may be refinanced, but may not go beyond 12 years from the date of the original note.

In order to meet postassistance requirements, annual delinquency reports are required from all lenders. HUD reserves the right to audit their accounts to determine compliance and conformance with FHA regulations and standards.

Urban Reinvestment Task Force

The objective of the Urban Reinvestment Task Force is the development and replication of programs that involve local citizens and governments in reversing the process of urban disinvestment. The task force will be involved in two separate programs, both designed to produce residential rehabilitation through such activities as home improvement lending and mortgage lending on existing housing. The two programs are the Neighborhood Preservation Program and the Neighborhood Housing Services Program, both aimed at revitalization and both focusing on the restoration of credit for homeowners in deteriorating areas.

Projects under the Neighborhood Preservation Program will deal with declining neighborhoods in attempts to renew the confidence of lending institutions, the real estate industry, city administrators, existing homeowners and potential homeseekers. The task force will identify and support innovative projects that bolster confidence in those neighborhoods.

The Neighborhood Housing Services Program will make credit available after an institutional decision to limit credit has been made. Projects under this program may include rehabilitating and financing multifamily units; revitalizing neighborhood business districts; purchasing, rehabilitating and marketing vacant properties; or other innovative approaches to stabilizing and improving neighborhoods.

The task force will disseminate information on successful programs for the benefit of other cities. A built-in evaluation system will determine the degree of program success or failure and will generate the type of information that can be disseminated to insure widespread knowledge of these demonstrations. Programs will receive modest demonstration grants for data collection, documentation and support of their activities.

The Urban Reinvestment Task Force has selected five programs for support in 1975.

The first is the Berkeley, Calif., Housing Conservation Program, which has focused its conservation efforts in three neighborhoods. By providing municipal services and public improvements and by assuring the availability of high-risk loans, Berkeley will obtain the information and experience necessary to expand this conservation effort to a citywide program. The city has committed revenue sharing and operating funds to the effort: $550,000 to a revolving loan fund and $750,000 for park improvements.

The second program is the Hoboken, N.J., Multifamily Rehabilitation Project, which provides below-market-rate funds for rehabilitation to owners of six to ten multifamily units located in central Hoboken. Funds will be provided through a combination of private lending institutions, interest-reduction grants financed through state funds from the New Jersey Department of Community Affairs and community development funds. An innovative municipal mortgage insurance program to insure multifamily rehabilitation loans will also be tested. This program builds on the success of Hoboken's Project Rehab and its Home Improvement Program.

A third effort is the Greater Hartford, Conn., Process Commercial/Revitalization Project in northwest Hartford. This program is designed to improve the appearance and consumer appeal of a four-block central shopping area along Albany Avenue, adjacent to a $3.2 million shopping center site and an existing rehabilitation project. The city has allocated community development funds and Comprehensive Employment Training Agency personnel to implement this program.

The fourth activity is the Oak Park, Ill., conservation program. This effort calls for single-family and multifamily property maintenance, public safety and crime prevention activities, a villagewide elementary school strategy, revitalization of the commercial district and an effort to increase the availability of conventional mortgages and home improvement financing. In addition, an equity assurance proposal to insure homeowners equity development has been recommended by a group of lenders in Oak Park and will be tested by the village. The neighborhood selected in Oak Park is just west of the Austin National Housing Services Program area in Chicago.

The fifth program supported by the Urban Reinvestment Task Force is the Yonkers, N.Y., multifamily rehabilitation program. This involves a partnership of property owners, tenants, the city building department and lenders cooperating to upgrade large apartment buildings in order to stabilize the surrounding neighborhood. The city has committed $350,000 in community development funds to the local building and housing divisions; part of those funds will be allocated to this effort. In addition, the city has agreed to a tax-abatement program to enable building owners to allocate additional revenue for property rehabilitation.

Urban Homesteading

Still another recent HUD activity is the Urban Homesteading Design Program, which supports demonstrations to encourage investment in urban neighborhoods and to better utilize the existing housing stock. The use of HUD properties in local urban homesteading programs should serve as an incentive to localities to mobilize a range of resources, public and private, to focus on the preservation of target neighborhoods.

Neighborhood preservation tools such as urban homesteading are consistent with the national housing goal set forth in section 801 of the Housing and Community Development Act of 1974. That goal states that a greater effort must be made to encourage the preservation of existing housing and neighborhoods in conjunction with the provision of adequate municipal services.

The demonstration design is based on the assumption that urban homesteading must be part of a program of neighborhood revitalization. The sale of properties held by HUD is intended to be used by localities as part of "a coordinated approach toward neighborhood improvement," as required by section 810 of the 1974 act. HUD is interested in homesteading programs in cities that are willing to specify the neighborhoods in which they will coordinate conservation efforts and provide the public services and amenities commensurate with the need to arrest decline and encourage private investment. The active participation of the private sector in a city's homesteading demonstration, especially in the provision of interim and permanent mortgage financing, is important to the formulation of a balanced demonstration plan.

HUD will work with cities in selecting the properties to be transferred to them and subsequently conveyed to homesteaders. HUD will also cooperate in the disposition of other properties it is holding in homesteading neighborhoods in order to optimize the impact of local preservation plans.

The program will be a one-time offering of properties. The legislation authorizes $5 million in fiscal year 1976; this can be used to provide technical assistance and to reimburse the FHA insurance fund for the properties transferred to cities. The department has determined that the full authorization will be used during the coming year for 1,000 properties. No technical assistance funds will be provided. Given these constraints, the number of cities that can participate will be limited; however, cities from the entire country will be selected.

All vacant, one to four–family properties in the process of becoming HUD owned will potentially be eligible for transfer, and there is no maximum value limitation for eligible properties. HUD will work with the cities in determining which properties are most suitable for transfer and will also coordinate its other disposition techniques to support the target neighborhood preservation effort.

Comprehensive Planning Program

Another HUD aid is the 701 Comprehensive Planning Assistance Program. It aims to strengthen the planning and decision-making capabilities of state governors, local governments and area planning organizations, thereby promoting more effective use of the nation's resources. Grants of up to two-thirds of the planning project's cost are made to supplement state and local funds for comprehensive planning for areas having common or related development problems. Eligible activities include the preparation of development plans, policies and strategies and implementation measures and the coordination of related activities being carried on at various levels of government.

A broad range of subjects may be addressed in the course of the comprehensive planning process. These include land development patterns, housing and community facilities, development of human resources and protection of natural resources. Also covered are the identification of historic structures and districts and replanning of whole districts that appear suitable for conservation and preservation.

Applicants may be state agencies designated by the governor; metropolitan, nonmetropolitan or regional planning agencies, including councils of governments; counties, cities and development districts; Indian tribal bodies; and interstate regional commissions.

State, metropolitan and regional planning agencies should apply to the appropriate HUD regional or area office directly. All other jurisdictions apply through the state planning agency.

New Communities

Still another HUD program of interest is the new communities loan effort. It provides guarantees that encourage the development of well-planned, diversified, economically sound new communities or major additions to existing communities. HUD provides financial and other assistance to private developers, who may receive guarantees for amounts up to 80 percent of HUD's estimate of property value before land development and 90 percent of actual development cost. The guarantee limit for any one community is $50 million.

Unfortunately, no new applications for this program are being accepted at this time.

Other Funds

Finally, although categorical grant programs have been superseded by the community development block grants, there are more than a thousand urban renewal projects and model cities programs still ongoing and providing great opportunity for economic investment in old properties. They offer many financial incentives, including the ability of local agencies to write down to as little as $1 the cost of historic properties listed in or eligible for the National Register; the ability to make additional cleared land around historic properties available at a written-down cost; or the provision of up to $50,000 for moving and up to $90,000 per structure for rehabilitating historic properties of National Register quality (with provision for a waiver of these limits in unusual cases).

HUD will entertain project amendatories to fund such activities, provided the amendatories can be accomplished by reallocating existing funds, as there have been no new funds since December 31, 1974. Of course, additional HUD funds can be put into an existing project if a locality chooses to use some of its community development block grant funds for that purpose.

To summarize, there are federal funds available to assist in the preservation of the nation's historic patrimony, many of them from HUD, and most of them administered by local governments. There are also other HUD programs that guarantee private mortgage lending on historic structures and provide for funding of historical surveys, plans for conservation of whole neighborhoods and districts, and identification of historic districts and properties eligible for National Register listing. The National Trust for Historic Preservation has received HUD research and demonstration grants, as have many other groups, both public and private.

These funds continue to be available for innovative projects that can demonstrate new and unusual ways to preserve the urban areas of the United States.

Integrity:
The Foundation of
the Preservation
Process

Cast-iron railing adorns Gallier House (1857-59, James Gallier, Jr.), Vieux Carré Historic District, New Orleans. (Richard W. Freeman, Jr.)

Integrity in the Vieux Carré

RICHARD W. FREEMAN, JR.

Richard W. Freeman, Jr., is chairman of the Vieux Carré Commission and a member of the National Trust Board of Trustees. He is president of the Louisiana Coca-Cola Bottling Company.

The Vieux Carré, and in a sense the whole of New Orleans, represents a special set of qualities that together create the identity of the place. Oh yes, one says, New Orleans can easily be identified, but so can Chicago, Jackson, Dallas, Denver, Orlando and Atlanta. Anyone who has been to a particular city can recognize it on returning. But suppose the city had changed and yet could still be recognized?

A city or part of a city that has kept its special quality has also maintained its integrity and has been true to its identity. It is identifiable not only because of today's landmarks, street scenes or street names but because the scale, the character, the land use, the diversity of the place have maintained a consistency that develops into an organic whole. This organic whole is recognizable, has value, is sought after. It is the importance of the place.

All developers seek to produce a recognizable difference between their efforts and those of others. It is this difference that makes clients out of prospects, and each development must have a special character in order to create interest. This special character can result in a value that allows the developers to recoup their initial cash and credit outlay and earn a profit.

Any vital city is under pressure to change. Not to change is equivalent to failure. New technologies, transportation systems, distribution patterns—all these require the adaptation of an earlier pattern to a future one. The challenge is to manage that change, for if change destroys the special quality of a place, the potential value is lost. But the special characteristics that together create a market value are not easily identifiable. These elements of specialness are not clearly written on the pavement.

THE VIEUX CARRÉ EXPERIENCE

Fortunately, the Vieux Carré resident is not concerned about the national image of the area when appraising its value. This diverse and vital area is more than the stereotyped cast-iron balcony studded with southern belles or Bourbon Street, a great honky-tonk extravaganza. The local knows that the Vieux Carré is home to 10,000 people—upper-middle-class and pro-fessional people, artists, recluses, shopkeepers. Such variety among the residents of the Vieux Carré must mean that diversity is integral to the place.

The Vieux Carré is controlled by a historic district commission created by the New Orleans City Council with authority from the Louisiana constitution. Before a property owner can change the color of his front door, permission must be granted by the Vieux Carré Commission or its staff. Yet property values have not been undermined by this control. Instead they have risen at least as fast, and in areas faster, than those of the city as a whole. High rents for ground floor retail space as well as upper floor residential space support land and building values. This can only mean one thing: The process works.

What is that process? First, it is based on research. In December 1968, *The Vieux Carré Demonstration Study* was released by the Bureau of Governmental Research, a New Orleans institution. This study combined economic, legal and architectural history consultants into a team that examined such Vieux Carré characteristics as physical and social change, economic trends, architectural styles, land use, leadership attitudes and administrative practices.

As a result of this study, guidelines for the future of the Vieux Carré are set, and a systematic approach to preservation of the area has been established. But this preservation does not attempt to stop the clock. Doing that would assure that the order and stability of the old would be retained by preventing the unknown consequences of the new, but stopping the clock would also eliminate an important element in the mix—utility. A freeze would deny the fact that all events are interconnected. As the Vieux Carré demonstration study says, "The past creates the present which, in turn, shapes the future. Contemporary identity can best be understood as the product of historical continuity." With that in mind, the successful developer in the preservation field must assure the extension of the past into the future.

Research is now beginning on the other side of Canal Street, in the American Sector, the central business district. This area currently has a large collection of 19th-century buildings that create an urban place of special qualities, but the sector does not have the protection of a historic district commission. The current research effort, the Growth Management Program, was begun in an effort to coordinate earlier studies of the central business district. The study group involved in this project quickly realized that the special qualities of the district were the type of land use and the character and diversity made possible by the large number of old structures.

Research efforts such as this have a continuing impact. For the central business district, the study begun by the Growth Management Program will lead to such results as special taxation, historic districts and transfer of development rights. For the Vieux Carré, the study was a starting point in the information-gathering process, which repeatedly is set into motion when the commission receives an application from a property owner who wishes to change a structure or the use of a structure.

The Vieux Carré Commission meets once a month in a public meeting. No decision is made in executive session or without soliciting comments from interested citizens. Before the meeting, specific research is done on the history of the site to be discussed. Staff reports cover the age, condition and use of the structure, as well as density and open space in the area. The zoning of the site is compared to the proposed use of the structure. Thus decisions are based on research. Where conflicts in philosophy exist, they are examined in the context of all the information and opinions available.

Of all the structures in the Vieux Carré, only a small fraction are of national importance—14 among more than 3,000 buildings included in the 1968 survey. This fact generates two important conclusions: (1) that most of the structures are legitimately subject to change and (2) that the Vieux Carré is important as an urban place, not as a collection of great buildings.

The process of dealing with the most important category of structures is easy: Permit the least possible change. For the rest of the buildings, the commission must exercise its judgment when an owner makes a proposal. This means assessing such factors as the impact of the proposed change on the land use of the area, the relative importance of the site, conditions in the building and in nearby structures and the amount of open space and residential density involved. These decisions must be made for a particular site, but with enough of a systematic approach to maintain a legal basis in courts of law.

Some Important Questions

Changes in the public spaces are possibly the most dramatic of all and have the most potential. For example, Jackson Square is a classic area laid out by the French engineers who designed the original grid of streets at the river bank. This square has seen the most important events in the history of the city. It has been the site of governments, the church and the military and has served as a parade field and as residential open space. The elimination of the streets that surround Jackson Square provides a good illustration of the questions raised in changing public space. Should the area remain an island surrounded by asphalt paving or should the square and the streets be looked at as a unit? Should the whole area be regarded as a place where people can congregate? If Jackson Square is a people place, and the auto has been banned from three of the streets that surround it, should the land use of the streets be changed? Will this change do serious damage to the square? These are the issues raised by a proposal of the city administration to do away with the asphalt paving and install stones similar to the ones in the cathedral and square sidewalks.

An illustration of a different character is Gallier House. This former residence of James Gallier, Jr., is another example of a research-based project. Gallier

constructed this Italianate style house in 1857-59. The structure stood relatively unchanged until the mid-1960s. Little was known about how a family of the mid-19th century functioned when the Ella West Freeman Foundation set out to make the structure into a museum depicting Gallier family life in the 1860s. Research has focused on archaeology, paint scraping, private collections and contemporary periodicals. Some of the questions raised here are: Should the stove be constructed to burn coal or wood? Should the floors be varnished, waxed or bare? Should they be carpeted wall-to-wall or covered with rugs?

A project like this goes through phases of physical change. Each change is based on the best information available at the time, and visitors can spot areas that are still to undergo change. The success of this authentic restoration might serve as a thought starter for developers who have large-scale projects with valuable structures on the sites.

People appreciate and recognize a quality preservation job. The well-done, authentic restoration can serve as a focal point to create value in a mixed-use development. Such a structure provides a difference unobtainable by the competition across the street.

Another example is San Francisco Plantation. This 19th-century plantation house stood as part of a large plot of land still worked as a sugar plantation when the land was recently purchased for use as an oil refinery site. The owners, Energy Corporation of Louisiana, see an exciting use for this structure. As an authentic museum of the period in which it was constructed, this is a symbol of corporate responsibility. Also, as research unfolds the details of both Gallier House and San Francisco, the facts are far more fascinating than any construction by decorators and architects of "what the place should look like."

Falling into the trap of fulfilling the taste dictates of the 1970s is a real danger. Research into finishes, paving, paint colors, use of lighting and other important details that go into a finished project can bring some surprises and create some initial disappointments. Some people are disappointed or shocked by color used in earlier eras. But authentic reproduction of such elements can lead to education, enthusiasm and a quality not found in a job done to suit the taste of 1975.

How should new construction be treated? Suppose the site under consideration for development includes both important and objectionable (and unimportant) structures? After the latter are demolished, how should the development proceed? The answer is: Let quality speak for itself. The design of the new should represent the world of today. Historic areas need historical continuity. To discontinue the design development of an area and to choose instead to replicate the past is a decision that automatically eliminates the possibility of adding value to a project or area through sensitive and high quality new design.

In addition, the construction of new buildings in an earlier style creates further problems. If a replication is

*Several commercial buildings in the Vieux Carré, New Or-
leans: Place d'Italia (top), Henry Sciambra Produce Market
(left) and Turci's restaurant (right). (A. Masson, top and
right photos; Richard W. Freeman, Jr., left photo)*

LAFITTE'S BLACKSMITH SHOP, *example of a French Colonial building in the Vieux Carré Historic District. (Vieux Carré Commission)*

well executed, even experts will have a difficult job distinguishing the real from the reproduction after passage of time. If it is poorly executed, the reproduction will be a sham that undermines the setting of nearby structures.

If the work is to be new and will represent a current solution to a design problem, how do you solve that problem in a way that is sympathetic to the older, more important structures? A number of alternative solutions must be considered, but the successful designer will find a combination of elements that together suit both the client's needs and the needs of the site.

Conclusion

To continue to be real, vital and functional, a city must change. If stopping the clock is not the answer, how should change take place? A process that seeks to develop the site, its land use and its character into an organic whole is one answer. The process demands a definition of the place, which is necessary before any change can be made. Once an understanding of the place is refined, the project can proceed.

In the continuum of the urban environment, the structures that are best integrated will be the ones most used and most sought after, and they will command the highest rents because they represent what people expect to happen at that site.

Writing in *The Vieux Carré: A General Statement* (Tulane School of Architecture, 1966), Bernard Lemann summarizes the integrity of the preservation process: "As an historic store-house the Vieux Carré represents a cumulative effect, not an isolated moment of history, but a kind of mobile movement ever receding into the background, or moving forward, depending on how one prefers to see it."

Old City Hall, *Boston. (Boston Redevelopment Authority)*

Overcoming Preservation Problems

ROGER S. WEBB

Roger S. Webb is founder and president of Architectural Heritage, Inc., in Boston, a nonprofit consulting corporation working in the area of historic preservation and adaptive use.

The preservation process is a complex operation requiring the skill, sincerity and cooperation of many professionals from both the public and private sectors, as demonstrated in Seattle. Unfortunately, one participant can derail the common effort. For example, in Boston communication between the public and the private sectors became so poor that a landmark was repeatedly set on fire during the past three years to prevent its reuse.

Successful preservation and reuse of old structures is difficult, compared to new construction. For example, the Hotel Vendôme in Boston collapsed during renovation and killed seven fire fighters as a result of structural alterations made 75 years ago. Those alterations probably did not meet the code standards even then, but this fact only became evident when a fire broke out, water was poured into the building and a section collapsed. There was no way the architect or owner could have predetermined the structural weaknesses, and this type of risk is an unavoidable part of the preservation process. However, that is the kind of problem one does not have in new construction.

There are also additional complexities in terms of cost estimating for preservation efforts. Therefore, it is a long-established tradition that the preservation process must have available large contingency funds.

Another problem is that of securing firm leasing commitments from tenants before renovation of what often appears to be a hopeless derelict. Boston's Old City Hall was unrentable at the time the city vacated the building, and no tenants could be attracted to sign leases. This year space was relet for $11 a square foot, but when renovation was first considered in 1970, $6 a square foot was conservatively projected for this same space.

Preservation successes have been the exception rather than the rule. Today, in both New York City and Boston there is widespread availability of excess office property, some selling at depressed prices. Occasionally the preservationist is fortunate enough to encounter projects where rehabilitation and preservation are substantially less expensive than new construction or the use of existing surplus and unrented new properties.

These problems indicate that the preservation process

can be difficult, but it has become recognized as being well worth the effort; the long-term benefits derived from that process are real and measurable. Such areas as Beacon Hill in Boston, Georgetown in Washington, D.C., and the Vieux Carré in New Orleans all have achieved national recognition for their successful economic regeneration, and each city has become more livable in the process. These historic areas have contributed to the economic strength of the cities and are now recognized as valuable amenities. In Boston, historic preservation processes in the new Waterfront, the North and South Ends, Charlestown, Back Bay, Beacon Hill and downtown are acknowledged to be major factors in a reversal of the exodus from the city.

Feasibility Study

The preservation process is risky even when successful, and a high degree of integrity by all participants is essential. Therefore, the preservation project must include an honest assessment of the economic feasibility of continuing use or reuse of the structure. Many may admit to having been tempted to "save" a landmark by loudly proclaiming its potential for reuse. On the other hand, preservation opponents often bypass the feasibility study process completely and proclaim a landmark "unusable" in very general terms.

A case in point is the Tweed Courthouse in New York City. The building continues to be used for municipal offices, but in 1974 the Beame administration decided that the undesirable historical and political association with the name *Tweed* was enough in itself to condemn the reuse of that interesting 19th-century courthouse. No amount of persuasion or public outcry could convince the Beame people to assess objectively the economic feasibility of reusing this landmark, although numerous experts assured them that the courthouse was an excellent candidate for recycling. Neither did they accept a suggestion to change the name of the landmark to Beame Courthouse.

A similar situation almost developed in Boston when the Old City Hall was no longer needed after the new one was finished around 1970. Many persons associated the 19th-century Boston city hall with decades of corrupt city government, symbolized by Mayor Curley, who served several days in public office while in jail. Fortunately, the desire to tear down the landmark that symbolized corruption to many did not prevail, though the vote to save it was only 3–2. Also, Mayor White's administration assisted by allowing sufficient time to devise an alternative use.

The previous administration considered recycling this landmark but had concluded that the reuse was too costly. The renovation cost in 1970 was estimated at $50 or more a square foot. In fact, costs were little more than $30 a square foot.

Design

There is often controversy about design between the advocates of restoration and members of the "leave it alone" club. A project that evoked substantial debate in Boston was the restoration of the 19th-century Faneuil Hall Markets, a unified urban area near the new city hall, and perhaps the first redevelopment project using urban renewal and eminent domain. Certainly—in 1824—it was the first such renewal in Boston.

The developer and architect of the project were strong advocates of leaving the structures in their much altered 20th-century condition as examples of the organic growth of architecture. Others advocated restoration of the exteriors to their original 1826 roof lines and granite facades, to conform with the design of Alexander Parris, the architect of the 1824 plans. Among the questions raised were the following: Should the original massing and pitched roofs be restored and retained for posterity as an example of the first major urban renewal project in the city of Boston? Should the landmarks be further altered by contemporary and successive renovations now and in future decades? Will Alexander Parris' plan for the Market District be recognizable to future generations? Is rehabilitation or preservation justifiable?

Ada Louise Huxtable, architectural critic for the *New York Times*, has eloquently stated that the rehabilitation process is most successful when it combines the best of the past and the present: "And so it is really very simple. To thine own self be true, as Shakespeare put it with tremendous style, and to your own time, as well. The best of the past deserves the best of the present, not some make-believe muck. . . . Suppressing today and stage-setting yesterday is false to both, and nothing meaningful happens behind ropes." (October 22, 1972)

The question of whether or not to restore the exteriors of Faneuil Hall Markets had strong proponents on both sides of the question. Each point of view had excellent justification. Architects, historians, planners and conservationists divided as they argued opposing viewpoints. This honest debate was useful, and the final design solution adopts the best of each side. This year will mark the completion of the restoration of the market roof lines, but the interiors will be renovated in imaginative contemporary designs.

The negotiations on this project were complex, and the process could have failed. In the end, the developer accepted less square footage and therefore less profit by having the roof lines lowered. On the other hand, the city was forced to find additional funds to complete the exterior restoration of the original slate roof lines and trabeated granite facades. This solution achieves more than just rehabilitation, because the integrity of the original design has been successfully preserved.

Marketing and Leasing

In Boston there is a proven demand for space in historic structures. Two cases in point are the Record American Newspaper Building and the Old City Hall, where tenants selected these landmarks over alternative locations in numerous neighboring skyscrapers.

The Old City Hall enjoys full occupancy while many buildings in Boston experience severe vacancies. This

BONWIT TELLER *department store, Boston, former Museum of Natural History. (Architectural Heritage, Inc.)*

fortuitous situation of a fully leased landmark resulted in part from the marketing and leasing strategy adopted for this project. First, treating the age of the landmark as an asset rather than a liability attracted tenants who expressed a preference for the historic value of the building. Second, rejecting tenants whose purposes are in conflict with the historic character of the landmark and seeking those who reinforce that character has resulted in a prestige and quality image that helps keep the landmark fully rented.

Sometimes one encounters leasing opportunities that violate the historic character of the preservation project. A case in point was the offer by McDonald's hamburger chain representatives. They wished to lease a large portion of the Old City Hall and to erect a golden arch across the front lawn. Other prospective tenants were a wax museum, an adults-only cinema and the inventor of a new, vertical car-parking system that would stack automobiles on the front lawn. Needless to say, these leasing opportunities were rejected.

Investors and Lending Institutions

Often in recycling landmarks the investor and lending institution are confronted with a degree of risk that is greater than that encountered in alternative real estate investment opportunities. Contributing to the higher risk factor is the likelihood that the landmark developer is comparatively inexperienced and smaller than the established developer of new properties. Moreover, as previously mentioned, unforeseen difficulties in rehabilitation will require larger contingency funds, and tenants must be found to utilize existing conditions. It is an unfortunate fact of life, but these factors and others

Faneuil Hall (1722) and Marketplace (1826), Boston. (© 1967 Wm. W. Owens, Jr., courtesy of Boston Redevelopment Authority)

increase the risk to investor and institutional lender. However, in the long run, it is the acceptance of these risks that preserves historic buildings and makes cities more livable and viable. This revitalization of our cites is a major objective of many institutional lenders and investors.

An interesting example, again, is the Old City Hall, where six Boston savings banks participated in the mortgage and shared the risk. The developer, Architectural Heritage, had no record as a real estate developer and no tenants were committed to sign leases. It took courage for those lending institutions to participate in the loan. However, the project was successful, while many other real estate projects went sour in the last few years.

It is interesting to speculate on the motives that led these six Boston savings banks to pool their risk and participate in the mortgage. Perhaps the decisive factor was a commitment to their community and a belief that, in the long run, they would derive economic benefit by contributing to the historic character and livability of Boston. Their decision to invest was based on a long-term interest in Boston that did not necessarily relate to the higher risk factor of renovation projects.

Summary of Needs

The preservation process requires an honest appraisal by all participants. Otherwise, the negative short-term implications of rehabilitation will predominate and insure the project's failure. Snap decisions by the public sector to "save" a landmark can unduly burden a community. Conversely, a declaration that a landmark is too costly to reuse without a genuine cost appraisal and feasibility study could allow an irreplaceable historic asset to be destroyed.

Planners can redesign a community so completely that there is little trace of its heritage, or they can embalm it with its history. To achieve a vital compromise between these opposing extremes is a desirable goal. Brokers should not dilute the historic value of a landmark by leasing to incompatible tenants. Finally, investors and lending institutions should be encouraged to commit capital to the preservation project as a way of achieving their objective of making cities more livable and viable.

Private Financing
for Preservation

LARIMER SQUARE, *a collection of restaurants, night spots, galleries and shops in restored area of Denver. (National Trust)*

Thoughts on Preservation, Past and Future

BRUCE M. ROCKWELL

Bruce M. Rockwell is president and chief executive officer of the Colorado National Bank of Denver.

Denver is just 116 years old, and I have been a participant in almost half of its history. My mother and father were born there of parents who came west in the late 1860s from New York and Indiana. I grew up in a city that had no "history." History to us was Yorktown and Boston, Shiloh and Gettysburg, not the opulent old Manhattan Restaurant on Larimer Street, where families went for special Sunday dinners. Built in 1870, it succumbed to the wrecking ball in 1968 as an action of urban renewal that I helped administer.

Urban Renewal and Preservation in Denver

I was the first chairman of the Denver Urban Renewal Authority and served in that capacity from 1958 to 1968. The commission was essentially of the bulldozer mentality; we really believed that not much over 50 years of age was worth saving. That seemed to be the mood of the city and of Congress at the time, so we designed a 27-block urban renewal project known as Skyline in lower downtown Denver. It obliterated the deplorable skid row area and with it most of Denver's original downtown commercial buildings dating from the late 1860s and 70s.

In the midst of the planning for Skyline a young upstart announced plans for a two-block restoration in the project area. The commission did its best to ignore Dana Crawford and her brazen scheme, but she would not go away. To avoid a public fight in the early, tenuous days of urban renewal, we planned around her with the certain conviction that her plan would fail and her property would be picked up at some later date for incorporation in the clearance area. Those who know Denver, Dana Crawford and Larimer Square know that did not happen—most fortunately.

The rest of the project area was almost totally cleared, without the shedding of a tear. The project was criticized and forced to a municipal referendum, which carried 70–30, but the challenge was political and based on questions of municipal finance, not historic preservation.

The wisdom or folly of the Skyline project is not yet clear. A serious blight was removed, and a revival of the area is in progress. Several hundred million dollars of new construction has taken place, but a dozen blocks are covered in asphalt awaiting redevelopment. Larimer Square is the strong anchor of the entire project, a magnet for people and investment.

The experience with Skyline brings mixed emotions. The area in question was untenable—block after block of dilapidated old buildings occupied by cheap bars, flop houses and pawnshops, a heavy creeping blight on downtown Denver. There was obviously no way to replicate Larimer Square 10 times over, but on balance, it must be concluded that we were overzealous in the clearance program. The commission should have saved at least a few of the representative structures. However, in the main, the area had no economic or social viability and the city is better off without it.

Larimer Square awakened in many Denver residents an interest in their own history. Up to that time, the historical movement had meant an obsession for Indian jewelry and gold-mining paraphernalia, of concern to a few almost as old as the city itself. But the easterners who moved into Denver by the thousands in the 1950s and 60s were mostly young people with a keener sense of history from their backgrounds in, say, Massachusetts or Virginia. As a result, the historic preservation movement began to bud and finally to flower. At the outset it was elitist and artistic, and it still is to some extent. It really did not then and does not yet address the difficult problems of the inner city. But the movement has imparted a deep sense of public consciousness not only of the western heritage but of the intrinsic values of historic preservation. The bulldozer days are dead in Denver, though urban blight is alive and well.

Old Notions and Practices

An American notion embodied in most of the postwar federal housing acts holds that the old housing inventory of the cities can and should be replaced. This is a bankrupt theory because replacement has not happened and is not going to happen. Americans must Europeanize their thinking about their cities. Restoration, renovation and rehabilitation are the housing challenges of this nation, and preservationists can continue to play a leading role in this thought revolution. However, both preservationists and business people must abandon the one-house-at-a-time syndrome and think in terms of entire neighborhoods—indeed entire cities. The tools and the programs to get the job done must be fashioned.

The Federal Housing Administration and the old urban renewal mentality are anachronistic, and the schizophrenia of the Department of Housing and Urban Development and urban housing bureaucrats is counterproductive. Finally, the negligence of the private sector is like a death wish.

Much is heard in Congress these days about red-lining. While I have never actually seen maps in banks and savings and loans marked up in red, it is well known that the mentality of red-lining is a fact of life, a natural economic phenomenon. Mortgage money flows along the path of least resistance to investment sources

DENVER CITY CABLE RAILWAY COMPANY BUILDING *now renovated for use as a restaurant.* (Roger Whitaker)

of least risk. It is easier to justify a 30-year loan on a new house in a safe suburban setting than one on a 50-year-old house in an uncertain environment of the inner city. Also, it is easier for appraisers to work from builders' cost figures than to assess the physical and locational values of inner-city property. And the politicians who most ferociously deplore this process are the same ones who created HUD and the FHA and who have tolerated the fixation on suburban development.

Suggestions for the Future

Both the public and private sectors in the housing business must drastically change their focuses. On the public side, new or expanded federal programs are needed for rehabilitation loans, grants and mortgage insurance. Further, the historic ad valorem property tax structure, which rewards the negligent owner and penalizes the prudent conservator of property, needs substantial modification.

On the private side, banks, savings and loans and insurance companies must show leadership and must put together teams of contractors, architects and investors to do red-lining in reverse. They must designate target areas or neighborhoods to be treated and re-

stored. They must team up with public officials—local, state and federal—to bring to bear all the resources necessary to revitalize inner-city neighborhoods. In the process, we can restore and preserve land and property values against which we can prudently lend our depositors' dollars.

This is not an assignment for lazy or complacent lenders; it requires tough, demanding and specialized lending. Those who do not know what they are doing can get burned. And why, one might ask, should bankers assume such a burden when there are so many safe, easy places to invest funds? The answer is simple, and absolutely true: because institutional life depends on it. Banks and savings and loans mirror the communities in which they work and on which they totally depend. Their vitality and growth is but a reflection of the vitality and growth of the city.

The slogan "Preservation is for People" is much in order, but it might be added that preservation is for *all* the people. It will not do to convert low-income housing to luxury housing through concerted public and private activity. Low-income people cannot, should not and will not be driven from their neighborhoods. We must learn to restore with the greatest possible economy, a choice that may offend artistic tastes and building code inspectors. But if preservation is to be more than an elitist fad, it must carry with it deep social commitment to all urban dwellers.

Examples of Financing Packages

A few examples of specific financing packages will give some idea of the variety of financing approaches. There is, however, one element in historic preservation financing that is constant: No two deals are alike. You have to know the investor, the architect and the contractor. It is no game for amateurs, and everyone starting out is burned once or twice, but in most cities the team of specialists needed is developing.

The Ninth Street Project is a Denver residential area principally dating from the 1870s. One hundred acres within the area are being cleared for the construction of three college campuses. Through the efforts of an organization named Historic Denver, a block of 14 houses will be turned over to the institutions involved. The available 35,000 square feet of space will be occupied by such facilities as conference rooms and faculty offices, and a park will be built around the buildings in the middle of the new urban campus. There was no private financing per se, but the project was carried out with a number of private donations.

The Denver City Cable Railway Company Building was a dilapidated 1880s structure in the center of the Skyline urban renewal project. Historic Denver raised $150,000 to purchase the property from the urban renewal authority, but before such a purchase can be made, a use for the property must be demonstrated. A large restaurant chain was interested in a long-term lease, and an architect who had worked on plans for the building agreed to rent half of the second floor. The

LARIMER SQUARE *outdoor art show. (Roger Whitaker)*

bank loaned $450,000 for renovation and there is now a new loan of $550,000, a figure that indicates the success of the project.

Historic Denver maintains its headquarters in the Molly Brown House, which has also become a tourist attraction and produces $40,000 to $50,000 a year from admission fees. Again there was no private financing for this building, only donations.

There is a large mansion in Denver that, although in an area zoned to allow 40 apartments on the site, was still a private residence. The property was owned free and clear and the owners were able to borrow $300,000 to convert it into seven luxury apartments. Today the return is approximately 18 percent.

Larimer Square is a well-known two-block project with principally retail space at the street level and offices above. Although Larimer Square is a financial success now, there was no conventional financing available at the outset because no conventional lenders believed that the plan would work. Properties were purchased one by one, with the developers searching for funds as work proceeded. Conventional loans have now become available for continued work.

Two old mansions in Denver were bought from the Catholic archdiocese for approximately $150,000 each. Because the archdiocese repaid the mortgage during rehabilitation, construction loans of about $150,000 became available for each building. The mansions, now

office space leasing for $12 a square foot, were restored with a quality not economically possible for conventional private contractors. The owner advertised for skilled crafts workers in 20 college newspapers. He offered to pay $2 an hour and had 400 responses. The restoration included such details as creation of new stained glass windows and sand casting of missing hinges. Now the building is 95 percent occupied and has a three to one cash flow coverage on a 50 percent mortgage.

As is obvious from even these few examples, with imagination, intelligence, effort and hard work the job can be done. But a building-by-building approach is not sufficient; we must turn our attention to entire neighborhoods. For that to be done, some long-standing American ideas must be changed.

Giving Lenders What They Need

RICHARD CRISSMAN

Richard Crissman is director, project mortgages, Ralph C. Sutro Co., Los Angeles, Calif.

Most people probably would agree that it is difficult to borrow money on old buildings, and it is more difficult in some places than in others. For example, rehabilitation financing for old buildings in San Francisco or New York City is not unusual. It may be that when a city is virtually an island and when there is an intense demand for land, the age of the structure does not make much difference in access to financing. The geography of Seattle suggests that similar factors may be at work there.

The real borrowing difficulties arise in those cities where there is an infinite supply of new land at the outskirts, and the suburban shopping center has come to dominate the old retail districts. Even so, there are plenty of people interested in the old retail districts. Certainly there is a huge market for all goods and services just among government personnel and financial employees, whose firms are permanently attached to the central business districts. It is this special segment of the market at which restoration buildings are usually aimed, but it is not certain that lenders understand the character of that market.

Almost every financial institution in the United States has the bulk of its investments in aging real estate. That fact ought to encourage lenders to put maximum efforts into the restoration of such structures, in order to increase the life of the buildings and the probability that present loans will be fully amortized rather than foreclosed. But that is not the way lenders usually think.

POPULAR VIEWS AMONG LENDERS

Two points of view have gained ascendancy in the lending fraternity: (1) that new is good and old is bad, and (2) that the central city is going down the tube and suburban areas are where everybody wants to be.

From time to time the journals read by lenders make a bow in the direction of correcting these impressions. For example, the Mortgage Bankers' Association magazine, the *Mortgage Banker,* carried a complete story on the Back to the City conference sponsored in 1974 by the Brooklyn Union Gas Company and the Brownstone Revival Society of New York City. This meeting drew about 600 people to the Waldorf for a three-day session. Another example of coverage read by lenders is the May 1975 issue of *Fortune.*

These efforts help, and they even create a small coun-

tertrend among the bright young people in lending institutions. The problem may be that by the time those people get to be in charge of policy, all the courage is washed out of them by the institution.

PRINCIPAL MORTGAGE CRITERIA

If one must work against prejudice—and by and large that is the issue—the way to win lenders to the desired point of view is to structure loan requests to their system as much as possible. To do this, it must be recognized that the principal factors can add up to an assured loan when they are arranged in proper fashion. Financing can be made much easier if the answers are designed to fit the lender's needs.

The demonstrations in the remainder of this presentation are a guide that might be entitled "Help Yourself to a Loan." Table 1 gives a list of documents needed to prepare the "ideal" loan application.

A SHORTCUT TO FINDING HOW MUCH YOU CAN BORROW

The ability of a property to repay its loan, with some margin, is the *debt coverage.* All too often, loans are thought of as some stated percentage of an appraisal, when the appraisal actually is only helping the lender evaluate a loan request. In short, it validates the debt coverage.

Assume that costs have been determined and that with the "as is" acquisition price, $600,000 is needed. When rates are 9 percent and lenders give loans for 20 years, the payments will be $64,800 a year. Most loans are 75 percent of value; therefore, the value of the subject project must be $600,000 divided by 0.75, hence $800,000. The difference between the value and the loan is *equity,* or $200,000 in this case. Most lenders think that when mortgage rates are 9 percent, return on equity is probably 1.5 percent more, for a total of 10.5 percent. These figures work out as follows:

Loan payments at 9% over 20 years	$64,800
Return on equity at 10.5%	21,000
Net income (required to justify the loan)	$85,800
Operating expenses of, say, 35% may be low for apartments and high for single-tenant buildings; here, divided net by 0.65 to get effective gross	$121,200

(A good source book is "Financial Constant Percent Amortization Tables," publication 187, available from Financial Publishing Company, 82 Brooklyn Avenue, Boston, Mass. 02215, for $2.35.)

The estimated vacancy factor of 5 percent is reflected by dividing the effective gross by 0.95 to obtain the annual scheduled gross rent, here $127,000. This is divided by the number of apartments (or offices, or rentable area) to get the annual rent required to support the loan. Then ask whether this figure is above or below competing rents. Some say adapted commercial and office space should rent for 80 percent of the amounts charged in new buildings, but a careful comparison should be made. If necessary, ask what can be done to adjust the data. Should costs be reduced, rentable area increased or design modified?

A conventional test of the process is to put the figures into the appraiser's format, provided the rents stood the market tests (figures are rounded):

Annual scheduled rents	$127,000
Less 5% vacancy	7,000
Effective gross	$120,000
Less expenses (itemized)	35,000
Net annual income	$ 85,000

When $85,000 is capitalized at 10.5 percent, the value is $800,000. But double check, as most lenders are limited by policy or regulation to loans of 75 percent of value. In this case, 75 percent of $800,000 is $600,000, the amount needed for the project.

How Much Cash Does It Take?

Almost any project requires some cash. Nearly all lenders expect a borrower to have equity in a project, and they would like to equate equity with cash. Here is the easy way to please a lender:

Price	$300,000
Cost of alterations	500,000
Cost	$800,000
Less loan	600,000
Cash deposit (equity)	$200,000

Table 2 illustrates the cash flow.

In the halcyon days of real estate financing, the early 1970s, developers generally were able to persuade lenders that they could contribute services and skills or "sweat equity" to projects rather than cash. Then, even some of the purchase price would be financed by the seller, who would hold a note or a second trust deed for some of the difference between the first mortgage and the price. Sweat equity is sensible when it works, but it has also been the source of many frustrations and failures in real estate development projects. Until the lenders' confidence returns, it is unlikely that much will be seen of this idea. But here is the imaginative, desirable and unlikely scheme of shoestring equity:

Price	$300,000
Cost of alterations:	
Materials and labor	300,000
Architect	20,000
Rental commissions	40,000
Supervision and labor	
of borrower	40,000
Developer's profit	100,000
Cost	$800,000

The cash flow is illustrated in Table 3. Note that 100 percent of the equity is earned from the project.

The third explanation, in Table 4, is the pertinent example, given the lender's current concerns with safety. The middle way allows credit for contributed services but also requires substantial cash investment. A lender would probably see any concerns about the adeqacy of equity as satisfied in this example. Price and costs are as in the previous example.

The sweat equity is $130,000 and the cash a healthy $120,000, or just shy of 20 percent of the project cost. As is typical of today's loans, the cash requirements allow comfortable margins for startup operating deficits.

It is appropriate and important to stress that no matter how loans are determined, lenders will insist that there be enough money within their control to guarantee the completion of alterations in the project. The lender's position also works to the advantage of the borrower: An unfinished building never has tenants, and vacancy democratically wipes out both sweat and cash equities.

Two loans, construction and take out, are usual in these projects. The take out is a commitment from a lender for a long-term amortizing loan, to be funded when construction is complete. Some take-out loans require that most tenants be signed up before loan funds are provided. When a builder can supply services, a contemporary construction lender's idea would be to fund with a smaller loan:

Loan		$450,000
Second		150,000
Services		75,000
Cash		125,000
	Total	$800,000

The take-out lender, who commits on the appraised value of the income stream, comes in at 100 percent completion and an occupancy of around 70 percent.

At a value of $800,000 and with a 75 percent loan ($600,000), $450,000 pays off the construction lender and the balance pays off the second holder. In either case, the owner has substantial cash equity going into the project.

Will You and Your Tenants Qualify for a Loan?

The matter of credit is simple and complicated at the same time. Obviously, institutional lenders cannot make unsafe loans. It is not so obvious that part of a lender's expectation is that every loan will be 98 percent easy to collect. If it is not, the rate of the note will not be enough for the money put out. Consequently, lenders measure both a borrower's ability and willingness to pay.

Ability to Pay

Lenders are constantly amazed that real estate developers submit balance sheets that show no cash. As a banker might say, the net worth can't make loan payments. A balance sheet is a record of how someone accumulated money in the past. The sheet may show that a person has been relatively acquisitive, but if there is not a healthy amount of cash in relation to the other items, it also shows that person has not been prudent, especially in the recent past, and may not qualify for either a long-term or development loan. Current cash ought to be at least equal to current liabilities, which are expected to include 12 months of payments on a mortgage or other long-term debt items.

No matter how great the assets on a developer's balance sheet, lenders generally suspect that the equity in real property is inflated by the enthusiasm and imagination of the developer and does not represent market values.

There may be no direct way to change that view, but a balance sheet that would encourage a potential lender of $600,000 to say yes follows.

BALANCE SHEET, 7-31-75

Assets

Cash		$ 27,000
Stocks		90,000
Real estate:		
Land		400,000
Rental property		1,000,000
In construction		500,000
	Total	$2,017,000

Liabilities

Personal note		$ 10,000
Trade accounts		16,000
Real estate:		
Loan payments 75-76		90,000
Land		150,000
Amortizing		700,000
Construction		300,000
Total liabilities		$1,266,000
Net worth		751,000
	Total	$2,017,000

The balance sheet shows the source of the equity, a one-to-one relationship of cash to current bills (including secondary liquidity in the form of stocks) and a net worth that exceeds the loan request. All these are the important measures to a lender.

Willingness to Pay

Lenders also are concerned about the willingness to pay and the problems with solvent borrowers who sometimes prefer to use their money for new ventures rather than paying for old ones. Everyone knows those hard-headed and practical developers who only make loan payments as long as their projects appear likely to yield profits; the moment they do not, the developer stops paying, regardless of ability. Lender's measure willingness to pay by a credit report showing the way in which previous indebtedness has been discharged and

by talking with other lenders given as references by the borrower.

In summary, the developer's credit is measured first by ability and second by willingness. Failing to pass these tests, the developer had better find a new and solvent partner, who will get the lion's share of the profit in return for the use of his credit as the borrower.

Importance of Rental Income

Another aspect of ability to pay is the sure flow of rental income to make the loan payments. No doubt a lender would provide long-term money for the renovation of a subterranean cave if the space were rented to Campbell Soups for a long period of time. Even caves have their uses to the makers of mushroom soup, especially those as solvent (dare I say as liquid?) as Campbell. The fact is, however, that many buildings to be renovated will have multiple occupancy. Therefore, the credit provided to the loan application by the tenants will be mixed at best.

The chances of getting financing are greatly helped by long-term leases. A good mixture of leases for a building that contains a ground floor of retail space and five or six stories of general office space is illustrated here:

Area (sq. ft.)	Tenant Type	Term (yrs.)
Ground Floor	(10,000 sq.ft., 100% leased)	
1,500	National chain	5
6,000	Regional chain	25
2,500	Strong, established local	15
2nd–5th floors	(40,000 sq.ft., 50% committed)	
10,000	Regional and local	5
10,000	Professional	3
20,000	Uncommitted	

The financial statements for all committed tenants should be included in a loan application. As was said at the outset, financing for a speculative building is unlikely in this year or the next.

When there is a single tenant for a building, the loan will be directly related to the credit of that tenant, because the developer's credit does not make much difference after the building is completed.

The general rule is that a lender's debt coverage concerns will be calmed when the rents on preleased space equal the loan payments; those concerns will vanish when the rents on space leased for 25 years equal the loan payments (providing the tenants' ability to pay is supported by their business history).

Nothing said here should lead one to believe that a loan cannot be gotten without following these rules. However, the closer a borrower can come to meeting criteria like these, the more certain achievement of the loan objective will be.

WHERE TO APPLY AND HOW TO BE INTRODUCED

The best source of loans for those who have rehabilitated buildings successfully is the lenders who have cooperated in those projects. If they are out of the market, or if the previous projects have not quite had 100 percent success, look elsewhere. Developers should remember that life insurance companies make the bulk of all loans on income-producing property throughout the United States and that savings and loan associations provide more than 80 percent of the residential financing in the country, excepting only large apartment developments.

As most borrowers know, savings and loans have open front doors, and almost anyone can walk through them. Life insurance companies are more selective, and the best entrance probably is through mortgage banking firms that service loans for the target life insurance companies. A mortgage banker often will know who is willing to entertain loans on rehabilitation projects even though they have not themselves given much publicity to this willingness.

Do not absolve mortgage bankers of the prejudice in favor of newness and remoteness. Developers should assume that both the loan finder and the lender will be at best indifferent to the merits of rehabilitation projects over those of new construction. The best tactic a sponsor can take is to analyze and present the project on the basis of the concepts of debt coverage, equity and credit. Make the presentation look as much as possible like a standard project. In the loan request, avoid any words about the romance of the old building, its history or its distinguished architecture.

Keep the presentation simple and in accordance with popular prejudice. The ideal loan package should contain most of the documents listed in Table 1. This list should help with apartments, condominiums and commercial projects.

BUNT WHEN YOU CAN'T HIT

When everything else suggested here fails and no lender seems likely to take a serious look at a project, remember these last words: Greed is not dead. Show lenders that they can make more money doing this project, and not have any greater risk, than if they choose some other project. Pay them a slightly larger fee or a higher interest rate, and give them something they can make money with—sometimes in the form of compensating balances.

New accounts offered to a bank lender need not be the borrower's money, and certainly should not be pledged as additional security for the loan. Compensating balances can sometimes be bought, and sometimes friends who control substantial funds will place them in the bank to help a project. New deposits ought to cause a shine in a banker's eyes even when nothing else does.

Sometimes it is necessary to be so underhanded as to put pressure on the carrier of a group insurance program for some nonprofit organization to which one belongs. Remind the insurance lender that the organization is most interested in the lender's participation in

this particular loan. Sometimes that will not work, either because the right connections are not available or because the lender is not susceptible to that kind of pressure.

When all else fails, follow the advice Little League baseball coaches give to their weaker batters: Bunt. The advantage of a financial bunt is that it makes people scramble; someone may get confused enough to do what you want.

Confusion might be precipitated by securing an official historical designation for an old structure, accompanied by an urgent request from the mayor of the town that someone get on with the rehabilitation in the community interest. Then get a vote of the chamber of commerce members saying that the building in its present condition is damaging the financial stability of the central business district and that it is imperative that plans go forward to "save" the business community from the embarrassment of the disreputable building.

Go armed with a few documents like this, and perhaps with a letter from the director of the redevelopment agency indicating that the agency is going to redevelop the lender's home office site along with the subject project. That might cause enough confusion that the bank will fund the loan in the "broad community interest," and will charge no more than 10 percent over what the loan would have cost if it had been made in the first place. That is financial bunting.

CONCLUSION

Lenders want every loan to have three ingredients: The project should have enough net earnings to insure monthly payments. The borrower should have enough equity to make loan payments worthwhile even if the property fails for a time to meet the projected earnings. And, both the borrower and tenants should have good enough credit to justify the lender's confidence. If a loan request meets these measures, much of the difficulty of finding a loan for an old building will disappear.

TABLE 1

DOCUMENTS OF THE IDEAL LOAN APPLICATION

	Commercial	Apartment	House and condominium
Items defining scope of project for lender:			
Brief project description	x	x	x
Area photos (dim as to subject)	x	x	x
City map showing project location	x	x	x
Key floor plan	x	x	x
Plat map (as from title report)	x	x	x
Items relating to lender's debt service measurements:			
Schedule of income and expenses	x	x	
Schedule of competing rentals	x	x	
Map of competing rentals	x	x	
Market study with comparable sales			x
Map of comparable sales			x
Summary of committed tenants (prices)	x		
Summary of declared buyers (prices)	x		
Appraisal or study of values	x	x	x
Items relating to lender's measure of equity and ability to finish project:			
Purchase documentation	x	x	x
Alteration drawings	x	x	x
Alteration building permit	x	x	x
Engineering, soils, seismic studies	x	x	x
Specifications, materials lists	x	x	x
Cost breakdown (signed)	x	x	x
Building contract (signed), subject to loan funding	x	x	x
Items relating to borrower's (developer's) ability and willingness to pay:			
Background and applicant's capabilities	x	x	x
Financial statement (balance sheet)	x	x	x
Cash flow projection	x	x	x
Credit report or authorization	x	x	x
Items relating to tenants' or buyers' abilities to pay:			
Annual reports	x		
Financial statements of buyers			x
Deposit receipts	x	x	x
Letters of lease intent	x	x	

TABLE 2
CASH FLOW IN LOAN WITH $200,000 CASH DEPOSIT

	Loan	Cash	Cost
To seller	$200,000	$100,000	$300,000
Alteration money held by lender	400,000	100,000	500,000
Total	$600,000	$200,000	$800,000

TABLE 3
CASH FLOW IN LOAN WITH MAXIMUM SWEAT EQUITY

	Loan	Seller's Second	Cost
Price	$225,000	$75,000	$300,000
Materials and labor	300,000	0	300,000
Architect*		Takes % of ownership	20,000
Rental commissions*	0	"	40,000
Supervision*	0	"	40,000
Developer's profit*	0	"	100,000
Payment to second, when work is complete	75,000	(75,000)	0
Total	$600,000	$ 0	$800,000

*In this ideal situation, payments go to the owner.

TABLE 4
CASH FLOW IN LOAN SWEAT EQUITY AND CASH DEPOSIT

	Loan	Cash	Sweat Equity	Cost
Price	$225,000	$ 75,000	$ 0	$300,000
Materials and labor	300,000	0	0	300,000
Architect	0	20,000	0	20,000
Rental commissions	40,000	0	0	40,000
Supervision and labor of borrower	10,000	0	30,000	40,000
Developer's profit	0	0	100,000	100,000
Reserve for startup costs	25,000	25,000	0	50,000
Total	$600,000	$120,000	$130,000	$850,000

THE CENTURY THEATRE *(1924), Chicago. (John Sower)*

Financing and Developing Large Commercial Preservation Projects

JOHN SOWER

John Sower is a mortgage banker and development consultant in Washington, D.C.

Historic preservation is in many ways a sophisticated type of real estate development. Thus it is important for historic preservation groups, public officials and others in the field to understand as much as possible about the development process so they will be better able to work in their respective home areas. It is important to know both the players and rules of the real estate game.

Another important point, particularly for developers and officials of financial institutions, is that historic preservation financing and development are major league efforts nationwide. The stereotype of the local ladies club attempting to save some old building is long out of date. The projects to be described here involve some of the largest developers and financial institutions in the United States, the investment of many millions of dollars and some of the most sophisticated development and financing techniques available. It is possible to identify several *billion* dollars of historic preservation projects in the portfolios of financial institutions in this country.

Those preservationists who have bemoaned buildings that could be preserved "if only some bank would lend the money" do not realize that many of their problems are due to a lack of knowledge of financial institutions. For example, commercial banks generally do not lend for long-term projects and generally do not invest heavily in real estate.

Following is a brief description of the types of financial institution involved with historic preservation, how they are involved and why. It is important to keep in mind that each project is unique and may require some combination of financing from various types of institutions.

1. *Commercial banks.* The main sources of funds for commercial banks are the checking accounts or demand deposits of individuals and corporations; generally these are fairly volatile and subject to short-term fluctuations. Consequently, banks usually make short-term loans. For real estate-oriented preservation projects, banks are most interested in construction loans against permanent mortgage commitments from long-term lenders or in medium-term loans for companies that have historic preservation projects. They are generally not a primary source of funds for either home mortgages or long-term mortgages for other projects.

2. *Savings and loan associations* (S&Ls). These institutions get most of their funds from individual savings accounts, which are more stable over the long run than checking accounts. Thus they are more inclined to long-term mortgages. Savings and loan associations, in some areas called savings banks or building and loan associations, are a primary source of mortgage financing for historic preservation projects, both single-family residential and larger commercial projects.

3. *Insurance companies.* Life insurance companies have steady cash inflow from premium payments and are interested in long-term investments for their capital. They are therefore a good source of mortgage financing for larger projects. They operate both independently and through mortgage banking companies, which arrange financing for individual projects and sell them to the insurance companies.

4. *Real estate investment trusts.* REITs, as they are commonly known, have fallen on hard times recently and are not a likely source of financing for any projects in the near future. They raise funds from stock sales and short-term borrowings and primarily invest in short-term construction loans. They also do some specialized financing, such as standby take outs and standing loans.

5. *Other.* Other financial institutions in the real estate market include pension funds and credit companies. Several government agencies are also active in historic preservation financing, as will be demonstrated in the projects described here.

The project descriptions that follow focus on the financing and development strategies that were used, saying little about the historical importance and design and structural characteristics. They represent a mix of different types of projects, including retail, office, high-rise residential rental, lowrise residential condominium, single and multiple-owner shopping areas and of course a couple of railroad stations.

These projects also encompass a variety of financing techniques, including long-term mortgages, short-term construction loans, standing loans, tax-loss syndications, standby take outs and government loans. They represent significant and profitable investments in historic preservation projects by each type of financial institution, including commercial banks, savings & loans, real estate investment trusts, insurance companies, mortgage companies, Wall Street investment firms and government agencies.

Nine states are involved here, all of them east of the Mississippi River. (Western projects are covered elsewhere in this book.) The projects are briefly outlined in table 1.

Gandy Dancer, Ann Arbor, Mich.

The old Ann Arbor railroad station, now the Gandy Dancer, is one of the best restaurants in Michigan, adapted to that use by Chuck Muer, of a long-established Detroit restaurant family.

The 80,000 square feet of land and 5,000 square feet of usable building space were purchased for $175,000. $450,000 was invested in improvements, a large part of which were electrical and mechanical, including concealed duct work. The project was financed by a local commercial bank strictly on the basis of Muer's success in the restaurant business. The loan was a business loan to a restaurant, not a real estate loan or a railroad station preservation loan.

The first financing from the bank was for only $250,000, less than 50 percent of the project cost. The loan was made on a five-year installment basis with 60 monthly payments at an add-on rate, resulting in a simple interest rate of 10.85 percent. The loan was secured by a first mortgage on the property, and the company had to raise the balance of the needed funds from internal sources. Fortunately, there was no prepayment penalty. After a year, when the restaurant had proved to be successful and grossed $1.4 million on its 125 seats, the bank agreed to refinance the loan and increase the amount to $350,000, changing the rate to a flat 10 percent with a five-year note payable on a 12-year amortization—in other words, a 12-year note with a five-year balloon.

The bank loan officer says that the bank officials regarded the building as a slight headache because it was a limited-use, single-purpose structure. They almost would have preferred a conventional building that would have been easier to resell or lease to another user had the project been unsuccessful. However, in the end they were generally pleased with the loan because of the success of Chuck Muer's operation and the consequent payoff of the investment.

Chattanooga Choo Choo, Chattanooga, Tenn.

The Chattanooga Terminal Station was completed in 1909, lost its trains in 1970 and was scheduled for demolition soon after. A group of local business people led by B. Allen Casey, Jr., an established restauranteur, organized the Chattanooga Choo Choo Corporation to buy the station and an adjacent 24 acres of land.

Today this is one of the best known large preservation projects in the country. The great domed waiting room is an elegant restaurant, the passenger and baggage areas are bright, attractive eating or drinking places and 24 old railroad cars have been converted to motel bedrooms. There is also a new 103-room Hilton plus a group of shops, trolley cars, exhibits, museums and walkways.

Twenty-four local business people invested $2.4 million, a reported $100,000 each, in stock in the new corporation, and intermediate-term loans from local banks completed the capitalization of the new company. An important point is that the intent from the beginning was to start a new and profitable business—not just to preserve the station. As a result, some preservationists have criticized the emphasis on standardized high-volume menu fare and the obvious "sell" to the 10 million tourists that pass by annually on the interstate highways between Florida and the Midwest.

The restaurant seats more than 1,200 people and averages 1 million visitors a year. The Chattanooga Choo Choo has been successful and may represent the largest startup capitalization for any historic preservation project in the country.

Chickering Piano Factory, Boston

When the Jonas Chickering Piano Factory building opened in 1853, it was the largest building in the country except for the U.S. Capitol in Washington, D.C. Robert Gelardin, Simeon Bruner and Leland Cott, architects and developers, have adapted this structure into 174 apartments and 30,000 square feet of commercial space for use by painters, sculptors, dancers, musicians, photographers and others active in the arts and crafts. The building is only 10 minutes from the Back Bay in Boston's rejuvenated South End, and it is shaped like a square doughnut with an interior courtyard.

The project was financed by the Massachusetts Housing Finance Agency, a state agency that provided both construction and permanent financing under a somewhat complicated formula that allowed for market, moderate-income and low-income housing—similar to the old Housing and Urban Development 236 program.

The property was purchased for approximately $500,000, and an entire paper could be written on the developers' efforts to vacate the building of small manufacturing and storage companies and other users. A permanent mortgage commitment was issued for

Chattanooga Choo Choo (1909), Chattanooga, Tenn. (John Sower)

CHICKERING PIANO FACTORY *(1853), Boston. (John Sower)*

$3,392,000, 90 percent of the appraised project value. The interest rate is 0.5 percent over the state tax-exempt rate for 40-year bonds, and an interest subsidy paid to the developers (actually deducted from the loan amortization) is passed through in lower rents to moderate and low-income artists.

One-fourth of the apartments (the average size is 1,000 square feet) rent at the market rate of approximately $340 a month; 50 percent of the units are at a subsidized rate for moderate-income people and average $160 a month; and the remaining 25 percent are rented for a figure equal to 25 percent of the tenant's income. The interest subsidy for the moderate-income units is set to be equivalent to a permanent interest of 1 percent, and the resultant $60 to $70 a month is deducted from the debt service.

The interest rate on the construction loan, also from the Massachusetts Housing Finance Agency, was 6.9 percent. The developers converted most of their equity above the permanent mortgage into cash by selling most of their interest to a syndicate of limited-partner investors, who were interested in the tax shelter of the depreciation and interest writeoffs. Under this arrangement the developers will regain partial ownership after a fixed time period. The ability of the developers to hold hard costs to a minimum in the renovation was important in the project success.

Flat Iron Building, New York City

One of the largest remaining cast-iron buildings in New York City, the Flat Iron Building was preserved by Rockrose Associates, an experienced renovation firm headed by Henry Elghanayan and his two brothers. This 1868 structure, a former shoe factory, was converted into a 144-unit luxury apartment rental building with 15,000 square feet of commercial space. It is located on Broadway in the New York antique district, near New York University and Greenwich Village.

The property was purchased with the development company's own funds for $600,000. An open-end construction and renovation loan of $3.55 million was obtained from First National City Bank, the second largest bank in the country. The rate was 1.5 percent over prime, with a one-point fee. This type of loan is riskier than a conventional construction loan, where there is a permanent commitment to take out or pay off the construction loan on satisfactory completion of the building. The risk is that adverse money market conditions could prevent the developers from finding permanent financing and thus force the bank to carry the financing itself.

Later, after a revised appraisal, Lincoln Savings Bank made a permanent mortgage commitment of $4.1 million, (75 percent of value) at a rate of 8.5 percent for 10 years plus 1 percent per year amortization. First National City Bank subsequently increased the amount of its construction loan to $4.1 million, thus reducing the amount of necessary cash investment by the developers.

There were design and technical problems in the project, as no two of the 144 units were exactly alike. However, the project was successfully completed, and it rented rapidly, with studio apartments costing between $250 and $340 a month.

The developers report that they had originally intended to demolish the building but that several community and preservation groups and city agencies worked with them in a cooperative manner, convincing them to renovate and preserve instead. As the developer explained, "This broad range of interested groups convinced us to try and save it." This cooperation between the developer and preservationist groups is particularly interesting because, as anyone who has been involved in preservation knows, this certainly is not always the situation.

The Cairo, Washington, D.C.

The 12-story, 80-year-old Cairo Hotel, close to downtown Washington, D.C., is being renovated and converted into rental apartments by the Inland Steel Development Company. In its heyday, the Cairo was one of the most elegant hotels in Washington and was also the tallest privately owned building in the city.

The property was purchased by Inland for $500,000 and is being financed under the Federal Housing Administration 221 d(4) program. The renovation program involved nearly gutting the building and is costing approximately $3.8 million following some delays in construction.

Permanent financing for 90 percent of the value, as appraised by the FHA, is for 40 years at the FHA rate of 7.5 percent in effect at the time of appraisal. Construction financing was provided by another Inland subsidiary, Inland Finance, at 7 percent. The company raised additional capital for the project by selling tax benefits to a syndicate organized by White Weld, a large Wall Street brokerage firm. Such underwritings often are for an amount equal to 10–20 percent of the FHA commitment. Negotiations with the FHA to increase the amount of the permanent mortgage commitment are currently under way.

Rents in the project will range from $220 a month for an efficiency or one-bedroom in the 700-square-foot size range to $450 a month for larger townhouses or multiple-level units. The building will have 170 apartments and is within walking distance of the business district.

The risks of renovation or preservation development are well illustrated by this project, which encountered unanticipated structural problems in the renovation, resulting in increased costs and time delays.

Inland is also converting the Woodley highrise apartment building into 73 condominium units. This project, which has been successful, involves the preservation of a 73-year-old building.

Inland Steel, with annual sales of $2.5 billion in 1974, is certainly one of the largest corporations directly involved in preservation projects. It has demonstrated an unusual sensitivity to preservation and an overall sophistication in community development.

Airy View Condominiums, Washington, D.C.

The 60-year-old Airy View condominium building, with 3 stories and 22 units, is located in Washington's intown Kalorama Triangle district. This project illustrates a standard financing formula for apartment or condominium conversion.

The property was purchased for $375,000 with interim loan financing from a local savings and loan at a rate of 10 percent per year, plus two points "up front." Marilyn Taylor is the developer, along with two out-of-state investors. They are renovating the property and selling the units as condominiums.

The same savings and loan advanced the balance of the construction financing at the same terms and issued a $750,000 commitment for end loans, the mortgages to the buyers of the condominiums. The interest rate for the end loans was set at the market rate (i.e., whatever the rate is at the time of closing) for a term of 30 years, with the buyer paying one point at settlement. The mortgages are for up to 90–95 percent of the purchase price of the units (up to $42,500), and they will be partially insured by the Mortgage Guarantee Insurance Corporation. The savings and loan may later sell the end loans to the Federal Home Loan Mortgage Corporation in the secondary market.

This financing was possible because of the record and strong financial statements of the developers. They were obligated to sign personally on the interim financing. Future projects of this type will be more difficult in Washington because of recent city legislation on rent control and condominium conversions.

Fairlington Village, Arlington, Va.

The 320-acre Fairlington Village complex straddles Interstate 95 just a few minutes' drive from downtown Washington, D.C., in suburban Arlington, Va. It is less historic than most preservation projects but is included because of the quality of the restoration and because it illustrates several financing concepts. Built as World War II–era housing for Pentagon employees, the buildings are of Georgian style architecture with brick exteriors and slate roofs. CBI Fairmac Corporation, owner of the project, is an affiliate of Chicago Bridge and Iron, a large corporation.

CBI Fairmac bought the 3,439-unit apartment project with financing based on its appraisal as a rental project. This financing was from Chase Manhattan and other banks in the form of a five-year standing loan at the prime rate of interest plus 0.5 percent per year. The buildings were redesigned from rental apartments into townhouse and single-level condominiums.

Construction funds were obtained from CBI's own resources, and a local mortgage company arranged end-loan commitments, originally from a local bank consortium and subsequently from Citizens Mortgage, a subsidiary of Manufacturers Hanover Trust Bank in

New York City. The most recent commitment for continuation of the renovation was for $45 million on a flexible formula whereby the developers can offer a range of end-loan interest rates to stay competitive with the local market. However, the developers must be prepared to make up the difference from the market interest rate. In other words, if an end-loan rate of 9 percent is set for a buyer but the market rate is 9⅛ percent, the developer must make up a one-point difference to the lender.

Citizens Mortgage services the end loans and "warehouses" them for potential sale to other lenders. One batch totaling $3 million was recently sold to a savings and loan in Miami. The Manufacturers Hanover Trust loan was made out of the commercial loan division rather than the real estate department.

The original standing loan agreement has a release formula with a 115 percent paydown per unit, resulting in its gradually being paid off as the condominiums are sold.

Renovation is averaging $20,000 in hard costs per unit, which includes total new wiring, plumbing, kitchens, bathrooms, central individually-controlled heating and air conditioning and other improvements. The units are retailing at $32 a square foot, compared with an estimated $45 a square foot to build similar quality housing in today's market. The project has won many awards, including the first in a new category created by the local chapter of the National Association of Home Builders—Revitalization of Community and Excellence in Restoration.

Faneuil Hall Marketplace, Boston

One of the country's oldest "urban renewal" projects is the Faneuil Hall Marketplace in Boston. Faneuil Hall itself was built in 1722, the first public market in Boston, and three long granite buildings were added in 1826. The marketplace has a long tradition in the center of the city's commercial life.

The city of Boston, through the Boston Redevelopment Authority, is leasing a group of the buildings, consisting of nearly 340,000 square feet of rentable space, on a net-lease basis to the Rouse Company of Columbia, Md. Rouse will redevelop the area into a complex of stores, restaurants and offices.

The city is utilizing funding from the Housing and Urban Development to fix the streets, bring utilities on site, renovate the facades and strengthen the buildings structurally. The 99-year lease agreement with Rouse stipulates a general development plan and a mutually determined timetable for redevelopment.

Rouse has the responsibility to find tenants for the project, arrange permanent and construction financing, supervise the actual construction and manage the project on an ongoing basis. The city will accomplish the renovation of an important historic area with minimum capital outlay and with the advantages of a partnership with one of the most successful and sophisticated development companies in the country.

Rouse obtained a permanent mortgage commitment from the Teachers Insurance and Annuity Association on conventional commercial terms, including interest rate, maturity and requirements for preleasing by acceptable tenants prior to take out. Construction financing has been arranged with 50 percent from the Chase Manhattan Bank in New York City and 50 percent from a consortium led by the First National Bank of Boston. This financing is secured as a general obligation of the Rouse Company; the permanent mortgage is secured by a first mortgage on the leasehold interest in the property and presumably by assignments of the rents from the leases.

This concept of a city government's net-leasing valuable historic property to a private developer, under a carefully prepared development plan and timetable, has considerable potential in other cities and towns.

The Century, Chicago

The Century Theatre, built in 1924 and known as the Diversey in vaudeville days, had a negative net worth when Sonny and Earl Malisoff, principals in the E&S Realty Corporation, decided to check into the property. The land was determined to be more valuable with the building demolished and the ground cleared for a new structure than with the old theater left on the property.

Fortunately, the Malisoffs had successfully completed other residential and commercial restoration projects in the Chicago New Town area. They decided to preserve the exterior facade and build a new interior, with 110,000 square feet of speciality shops and a "fashion mall" on a seven-level plan with an enclosed 70-foot-high atrium.

Financing for the project was difficult. Lenders are used to shopping centers anchored by one or more triple-A tenants paying enough rent under long-term leases to assure that the mortgages will be paid according to schedule. A local mortgage banking firm arranged financing for the project, which was described as "a typical REIT deal." The five-year standby permanent commitment that was arranged is the same as any other permanent commitment, except it has a shorter term and is at a higher rate. It offers the construction lender the security of knowing that when the project is completed, that lender will be paid off.

The permanent and construction financing was for $7.5 million, 75 percent of the appraised value, based on comparable rentals in the immediate area for similar tenants. The developers have already advanced approximately $1 million of their own funds in the project.

After construction is completed, the tenants have moved in and the rental and cost figures have "hardened" (i.e., after six months to a year of actual operating figures), the developers will probably refinance. They can then obtain a conventional permanent mortgage from a large savings and loan or insurance company in an amount equivalent to 75 percent of the reappraised value of the project. This refinancing should enable the developers to free their own invested

capital and realize additional capital based on the project's success. They have already completed the 550-space parking ramp and many tenants have signed leases. The project is scheduled to open in late 1975 or early 1976.

Some of the construction problems on this project were unique. The developers actually built a new building from the inside out—that is, they built a new core and moved out to the original walls. Construction was more difficult than on conventional projects because there was no standardization; each steel beam had to be individually measured, cut and put into place.

Oldtown Mall, Baltimore

A pre–Civil War, two-block-long shopping area in inner-city Baltimore is emerging and being revived,

thanks to a combination of private and federal financing and a tremendous amount of persistence and patience by the people involved.

Gay Street was the most important shopping area in Baltimore in the early 1800s, and the Belair Market, built in 1813, was the first public marketplace in the city. The redevelopment planning for the area started 17 years ago, and the project is now being completed. The slowdown in urban renewal funding for housing negatively affected the revival of the entire market area on the close-in Baltimore East Side.

There are 84 store buildings on the two-block section of the street, and they are owned by every imaginable combination of landlord, tenant, estate and absentee management. The city has developed a master plan, under which each of the 84 stores will be renovated and

QUAKER SQUARE, *Akron, Ohio, (facing page) and interior of Quaker Square. (Samaras Photography)*

restored to their original 1800s-era style. This will be done using city code enforcement pressure as the stick and such carrots as Housing and Urban Development 312 loans, Small Business Administration 502 loans, bank loans and private investment.

The city inspected each building and gave each owner a list of the improvements necessary to bring the building up to code. Throughout the city HUD 312 loans at 3 percent interest were made available for stores where only minor improvements were necessary.

The Oldtown Local Development Company was organized to provide financing to merchants wishing to make sizable improvements in addition to those required by code. This financing was through 15-year, 5.5 percent loans from the Small Business Administration and similar loans from the city of Baltimore. Some businesses, such as the financial institutions, are doing restoration with their own funds.

The city renewal agency, the Department of Housing and Community Development, is said to be one of the most effective in the country. This agency is investing money in closing the street to automobiles, creating adjacent parking lots and putting in trees, benches and a fountain. The basic idea behind the project is that, as an attractive and unified shopping area, the mall can provide better goods and services to residents of the immediate area. The area can also effectively compete with suburban malls by highlighting its historic preservation atmosphere.

This successful, multiple-store restoration project has

been the model for similar renovation projects in other old inner-city business districts, including both large cities and smaller towns.

Quaker Square, Akron, Ohio

Around the time of the Civil War, a German immigrant named Ferdinand Schumacher began milling oats in the back of his small store in Akron, Ohio, an enterprise that has since grown into the Quaker Oats Company.

The company's old brick buildings, located in downtown Akron, were purchased in 1973 by a group of local business people for $325,000 with a one-year loan from a local bank at 2 percent over the prime rate per year. (The loan has since been renewed for another year or two.) The initial financial strategy was to raise funds from a public offering—i.e., to sell 600 limited partnership units at $5,000 each for a total of $3,000,000. The developers had a formal prospectus prepared and distributed; however, in the summer of 1974, the stock market was down and still falling, and the offering proved unsuccessful.

The group then raised a total of $370,000, enough to get the project opened and four floors of shops rented and in operation. This was done by combining a unique and a common method of financing. The common one was an investment of $250,000 of the group's own funds; the unusual method was via scrap sales—selling old machinery and equipment in the buildings for an additional $120,000.

The project is attractive and thus far successful; the developers are now seeking additional financing in order to expand.

Traugott Schmidt and Sons Building, Detroit

Traugott Schmidt and Sons were tanners and merchants of furs and hides, and their firm was a pre–Motor City industrial giant. The building is now being converted into a complex of shops and restaurants, following its purchase on land contract by a group of local, predominantly minority group professionals and business people. (Under a land contract transaction, the seller provides financing to the buyer after a low cash down payment and retains title to the property until a certain amount of the principal is paid.)

Equity investments have been made and are being organized from the same investors and from several Minority Enterprise Small Business Investment Companies for approximately $500,000. Permanent financing will be sought after additional leases have been signed by tenants. In addition, a joint venture with an established development firm is being negotiated to assist in obtaining the financing, leasing and management.

Conclusion

Perhaps this has been an inundation of financing

TABLE 1

SELECTED LARGE COMMERCIAL PROJECTS
BY TYPE OF PROJECT AND FINANCING

	Type of Project	Types of Financing
Gandy Dancer *Ann Arbor, Mich.*	Restaurant	Bank term loan, Refinancing
Chattanooga Choo Choo *Chattanooga, Tennessee*	Restaurant, retail shops, motel	Common stock, Bank term loan
Chickering Piano Factory *Boston, Mass.*	Moderate-income housing	State housing loan, Tax-loss syndication
Flat Iron Building *New York, N.Y.*	Market-rate rental housing and retail	Open-end construction loan, Permanent mortgage commitment
The Cairo *Washington, D.C.*	Market-rate rental housing	FHA 221 d(4), construction loan, Tax-loss syndication
Airy View Condominiums *Washington, D.C.*	Highrise condominium	Construction loan, End-loan commitments
Fairlington Village *Arlington, Va.*	Garden condominiums	Acquisition loan, Warehousing, End-loan commitments
Faneuil Hall Marketplace *Boston, Mass.*	Retail, office	City-developer net lease, construction loans, permanent mortgage commitment
The Century *Chicago, Ill.*	Retail	Standby takeout and construction loan
Oldtown Mall *Baltimore, Md.*	Inner-city commercial revitalization	HUD 312 loans, SBA 502 loans, city loans
Quaker Square *Akron, Ohio*	Retail shops, offices	Public equity offering, bank acquisition loan
Traugott Schmidt and Sons Building *Detroit, Mich.*	Retail shops	Land contract, Small Business Investment Companies (SBICs)

strategies and techniques. However, two points should be reemphasized:

1. Historic preservation is a sophisticated form of real estate development; hence it is important for preservationists, both private and public, to explore fully the alternatives of development strategies, particularly the possibilities for obtaining private financing for different types of projects.

2. Historic preservation is now in the major leagues. Many of the largest developers and financial institutions in the nation are involved in preservation projects as good investments. It is time for all financial institutions to look seriously at these projects in their own areas.

But the best, and perhaps only, way to make what has been said here have real value is through application of the techniques or concepts to preservation projects throughout the country.

Preserved Buildings as Profitable Real Estate

Congress Street, *Savannah, Ga. (Mary Elizabeth Lattimore Reiter)*

Preservation as Profitable Real Estate in Savannah

LEOPOLD ADLER, II

Leopold Adler, II, is vice president of the investment banking firm Robinson-Humphrey Company, Inc., in Savannah, Ga. He is a trustee of the National Trust for Historic Preservation, treasurer of Preservation Action, chairman of the Savannah-Chatham County Historic Site and Monument Commission and past president of the Historic Savannah Foundation, Inc.

Reflecting on the past 20 years of involvement in historic preservation, I realize that the accomplishment in Savannah has allowed me to participate in the life of a city trying to solve its problems. Preservationists, as Arthur Zeigler has said, are doing something constructive about the environment, and doing it more successfully than any other group. The result is less crime and better housing on a scale that does not dehumanize. He adds, "We are using a valuable stock of housing that otherwise would be a wasteland—deteriorating and causing social problems from increased crime to falling tax rolls." Carl Westmoreland of Cincinnati puts it another way: "To revitalize a neighborhood, to bring back the middle class, one must increase ownership, reduce densities and add amenities."

One rule should be added to these preservationists' words. The work or subsidy (a word usually disliked) that is necessary in preservation is a far better and less expensive way to cure the ills of our cities than any other. A subsidy, whether in effort, money or time, is a necessity.

Founding of Historic Savannah

In Savannah, as in many other cities in the United States, the downtown became a slum and was badly deteriorated 20 years ago. Today this colonial city has had a rebirth, a reclamation of meaningful urban proportions. For instance, the Davenport House was in a slum two decades ago. Eleven families lived there, and it was to be torn down for a parking lot. Today it is the Historic Savannah Foundation headquarters.

Historic Savannah was founded 20 years ago in response to the destruction of 18th and 19th-century buildings. The group was founded by seven women who wanted to save the Davenport House. They were dubbed "hysteric Savannah," for they became frantic at the seemingly senseless demolition of irreplaceable and beautiful architecture.

These women bought the Davenport House and saved it from the wrecker's ball. They were afraid to own property (they promptly gave the deed to another organization), and they were naive about anything that involved real estate or financing. But they created enough interest that a group of far-sighted business people joined them to organize an effective force to deal with the situation.

Since then, the Historic Savannah Foundation has spearheaded a drive that has led to the restoration of 800 buildings and reclamation of nearly three square miles of downtown property. Today it is a major force in the city, and a consortium of commercial banks and savings and loan institutions sometimes provides up to 100 percent financing of the group's restoration activities.

From 1959 to 1968, these efforts resulted in $50 million in construction activity for restoration and approximately $18 million in related real estate activity, with attendant commissions and profits and an extremely active market, where values have often risen 10 to 20-fold in the period from 1960 through 1973. For example, in 1960 a four-story, stucco-over-brick house in Gordon Row could be bought for $2,500. Today a house there would be $30,000 unrestored—when you can find and buy one.

More than $35 million in public improvements has been spent in buildings alone, and this has attracted another $23 million in other private construction. Many of Savannah's parks, once dirt lots, are now flowering squares, and the historic riverfront, which lay fallow for years, has in the past three years attracted 60 shops and restaurants and a $7 million urban renewal improvement project.

In addition, the tourist business in Savannah has grown from less than a million dollars in 1962 to more than $50 million in 1974, with attendant increases for bank deposits, restaurant business, postal receipts, retail sales and filling station revenues. Two new hotels have been built and more are on the drawing boards.

These are dramatic results. The July 1975 *Fortune* magazine points out in an article on Savannah's accomplishments that "Savannah is still a charming place to visit, as well as to live and to work in. Anachronism can be made to pay off in urban civilization."

Now all the utilities are located in the historic district. The old gas company had reclaimed a 10-acre tract in 1945. When the Atlanta Gas Light Company bought the Savannah Gas Company in 1966, its first thought was to discard this rental project. The firm was principally a utility and did not think it wanted to own real estate. However, when the officials saw the rents and the commercial and residential mix, they changed their minds. They would sooner sell their gas business now.

The electric company built a compatible building as its headquarters in the shadow of the gas company reclamation. Recently the telephone company bought an old house for use as its downtown public office. The company paid $110,000 for the house in a nearly restored condition, plus $80,000 for the lot beside it and $40,000 for renovation. The first floor is the public office for customer use, the second floor a conference room for civic group meetings and receptions and the third floor the office space for the district manager and staff. The basement is storage space, the attic is for files and the courtyard serves as a lunch area for the people who work in the building. The telephone company wanted to fill its needs with a historic house to help preserve the central city but also found in doing so that the building was less expensive than constructing a modern nonentity.

So Savannah, the seat of the 13th original English colony, has preserved its past profitably and sensibly. However, this did not just happen. Although Savannah is a particularly beautiful city, it was not recognized as such a few years ago—not by its own citizens or the traveling public. In fact Tom McCaskey, vice president of Colonial Williamsburg and an expert in tourism, said 15 years ago, "Savannah is the best kept secret in the country—but spend $300,000 a year in restoring and promotion and you'll do at least $100 million a year in tourist and convention business." What a return!

Real Estate: The Name of the Game

Anyone who travels to consult or speak on preservation discovers amazing techniques developed on the local level. But the one consistent method that does not fail and produces tangible results is that of buying and selling properties. So, the name of the game is real estate. Until the Historic Savannah Foundation entered the real estate market, the development of downtown Savannah, as had happened in hundreds of other cities, had been left to the vagaries of urban renewal ("urban removal" as preservationists fondly call it) or to the confusion of local planners. Their deference to merchants made them try a variety of experiments that included malls, minibuses, phony storefronts, replicas of Colonial Williamsburg with Quonset hut housing or worse and unsightly parking garages and lots.

Now area restoration is being used in Charleston, Savannah, Pittsburgh, Annapolis, Albany, Galveston or any number of cities as a method of reclaiming both commercial and residential properties in downtown neighborhoods and transforming them into viable communities contributing to their cities.

The first problem is to identify the property. This sounds simple and does not take long, although one must have professional help in order to do it well. In the space of three months, Historic Savannah inventoried some 1,100 structures from a list of more than 2,500, with students taking direction from a team of architects and consultant planners. This provided information on the architectural and historical value of the buildings; the survey also was invaluable as a real estate tool showing what to buy, how much an effective program would cost and—after some thought—how to get people to move into a deteriorated neighborhood.

The Savannah survey, a Bible for the downtown property owners, is the basis of urban renewal programs as well as the historical zoning ordinances. It cost only $25,000 from start to publication but was a lever to accomplish $40 million in restoration.

The survey enabled preservationists to enter real estate with a vengeance. Other downtowns had problems; some had been wiped out. Savannah's was 75 percent intact, largely because that first great practitioner of urban renewal, William Tecumseh Sherman, did not burn the city when he reached the sea in 1864. In fact, he gave the city to President Lincoln as a Christmas present. At any rate, if what was valuable was to be saved, it had to be bought and sold to people who would restore with restrictions.

The preservationists were in competition with the homebuilders because the homebuilders would pay 10 cents for a Savannah Gray brick compared to 3 cents for a common brick. The Savannah Gray brick, soft and porous, could not be duplicated and a wrecker could make a profit of 50 percent on the brick alone and have a parking lot to boot.

The buying and selling of property by Historic Savannah—usually at little profit and marked up to cover legal, interest, insurance, tax and administrative expenses—became the turning point in the direction downtown Savannah was to take. Historic Savannah led the way and others joined to take advantage of an overlooked and underpriced situation.

Historic Savannah Success Stories

The Cluskey Building is an example of a success. This handsome double residence was slated for demolition to make room for a 14-story glass and concrete annex to the courthouse behind it. The foundation was able to acquire the Cluskey Building because, in order to get a high price of $162,500, the owner let the foundation name its terms: $1,000 down for a six-month contract with $14,000 more at the end of that time; temporary interest payments while more funds were being raised; and finally $1,000 a month for the next eight years with a balloon note at the end. It was thought that if the building was not sold by then the foundation almost did not deserve it anyway. But a purchaser came along, and although a $25,000 loss was sustained, that amount was considered a contribution of the foundation and its benefactors to the cultural heritage and urban vitality of the city. This demonstrated the basic reason for the existence of the Historic Savannah Foundation: to assume the financial burden of showing the way to practical modern use of fine old buildings—in this case as law offices.

The house at 18 East Oglethorpe Avenue is another example of the determination of the Historic Savannah Foundation to keep good historic architecture. This fine early 19th-century wooden house is located two doors from the Juliette Gordon Low birthplace, a restoration complex worth nearly a million dollars, and was slated for a parking lot. The roof had already been torn off when a bargain was struck for $50,000, including a loan company building in the side yard. The building was almost a total wreck. The foundation carried the property for two years, thanks to income of $350 a month from the loan company. Then a young real estate broker restored the house for his offices. He paid $42,500 and put $80,000 into restoration. He gets $15,000 in rent plus $4,800 from the loan company, and he has a floor-and-a-half to go. He also brokers downtown properties.

Other profitable commercial development occurred on entire blocks, such as Congress Street, where instead of demolition of buildings, as was planned, face-lifting occurred and values rose.

Over a three-year period, Historic Savannah raised $200,000 for a revolving fund; in 1965 an area restoration was launched in a blighted residential neighborhood that rated high in the foundation's professional inventory. The Pulaski Square–West Jones Street project began November 21, 1965, after the foundation bought key houses in the area. By buying only one of a pair (for who could then tear the other down?) or, better still, by optioning or buying only one of a row, the equity was stretched and to date more than 90 buildings in the area have changed hands. This was done with only $38,000 of seed money, and now more than $5 million in restoration has occurred. Here are some before-and-after situations:

1. A small West Jones Street townhouse was bought for $3,000. It was restored with air-conditioning, exposed brick walls and heart-of-pine floors for $14,000.

2. On Harris Street two young couples with small children paid $5,500 for a double house. One couple restored its part for $37,500; recently the neighbor sold for $100,000.

3. A year later, next door, another couple bought an abandoned house for $21,000 and restored it for $68,000. Today its appraised value is $135,000.

4. Across the square, a house on Charlton Street was bought for $12,000 by a couple that moved back to the city and restored it for $60,000, including a swimming pool in the back yard.

Restoration proceeded at a fast pace and the neighborhood was transformed into one of the loveliest in the city.

House on West Jones Street, Savannah, before (top) and after restoration. (Leopold Adler, II, Historic Savannah Foundation)

Urban Renewal Experiences in Savannah

Across the historic district to the east, just one square south of Columbia Square and the Davenport House, the first urban renewal effort made Troup Ward a pilot project in the use of Federal Home Administration (FHA) funds for restoration.

This problem was a little tougher, for the foundation now began to deal with the local and federal governments. But the group had a good record and, more important, determination. And it had learned to sell—with flyers, signs and action. So, the city was enticed to cooperate.

Savannah had the first urban renewal conservation program in the South. The urban renewal agency, which was under the aegis of the city housing authority, took the Troup Trust Area as a pilot project after Historic Savannah paid $24,000 for some abandoned buildings rather than see them torn down.

The area was stark: more than 15 acres encompassing 82 structures and 127 dwelling units. But the federal government came again, this time to cooperate, and work began. The housing authority–urban renewal team did a rehabilitation demonstration project that cost $141,550 for four units. It was sold for $93,500, a writedown of $48,000. The city contributed $96,000 as its one-third match for landscaping, paving, grading, drainage and lighting improvements, so a square was reborn.

With the private sector pitching in, 36 structures were rehabilitated with section 312 loans amounting to $1,007,000 from the U.S. Department of Housing and Urban Development (HUD). An additional one-third in cash contributions was required from the owners. Thirty buildings were privately restored at a cost of $551,000. In addition, 11 structures were brought up to code standards with $10,000 of private money. New construction was attracted to the area in the amount of $314,000.

A homeowner in the area could either borrow pri-

Savannah house saved by Historic Savannah Foundation. (Leopold Adler, II, Historic Savannah Foundation)

vately or get a subordinated 312 loan (one that can come after a first mortgage) directly from HUD: $17,300 per dwelling unit for up to five units or 90 percent for more than five units. This meant two important things: one, that FHA financing was available for downtown as well as in the suburbs and, two, that buyers in Troup Trust each could get a second or third lien of up to $52,000 to restore their property. All that was necessary was that their plans pay off. They did, and now urban renewal is joined with private preservation efforts to the enhancement of Savannah. Remember, here $24,000 of seed money produced $2.5 million, and today another $1.5 million has been spent nearby.

There is one more example of urban renewal done the right way. The Savannah riverfront spans nearly a mile where the city was founded in 1733. As Savannah grew, it depended on its port and prospered. Eli Whitney's cotton gin made Savannah the cotton port of the South and the cotton exchange reflected that fact. Ramps and retaining walls were built to preserve the 40-foot bluff along which the city was built. Freestanding warehouses were erected on the river level and joined to the top of the bluff, called the Strand, by a series of ramps and bridges that is a marvel to see—a double marvel because they are still intact.

Thirty years ago the Factor's Row complex, with its unique systems, was threatened with annihilation. This threat was fortunately forestalled then and again in the 1950s, but recently part of this amazing complex (two stories on the bluff and five stories on the balconied Savannah river side) was threatened by developers planning a 15-story highrise motel and apartment building.

To date, attempts at highrise construction on the river had been repulsed. In the past three years, 60 shops and restaurants opened along its length. A $7 million urban renewal program started in mid-July. It will buttress the edge of the river and repave the streets with block and cobblestone, thus restoring for Savannah a genuine part of her history. More than $4 million in private funds has already been attracted and certainly another $10 million will come soon. An example is one row of buildings two stories above the bluff and three below: It pays $100,000 a year in rent and has $250,000 invested in it. The net before depreciation is $80,000 a year; there are 30 tenants.

Other Successes and Future Plans

Most chambers of commerce celebrate the Fourth of July, occasionally do a fair job of industrial solicitation, have 25 irons in the fire and conduct annual membership campaigns for free enterprise. Savannah's was like that too, except there was a separate industrial solicitation group. In 1960 the Historic Savannah Foundation got interested in the Savannah Chamber of Commerce, particularly because it was not spending its $90,000 annual budget for tourist promotion. Today with advice from Tom McCaskey, the Chamber of Commerce occupies and has superbly renovated, at a cost of $250,000, the Central of Georgia railroad station. After Amtrak discontinued passenger service there, the station reverted to the city, which leases it to the Chamber of Commerce for $1 a year. Located at the intersection of I-16, it is the gateway to the city and its train shed may have a farmers market. Now the Chamber of Commerce, with an active visitors bureau, plays a vital role in a growing Savannah.

In Savannah, and often elsewhere, the private sector has shown the way to preserving old buildings profitably. Work was done through the private, nonprofit Historic Savannah Foundation. In this way a catalyst was provided. Had someone said that $1 million in cash and $4 million in loans would have to be raised in 10 years to effect a viable, vibrant downtown with some $80 million in restoration and new construction, I doubt that we would have even tried. But we were determined to keep the downtown vital with banking, shipping and retail interests—all contributing without losing the flavor that history had provided.

The subsidy was inexpensive. A million dollars grew to $80 million, and work continues. This is the subsidy mentioned earlier. It is necessary in every venture in some form. In Seattle the city leaders were smart enough to see that, as they do in Savannah today.

Historic Savannah has just raised another million dollars, and the city is working to improve the main commercial downtown street. The foundation has been dedicated, competitive and innovative. Now it has new projects, new problems and possibly some new solutions.

The preservation movement in Savannah is a success. When it started, it reused buildings that were empty, so there was no problem of displacement. The cost of restorations privately done at $40,000 for acquisition and renovation costs seems as good an investment today as Coca-Cola stock at $3 a share was 25 years ago.

The old city has regained a large part of its elegance, from high-stoop row houses to low ones. The Historic Savannah Foundation acted with ever-increasing vigor as successful techniques showed the way and the combination of nonprofit status, private enterprise and government succeeded through cooperation. A zenith was reached when the foundation stopped the state university system from destroying some great buildings in order to build mediocre classroom structures.

The Historic Savannah Foundation still owns and sells properties, including the commonplace and the unusual, even empty lots. All of this has received much publicity, aided by the fact that a newspaper headquarters has restored one of the oldest houses.

One resident, who was described at a recent fundraising luncheon as restoring more houses than the National Park Service, has replanted complete squares. He has also restored Victorian houses in an area that is fast decaying. Here 400 houses cry for help. This area poses the problem of displacing low-income residents. Many structures were to be demolished, and some in fact were, so concern was great. Private initiative restored one row for middle-income people at a rent of $250 a month per unit. Around the block is a row for low-income people at a rate of $75 a month per unit.

If these houses were 10 blocks away in the Pulaski Square–West Jones Street project, they would bring $15,000 to $20,000 unrestored. Here, two young couples bought at the ends of a row in the middle of a slum neighborhood. One restoration is completed. On the other the owners are doing the work themselves; they paid $3,000 for the shell and will restore it for $10,000. The slum landlord who owned the row has withdrawn the remainder from sale to wait for his killing; he does not care about any of the people or the buildings. So to help prevent displacement and the speculation that prevents restoration, and to effect a healthy mix for this Victorian district, a nonprofit group was formed to buy and option three rows of houses (some 60 units), with a goal of restoring 600 units.

The group will try to use federal community development funds—grants and loans to rehabilitate through a nonprofit organization. The grant would be modest: $1,000 to $3,000, dependent on acquisition costs. This would be coupled with a modest loan from community development funds—$8,000 to $10,000 to be repaid in five to six years by section 8 leased-housing assistance payments. That would enable the units to be brought up to code and provide some form of ownership for these low-income residents, some of whom have lived here for 30 years.

This is a subsidy, certainly. But, there is help from private sources (banks and individual mortgages), the National Trust for Historic Preservation, the National Endowment for the Arts and Humanities and, it is hoped, from HUD, so that these people might have the chance to live here. With other capital attracted, there will be a healthier, richer environment, one similar to the Mexican War Streets area developed so successfully by the Pittsburgh History & Landmarks Foundation.

Savannahians can take pride that their concern for people as well as buildings in this colonial city is in the tradition of the city founder, James Edward Oglethorpe, a humanitarian who brought more than 34 debtors among the first settlers. If his dream is realized, his city will be a national example of a place that has recreated an urban environment of the healthiest kind for human habitation. However, it is important to remember that only through the buying and selling of real estate did Savannah restore its invaluable historic downtown. It must be said that, were it not for the Historic Savannah Foundation and its syndication of real estate, this handsome Victorian city would not be as it is today: a testament to preservation efforts and benefits.

Headquarters for Victoria Station, a restaurant chain, San Francisco. (Carleton Knight, III)

The Realities of Renovation: Economics and Related Influences

RON KAUFMAN

Ron Kaufman heads the Ron Kaufman Companies, a commercial and industrial real estate firm specializing in downtown San Francisco properties and involved principally in the redevelopment of old industrial buildings. He is currently a general partner in 10 active real estate developments.

People who enjoy old buildings are not freaks or fanatics. They do not necessarily dislike well-planned, new highrise buildings. After all, these will be the restorations of the future.

The majority of my work involves the conversion of old brick industrial buildings located near downtown San Francisco to office and commercial space. Preserving old buildings gives me a good feeling, but it also provides a fine, long-term profit for my associates and clients and myself. And it is the economic aspects of real estate, which are vital for successful preservation, that will be discussed here.

PRESERVATION CRITERIA

In planning preservation projects, the factors a developer usually considers are as follows: Environmental factors, including the size, desirability, location, configuration and aesthetics of the site; financial factors, including land and building costs as well as total improvement costs, financing mechanisms available, marketability, return on investment, and growth and future development potential of the project; other factors, such as the availability of transportation, public facilities, housing and parking.

The most important of these factors are location, the aesthetics of the improvements, leasability or market acceptance, financing and, above all, financial feasibility.

Most of us are not in the real estate business as philanthropists. No matter how emotional we feel about a property, preservation will not be achieved unless the economics are at least competitive with other long-term investments. Long-term is emphasized because property development cannot be approached as an overnight, quick-buck investment. It is almost like raising a child, where a great deal of care must be given in the early, formative years.

STRUCTURING A PRESERVATION PROGRAM

Location

Staying close to the high-occupancy and high-rent office areas is beneficial. When a property is a considerable distance from downtown in an area that is normally not considered good, the project still can be successful if positive features overcome the locational deficit. Examples of such features are excellent bus or commuter train service, proximity to freeways, a large parking lot, a competitive rent scale and attractive design.

Physical Attributes

The basic original design of a building is important. Often basic lines have been covered by layers of plaster, wood and other materials put on top of the basic brick. To many people these buildings appear to be candidates for demolition. The key is to look under the surface and see what was originally created. It is also important to enhance the original design rather than make drastic changes and use slick coverups. This is an important part of the economics of preservation, as the Fibreboard headquarters office building in San Francisco will show.

Another important physical attribute is the volume of interior space. Often older buildings have ceiling heights or unusual ceiling configurations that provide exciting potential for both design and marketing.

A prospective development property must comply with structural and life safety codes at a realistic cost. Most code compliance requirements do not enhance the leasability or income potential of the building. Therefore, the cost of code compliance must be weighed carefully before deciding on financial feasibility.

Construction Costs

Construction costs are a major determining factor in the financial feasibility of a preservation project. The upper limit of costs is determined by the income and financing potential of the property and will have a direct bearing on competitive marketing and a satisfactory return. A knowledgeable contractor who can give reliable estimates quickly and perform quality renovation work at competitive prices is essential. Quality work and followup keep tenants happy, and in the long run this is a good investment.

Early in the analysis of a specific property, meet with the contractor and determine construction cost guidelines and a development program. I compare the quick estimates and basic drawings with construction budgets previously set from studying financial feasibility. If the contractor's budget is within the feasibility budget, you are ready to move further. If not, the development program must be revised and/or construction savings found.

A close relationship with a knowledgeable contractor can also bring help in the many surprises found in older buildings, such as aging mortar and bricks, decomposition of wood, rotten piles and special code requirements. Also, it is important to maintain the confidence of the investors and the users in the contractor.

Leasability

A project is successful only if the finished product is accepted by users. Do just enough work on a building to give the user a suggestion about the finished project and then stop. When tenants are interested, let them feel as if they are taking part in the design and planning. This makes for happier tenants who are "doing their own thing."

In most cities there is intensive competition for tenants, but conventional office or commercial space cannot compete with well-conceived historic preservation. The preservation project is unique; it has dimensions and ceiling heights that most new buildings do not have and an environment that is difficult to duplicate. This uniqueness adds to leasability and is therefore an important part of financial feasibility. Be aware of competitive space, but consider that there are two distinct markets: the new and the restored.

Specific Economics

There are many aspects of renovation work that have direct or indirect influence on the success of a project. Above all, the economics must make sense and the building or project must qualify as a feasible real estate transaction. Once it appears to pass the tests of the real estate world, the preservation items add appeal and desirability. However, an old building with "charm" cannot be a crutch or a substitute for sound real estate economics.

What do *make sense* and *feasible real estate transaction* mean? This can depend on the objectives of the owners, but to me they mean a reasonable profit for the risk involved, enough net income to justify a realistic loan and to service the debt, plus funds remaining to pay a distribution to the owners that is somewhat better or more attractive than that offered by other investments competing for their equity.

Economic feasibility is tested simply. Even though my formal training is in real estate research, my associates and I do not get involved with complicated tables, computer calculations and pages of formulas.

Table 1 shows our typical feasibility study form. The numbers are filled in based on experience and judgment. Each partnership has different long-term and short-term objectives for an acceptable investment return and how soon this return is wanted. The best attitude toward "attractive" real estate projects is that these are long-haul projects where cash flow in the beginning is not necessary, but where future income is possible.

The site, including the buildings to be restored, must provide a competitive base cost per usable square foot. Then when improvements and indirect costs are added to the base, the project can still be competitive. Unique aesthetics are not enough. Much will depend on construction costs that are competitive and still offer quality. Indirect costs will be detailed later but must be recognized at 10 to 15 percent of costs. They can be minimized by the timing of escrow closings, preleasing or speed of construction—i.e., by how astutely the development manager works.

Income can be calculated as a precent of costs to produce a net return. Add on expenses to arrive at a rent and see if that rent is competitive. I prefer to select a competitive gross rent and eventually see if the net income will be high enough to attract a lender and satisfy the investors. Vacancy and loss of efficiency is usually accounted for by reducing the leasable footage by 10 percent in the first calculations.

If the income does not justify cost or vice versa, then a careful examination is made. Can costs or expenses be reduced? Can income be increased?

Expenses are a critical ingredient of financial feasibility. They are influenced by careful building management, by leases that are explicit and well written and by design and construction that require minimum care and maintenance. Usually, expenses are carefully detailed, item by item, to test against the per-square-foot estimate.

The net income is arrived at by subtracting all expenses from gross income. The net income is what counts in arriving at return on total investment, cash for debt service, etc. A highly competitive rent may produce a lower-than-market gross rental, but the lease can be structured so the net income is equal to or higher than normal. A percentage rate of return should be at least a few points above the interest rate for long-term real estate loans.

An assumption of the value that will be assigned by the lender is made on the basis of past contact with lending institutions and the economy. This value may be different from market value. Then the potential loan and equity are determined. If the equity is unusually high, it is a signal that the economic feasibility and leverage are out of check.

The return on equity is a key factor. It should be higher than the overall project net return and will depend on such factors as risks, development time, speculation, personal signatures and leverage. Fifteen percent, more or less, is not unreasonable to expect as a net return on equity.

For the first test of economic feasibility, a developer should be conservative. If the project looks good with conservative input, that is tantamount to a go-ahead.

Another specific economic analysis concerns the development phases. Different phases involve different degrees of work and expenditure. Minimum preservation work may be feasible for up to 5 or possibly 10 years, with more extensive work to take the building another 10 to 15 years further. At that point, it might make sense (because of lot size and location) to demolish all or part of the improvements for new construction, if the investors agree this is the maximum use. Sometimes preservation feasibility studies indicate a minimal return, but investors will proceed if there is the

Offices for Victoria Station restaurant with London taxi in midst, San Francisco. (Carleton Knight,III)

"carrot" of a future higher use. The point is to get the project going now and assume that rent escalations over time will make net return attractive enough to avoid demolition 5, 10 or 15 years later.

Maximum renovation in the beginning should insure a long future for a particular property. Although it would be rewarding to see each preservation project stay in its restored form indefinitely, this is not always realistic to a lender or investor. Thus the more flexible and realistic the developer is, the more total preservation projects can be accomplished.

The end product is to create real estate with value that far exceeds actual cost. This can and must be done.

Financing

Financing is a key economic feasibility ingredient. Many lending institutions have been hesitant to lend on older property. They have wanted to see the finished, fully occupied product before considering a long-term loan. Because of a constant campaign of publicity, education and public acceptance, many lenders will now accept the permanency and feasibility of restoration properties. Some banks will provide two to three-year financing in amounts sufficient to complete projects and enable developers to seek permanent financing. This is

MONTGOMERY/NORTH BLOCK, *San Francisco. (Carleton Knight, III)*

not as desirable as having permanent financing initially, but it works.

Demands on today's economy created by external forces mean many traditional rate cycles, financing sources and loan amounts may not be available when wanted. Therefore, securing permanent financing before a project starts is even more important. In addition to physical values and financial feasibility, lenders give serious consideration to a developer's record and creditability and to the net worth of the backers.

Development Management Program

The development manager and contractor must set strict economic guidelines at the earliest stage of the project. A development concept should be established, with the emphasis on simplicity and preservation of the original structure. Only when every economic guideline is tightly established should other specialists be brought in to refine the concept, being careful to stay within the budget. In many cases this sequence will make the difference between success and failure.

The development management program means tight control of a project, with responsibility and authority vested in a person with a sound record. Decisions must be made frequently and quickly to insure momentum in the entire program.

Case Studies

The results of the various ingredients discussed here can be outlined briefly using the Montgomery/North block as an example. The block is located between Fisherman's Wharf and the San Francisco financial district.

The north half of the block was occupied by a semiabandoned corrugated-box plant, which dated from 1918. The building was badly deteriorated, but existing design, stairways, shafts and so on were used as much as possible. The windows were recessed and colors compatible with Telegraph Hill, which is immediately behind the building, were selected. Fibreboard now leases the entire building and adjacent parking garage (at 25 percent below market) and subleases excess space.

Approximately a quarter of the block was occupied by a granary which had been rebuilt after the earthquake of 1906. The building lacked natural lighting and workable dimensions. To overcome these problems, a portion

A building in the Montgomery/North block before (left) and after restoration. (Ron Kaufman Companies)

was demolished and a courtyard and provision for light and air circulation created. The 42,000-square-foot building is occupied now by Western Contract Furnishers.

Also on the Montgomery/North block is the Victoria Station headquarters. Built in the 1880s with six stories, the structure had been reduced to two stories in 1955 when it was renovated for use as a food-processing plant. The building had no natural light but was high ceilinged and spacious. Today, it has underground parking, a gymnasium, a sauna, a training kitchen and exposed brick interior.

Finally, the fourth building on the block is currently used by QM Productions to shoot interior scenes for "The Streets of San Francisco." It, too, will eventually be upgraded.

Work on the Montgomery/North block was done in stages; that is, enough work to show the potential of the space was completed and additional work was done later when rental budgets justified. Finishes are of various qualities, depending on these budgets. The lender agreed to reserve funds for all possible stages, and the leasing program started as soon as the acquisition escrow began. Thus the buildings were fully leased by the completion of basic (cosmetic) work. This program involved brochures, broker cooperation, open houses, articles and much leg work.

Preservation Attitudes

Community and User Acceptance

Community and tenant attitudes about renovated buildings are important feasibility factors. It is the developer's responsibility to present favorable impressions to the local and national press and the city government (especially the planning, assessor's and building permit departments) and to do a thorough job of marketing the space. In a way, developers are trying to create a Preservation Club which the entire nation is invited to join.

Successful renovation projects attract other developers, usually with economic motives. All renovation developers need to carefully cultivate the leasing agents in their communities for both general education and specific information about a property that is or will be for lease. This can be done through news releases, careful historical research, open houses, simple graphics and, above all, an ability and willingness to help the leasing community put transactions together—i.e., by showing brokers how to make deals and earn fees.

Creating this attitude of acceptance is creating excitement among the consumers and the community in general. Many tenants like the idea of having a building that not only fits their use and allows them to operate most efficiently and productively, but gives them a special identity. For some, preservation has snob appeal—that is, they will like the idea of occupying or owning a building that is unique.

High and Low Density

Low-density preserved buildings can and should live compatibly with high-density buildings in most downtown areas. In fact, a city can be exciting because of the variety of its buildings. A low-profile structure can create openness between large buildings, as well as a relief in the skyline and in the scale of the community. However, certain large users, especially corporations, need enormous office buildings to function efficiently. It is better for a community to have this user in a large highrise rather than creating an urban sprawl by having the user occupy fragmented sites and/or locate away from the downtown transportation core. Public and private owners benefit from the concept that highrise and low-rise buildings can live compatibly together.

City Attitudes

Many city planning departments encourage renovation projects. This same attitude can be transplanted to civic groups through careful work, including personal tours and meetings. On the other hand, city building codes and inspection departments are often rigid and lack understanding of unique renovation problems. This means extra time for the development manager, contractor and engineers to work closely with those departments. However, sometimes their requirements are so rigid and the cost of compliance so high that the project must be scrapped.

The city assessor's office is also important. There are many preservation tasks that, if done separately on a building, would not result in an increased assessment—for example, repainting and reroofing. Sometimes the assessor's attitude toward these items, when they are a part of a total project, leans to the creation of a higher tax base. The National Trust could perform a major service in this area by promoting state laws to prevent property tax increases for project activities relating to structural and earthquake compliance and life safety and other code matters that bring buildings up to the point where they can be developed for users.

Historical Designation

In some communities, when buildings are designated as historic, developers are limited in what they can do. I

THE ROYAL EXCHANGE BUILDING, *San Francisco, with interior bracing to meet code requirements. (Carleton Knight, III)*

find historical designations distasteful, a negative approach, and would discourage them. The positive method is for the National Trust for Historic Preservation and other individuals and groups concerned with preservation to show owners of significant historic buildings how they can profitably restore their properties and thereby assure a renewed life. One of the problems with historical designation is that well-meaning but possibly misguided groups or individuals sometimes can get hung up on almost any building that is pre-1930 and thereby ruin the credibility of true preservation work.

A Preservation Task Force

The National Trust might form teams of experts in various parts of the country to go into communities and show owners how to restore buildings profitably, enjoy the work and feel good about benefiting the future of the community. Certainly the basis for such task forces exists now, and there is no substitute for personal contact. For many suppliers this can also be a profitable way to spread the sales of services.

RECYCLING AND ENERGY CONSERVATION

There is a national responsibility to conserve energy, and the building preservation field is no exception. New and existing projects can be carefully examined for energy conservation principles, and by adherence to these principles an important service can be performed for our country and ourselves.

A project at 101 Vallejo Street in San Francisco demonstrates energy efficiency. This two-story and basement building was constructed around 1855 on what was then the San Francisco waterfront. The foundations were made of heavy rocks that were originally ships ballasts. In the 1906 earthquake some of the brick walls were partially destroyed, so the present building consists of both pre and post-earthquake brick work.

The major energy conservation features of the building are as follows:

1. Glass exposure was oriented to north light, glass size was limited and windows were set back from the wind and heat line. All windows open if tenants wish more air than is supplied by mechanical means.

2. Ventilation and heat systems are simple, with no air-conditioning. Gravity vents and pressure louvers were used.

3. Partitioning was kept mainly low and open to simplify lighting and air patterns.

4. Lighting utilized simple wood-trimmed fluorescent fixtures.

5. Exposed insulation panels were applied between the open joists of the high ceiling on the second (top) floor. This provided climate and sound insulation and is a design feature.

The end product was a recycled building that conserved construction materials and had long-term energy conservation features. The project received local

and national recognition, which in turn helped with leasing and financing.

Developers and/or building managers must meet personally with the head of each company that occupies a building to explain the importance of energy conservation. They must post reminders and stickers, and work with the janitorial staffs and maintenance contractors to be sure lights and equipment are promptly turned off when not needed.

When the long term implications for the United States are considered, energy conservation becomes as important as the concept of preservation itself. Furthermore, conservation provides an economic bonus for preservation efforts because it helps reduce expenses.

MANAGEMENT

The actual development work occupies a small percentage of the life cycle of a property. Therefore, careful property management becomes an important ingredient in the financial feasibility of a preservation project. Management includes the operation of a building on a day-to-day basis; careful purchasing of supplies; administration of leases; solving emergency situations; dealing with possible refinancing packages or assessment appeals; attention to preventive maintenance so major repairs can be avoided; and constant tenant relations so that when problems arise they can be solved on a quick and personal basis.

Usually not enough emphasis is given to property management, since some people in real estate look at it as a chore, like taking out the garbage. But buildings are major capital items and running them is like running a major business. The role of the manager is extremely important for the immediate and long-term profitability and image of a property. It is a distinct advantage for any developer to have property management input in the early stages of any development. This can save future headaches and expenses and usually means that 5-10 percent more of the gross income than that prescribed by lending institution formulas is added to the net income. Certainly that is a strong reason why an alert, well-trained building manager can be an important part of financial feasibility.

SUMMARY

One can theorize about decision-making criteria for building preservation, study a typical preservation program, examine attitudes that influence economic feasibility and talk about the many related factors. However, before a preservation project is started, one must establish, through the use of sound real estate principles, that the project is economically feasible and has profit potential. That is the primary reality in the renovation-preservation process.

TABLE 1
TYPICAL FEASIBILITY STUDY FORMAT

1. COSTS
   Land (____ square feet, including existing
      buildings of ____ square feet) $
   Construction, including garage and aver-
      age tenant finish $
   Indirect costs (see detail below) $ _____
                                    Total $

2. INCOME*   per month   per year
   North building: ____ ¢/square
                   foot x ____ square
                   feet $ $
   South building: ____ ¢/square
                   foot x ____ square
                   feet $ $
   Parking: 250 cars x $____ $ $
   Assumed ____ % vacancy, etc.
      (loss)   ($)   ($)
                                    _____   _____
                           Total $ $

3. EXPENSES (inclusive)
   North building: ____ ¢ x ____ square feet $
   South building: ____ ¢ x ____ square feet $
   Parking $ _____
                           Total $
                           NET INCOME $

4. OVERALL RETURN PERCENTAGE
   Net income before debt service ÷ total costs

5. POSSIBLE LOAN, ASSUMPTIONS, EQUITY
   $____ "income value" by loan appraiser x ____ %
      loan = $____ loan and $____ equity.

6. DEBT SERVICE
   ____ % over ____ years = $____ (per month or per
      year)

7. PERCENTAGE RETURN ON EQUITY
   Net income after debt service ÷ equity

8. AVERAGE ANNUAL EQUITY BUILT UP

NOTES: Economics are based on maximum costs, high rates and
bit contingencies. Equity should be less, interest lower, net
income higher, etc.; this would result in a positive effect on the
return on equity and cash flow.

Leasing of improvements can be considered to reduce equity.

*Income figured with average rents.

INDIRECT COSTS (estimates)
   Architectural consultation, excluding
      tenant layouts $
   Construction consultation $
   Development management program
      (full program, including concept,
      investors, loan package preparation,
      supervision, etc.) $
   Insurance during construction $
   Taxes during construction $
   Interim interest: $____ x ____ %
      x ____ months $
   Loan fees $
   Leasing fees $
   Start up, contingency reserve $ _____
                                    Total $

Conference
Summary

The Dangers in Preservation Success

PAUL J. GOLDBERGER

Paul J. Goldberger is architectural critic for the New York Times.

A number of fascinating things are said here in these papers, and even though some statements have been contradictory, one tends to feel that all of them are right. Preservation is now accepted as a positive good by a wide segment of the public, and the stigma of the quaint house museum, which held back the preservation movement for so long, seems shaken off at last. But there are several dangers in all this success.

An Unrealistic View of Preservation

First, because preservation is an accepted good, there is a tendency to slide over much of the hard data that is absolutely required to argue and cajole a project into existence and to fool ourselves into thinking that any good preservation scheme is a sure shot. We cannot do that; as Leopold Adler said in his presentation on the Savannah story, the name of the game is still real estate.

For this reason, Alan Black's remarks were also very much to the point. He is quite frank in stating that the Grand Central restoration at Pioneer Square was an "emotional and unprofessional purchase" of a building, saying "We signed the purchase documents . . . and wondered why!" I welcome his frankness in telling us this and in not pretending that Grand Central, for all its success, is ever going to make anybody rich. From the applause with which his admission of an "emotional" decision was greeted, I sense that most of the audience also found his remarks a refreshing change.

Similarly, the analyses of Richard Crissman and Charles Tseckares were equally welcome. They provided the kind of hard, unemotional data that we need and cannot afford not to provide. The public may have been won over to preservation, but the tenants and the bankers await the data, as they always have. Though a number of recycled buildings have added prestige value (rather than the less absolute value of their competition on the real estate market), this is a dangerous development to count on. I would guess that if Charles Tseckares had depended on prestige alone to sell One Winthrop Square, it would never have gotten off the ground.

Misusing the Preservation Movement

Second among the dangers of success is the tendency of real estate developers to use preservation sentiment for their own purposes. Now, I do not subscribe to the point of view that sees all developers as lurking villains panting to put an end to every good old building they can find. However, in general the development community—with obvious and happy exceptions—has not been preservation's closest ally. Now that it has become socially—and politically—acceptable to be a public advocate of recycling, preservation-oriented remarks are heard with increasing frequency from developers of new buildings.

It is a great tribute to preservation, of course, that it has been able to change the rhetoric of developers, but is it anything more than the rhetoric that has changed? For example, to look into a case now pending in New York City, developer Harry Helmsley has proposed to build a new hotel behind McKim, Mead and White's great Villard Houses, the U-shaped Renaissance brownstone grouping that has miraculously survived intact on Madison Avenue. Helmsley talks fondly about the Villard Houses, but his original plans called for an unsympathetic tower with silly arches at its base to simplistically echo the old building. The Villard Houses are to serve as the hotel entrance, but most of their rear was to be cut off and most of the interiors, including the incomparable Gold Room, were to be scooped out and demolished.

Helmsley argued that he is saving the buildings, but his position has an odd similarity to that of the American general who tried to explain his "pacification" mission in Vietnam by saying "We had to destroy the village in order to save it." Helmsley seems intent on destroying the Villard Houses in order to save them; moreover, he wishes to take advantage of their prestige at the same time he commits his act of destruction. He has now given in and submitted a more responsible plan, which includes preservation of the interiors, but the point—his desire to exploit the buildings rather than save them—remains.

In less dramatic cases, many have heard developers use preservation rhetoric to sell projects and convince local opponents that projected schemes will have smaller scale, more sympathetic materials and the like. Many of those amenities seem to disappear mysteriously once the project has passed the hurdles of public opinion.

Again, I do not like to foster distrust between preservationists and developers, because we need more, not less, dialogue. But I am concerned that preservation's success has led some to adopt its rhetoric without any of its values.

Closely related to this concern is the problem of speculators taking advantage of preservation's ability to cause property values to rise. This is a complex and delicate problem deserving more extended discussion than is possible here, but it must be cited as yet another potential penalty of preservation's success.

Relationship of Preservation and Modern Architecture

The third category is a continuing problem more than a result of preservation's success. It involves modern architecture and the relationship of the preservation community to it. As an architecture critic in New York City, I tend to be fairly negative about most of the new buildings I see. Nonetheless, when Bruce Chapman spoke about new buildings "that almost seem intended to make ordinary people feel unimportant," I suddenly felt a perverse urge to defend modern architecture.

Not that I really disagree. Looking around Seattle, one can see exactly what he means. But the sort of new buildings seen in downtown Seattle, and in virtually every other American city now, is only part of the modern architectural picture. Indeed, they are an outdated, obsolete part of the picture. The silly tower with the sprouting base next to the Olympic Hotel in Seattle is only now being constructed, but it is nonetheless a building of the past. Its architect, Minoru Yamasaki, is part of the rear guard, and he has created a piece of 1950s exhibitionism.

The point is that modern architecture has gone beyond this foolishness—in part because of pressure from preservationists to begin to include the sort of amenities, the livable space, the human scale, the associational values of old buildings. There is a new consciousness of what makes a city livable, and it has already trickled down into modern architecture, in the work of John Portman, the Atlanta-based architect who has done the Hyatt Regency hotels, or even of such a confirmed modernist as Philip Johnson, whose new IDS skyscraper complex in Minneapolis shows a real understanding of the same sort of urbanistic values found in places like Pioneer Square.

The best younger architects, firms like Venturi and Rauch, Hardy Holzman Pfeiffer and Davis, Brody and Associates, have made great strides away from the glass-box syndrome. When pressured, even a firm like Emery Roth and Sons, the New York City office-tower factory, can do better. Three buildings Emery Roth has done for New York developer Mel Kaufman have excellent amenities and lively, exciting public spaces, all done at the behest of the client.

So the point here is that preservation's success must not be allowed to make preservation parochial. This is a time when modern architects are finally beginning to learn about their failures, and to correct them they need help rather than catcalls from preservationists.

Elitism

A fourth problem, and one that I was also glad to hear mentioned, involves elitism. I was glad that Bruce Rockwell from the Colorado National Bank came right out and said that it will not do to convert from low-income housing to luxury units. This change is often seen as a sign of success, but it is not. One is tempted to say that any neighborhood should be lucky enough to be in such demand that real estate values soar, but there

is another side to this process, and preservationists must deal with it more fully than they have in the past.

Bruce Chapman also acknowledged this problem when he urged that preservationists not invite class antagonism. He made a superb point that is not adequately covered here—the fact that the poor often resent rehabilitation, even when it is clearly being done for them and not to remove them. This feeling stems from the belief that old buildings are in some way less valuable than new ones and that the poor are therefore being cheated by preservation.

Harmon Goldstone, former chairman of the New York City Landmarks Preservation Commission, once described an enormous battle with the Harlem community over a fine McKim, Mead and White library. The commission wanted to designate the library, and the city was prepared to offer funds for rehabilitation. But the Harlem community wanted the funds to go for a new building. Residents saw a new structure as a symbol of progress, and an old building, even one so fine as the McKim Library, as a symbol of being tied to the past. Eventually the community was won over, but it was difficult, and the dispute pointed up a crucial problem that preservationists have not adequately dealt with—namely, how to convince the poor that rehabilitation can indeed be in their interest.

This reluctance for preservation on the part of the poor is not all that surprising. Given how badly served they are by most of the old buildings they know, such as tenements and schools, it is logical that they should associate old structures with a holding back of progress.

Bruce Rockwell also said that "the bulldozer days are dead in Denver, but urban blight is alive and well." It is indeed, and while preservationists and urbanologists are correct in believing that the bulldoze-and-rebuild method of urban renewal has rarely worked, they must not fall into the equally simplistic trap of believing that the standard rehabilitation approach will by itself save our cities.

Design Excesses

The fifth and final trap of preservation's success is one of design. Just as there is a standard highrise office building vernacular that we are trying to get away from, so there is also a standard preservation vernacular. I worry that more success will lead us to follow formulas more and more, rather than to think through each project anew. Obviously, given the choice, we would take the standard formula recycling job over the standard glass office tower; the recycled building is still a lot more fun to be in. But we do allow ourselves to use devices such as exposed brick and cute graphics too often. Maybe that is why my favorite things about Pioneer Square are the offbeat elements, such as the old details and the views that contrast the square against the backdrop of other neighborhoods. These are the things unique to the place.

Similarly, Gas Works Park is exciting. Turning the great industrial shapes into sculpture is a brilliant idea, and it is as much a break from the standard preservation project as it is from the standard new landscape design project.

All this relates to the comments of another conference participant who said people will travel thousands of miles to see Disneyland and walk on a fake Main Street when there are so many real Main Streets being ignored. Well, people go to Disneyland precisely because it *is* fake, because it is an unreal place. Too many designers have been consciously trying to imitate Disneyland, to make places a little too cute and unreal. Those places could almost have been left alone, like the Gas Works structures, which possess tremendous power merely as objects in themselves. It is a terribly sad irony to see us trying to make the real Main Streets more attractive by prettying them up so that they look like the fake ones.

I do not mean to sound too sober and critical, because I admire enormously what has been done in Seattle—it is a lesson for all cities. But it is good enough that it should goad us on to another level of accomplishment. In other words, preservationists must learn that it is no longer enough merely to save buildings. The lesson of Seattle, and of this conference as a whole, is that preservation has indeed grown up; it has earned the right to be taken seriously as a tool of urban development. With that right comes still more work, and the demand to find new solutions that are free of either architectural or social formulas. From the serious, unsentimental tone of the Seattle conference, I think preservationists are ready to meet that challenge.

Strengths and Shortcomings of the Economic Benefits Conference

WILLIAM MARLIN

William Marlin is associate editor, Architectural Record; *architecture and urban design critic,* Christian Science Monitor; *and former editor-in-chief,* Architectural Forum.

One thing that came out very clearly in the conference on the Economic Benefits of Preserving Old Buildings is that the past is right on time. It is one of the few things that is on time today.

The conference is on time in the same sense. The presentations provide examples of preservation that have yielded appreciable returns to daring people. They are examples that many will write about in an effort to reinforce the courage of preservationists throughout the country.

Now, having appropriately praised the conference, it is also appropriate to suggest that one problem with preservation is that those who support it are often pretentious. Also, many have paid only peripheral attention to the mechanisms of money and decision making, which are responsible for the growth of cities, their character and their configuration.

Another problem is that, until recently, preservationists tended to be preoccupied with archaeological considerations. In the context of municipal government, more emphasis must be placed on the overall planning mechanisms so that in both new construction and attempts to resuscitate existing structures, there is the same consideration for human accessibility, the same relationship to people.

Consider the great and charming town centers of the European capitals or the hill towns of Italy. Look at Rabino and Spain and Morocco; there is no sense that those places simply happened all at once.

Cities and towns are incremental affairs that cannot be wiped away and built anew. The development of a society is reflected in a city—a composite of past and present.

If anything is learned from the conference, it should be a fresher attitude toward the value of standards, whether they are applied to the character and configuration of what is being built or whether they are guidelines and regulations to make the most of what already exists.

Preservation: No Longer Peripheral

The time when preservation was a peripheral indulgence of a few is over; it is now part of the societal process. In a wider sense, preservation has come to mean stabilization and conservation—the fullest use of the resources passed on by forebears.

Old buildings are structural and spatial resources, to be sure. However, it must not be forgotten that the fundamental resources at stake are the resolve, the competence, the staying power and, indeed, the buying power of ordinary citizens trying to experience and enjoy their communities.

The rampage to do away with old buildings has had the result of reducing or also doing away with the public commitment and tax base. On the other hand, preservation, as seen in Pioneer Square in Seattle, for example, is more than a resuscitation of a structure for new and timely purposes. It is the resuscitation of a sense of an entire city. As Louis Kahn said, that is fundamentally a sense of meeting, of bringing people, activities and periods of time into proximity.

When the past and present rub elbows, as in Pioneer Square, money is the result. But, refreshingly, Seattle has shown the nation that making money, making a difference and making sense can happen all at once, given the proper municipal direction.

The urgency of preservation has been underlined by the higher cost of energy, materials and labor; thus the existing stockpile of structures must be seized upon and used for the sake of the economy. For this reason, more conference discussion of the effect of energy and material shortages and how they underscore the urgency of preservation would have been beneficial.

Local governments know that large capital expenditures in blighted neighborhoods have often backfired and now demand a more thoughtful strategy, a more careful look at those areas on the brink of extinction.

Preservation can be a money-saving way to intervene in the extinction process because costs, as has been amply demonstrated, are often lower and the process commands more public attention.

The shift from federal categorical programs to block grants is allowing localities to develop programs and approaches tailored to local needs and to unique cityscapes. This, in turn, has created a demand for information and examples and has made meetings such as the Seattle conference highly practical and important affairs. From them can come examples to be used in evangelizing and creating leverage to make the most of the past.

Many clever examples of preservation were shown at the conference, but Paul Goldberger is correct in saying that the temptation to cuteness in adapting old buildings for human enjoyment must be resisted.

We are not in the business of being carnival barkers. We are in the business of making sensible use of structural resources for community gain. At the same time, there is a need for the P.T. Barnums who will evangelize and dramatize the values of preservation.

Schiller said of a friend's building, "If his idea were not so downright clever, I would be tempted to call it downright stupid." Schiller's perception of his col-

league's work is an indication of a design balance that must be struck in approaching the resuscitation of old buildings.

Conference Shortcomings

Numerous projects discussed here have dramatized the fact that preservation is not an embalming or archaeological function, nor merely the curatorial task of a museum director. It involves regulations, guidelines, statutes and a clear understanding of how various municipalities throughout the country have gone about organizing themselves to inventory and rescue their existing areas. I would like to have seen more examples and case studies of how that rescue has been accomplished, because in more than 600 American communities active neighborhood or downtown district renovation is under way.

At a conference on economic benefits, there should have been more discussion of fundamental strategies, as well as the procedural aspects of adaptive use and urban conservation. I would also like to have heard more about the decisions that led, one way or the other, to the successful process in which preservation has been able to make the past part of today's progress.

Reclaiming that history results in much more than just the isolated victory, the "fun" place to go, the bookshop in an old warehouse. Preservation is also a wakening and an understanding that what exists supplies a structural context, a cultural clue to the approaches that must be brought to building new things today.

It is also correct that the preservation movement has probably had more influence on new buildings than it has had, proportionately, successes of its own. Urban design and development guidelines are gradually being changed to adjust to the insights born of the increasing number of examples of rescued districts.

Conclusion

There is no longer any question that preservation is a practical activity. The U.S. General Services Administration testified before Congress that saving an old building employs five times as many people as building a new one of the same size. That figure has been verified by a number of labor organizations. Preservation results in economic use of energy and materials, and it can yield a positive result on the bottom line. However, the ultimate bottom line is whether or not what is built and what is saved from the past fit together to form a cohesive fabric, because, again, cities do not happen all at once but over time.

What is built today might be old guard or new. At the same time, what is saved from the past can continue to be old if preservation is aborted with design solutions that undermine essential integrity.

Ultimately, it is a matter of human as well as structural relationships. Frank Lloyd Wright once said that there could be no separation between architecture and culture, nor any separation of either from the happiness and productivity of a people.

The Seattle conference is a beginning toward documenting the arithmetic of quality, culture and happiness. To that extent, it is a start to be celebrated.

Demands for the Future

MRS. JOHN W. R. CRAWFORD

Mrs. John W. R. Crawford is president, Larimer Square Associates, Denver, and a member of the National Trust Board of Trustees.

Although the tone of the conference on economic trends for recycling the nation's old structures was one of welcome optimism, the truth is that facts and figures shared there are little known in the real estate industry and even less known among lending institutions. If the redemption of our cities is to be accomplished, preservationists must reach these groups.

The problem is dramatically demonstrated by a look at the professional involvement of those who attended the Seattle conference and, more important, those who did not. Approximately 400 participants were brought together by a common desire to understand the realities of preservation, but at a conference originally designed for the banking community, there were only 10 or 11 bankers, 2.5 percent of the registration.

In a summary of the meeting, the bankers' wisdoms should be remembered. They said that preservationists must work first on the lenders at the local level. The National Trust can be supportive on the national scene through contacts with such organizations as the American Bankers Association, Mortgage Bankers Association and the Urban Land Institute; however, the real challenge is at home, where each preservationist has an educational mission. The lenders in our cities, large and small, must become believers in the profit potential of reuse. They have been thoroughly conditioned over the last 25 to 30 years to be wary of the inner cities where old buildings are congregated. The safe property prospects have been in the suburbs.

Preservationists must understand that few bankers can really "see" the city. They recognize only existing conditions—grime, blight, decay—and cannot visualize a physical transformation that automatically routs the pigeons and pensioners, soon spelling profits for the developer and the lender, with a simultaneous boost to that all-important tax base.

Currently, the real estate community and the bankers are convinced that renovation of old buildings costs a great deal more on a comparative basis than demolition and new construction. Now, with presentations from this conference, it will be possible to tell lenders that case studies demonstrate that the cost for renovation is running a quarter to a third less than the cost of new construction—and the quality of the projects is frequently superior. We can also say with more confidence that the marketability of recycled buildings is proven, often exceeding that of conventional development.

Probably the most compelling argument for the cause of preservation is the Pioneer Square statistic of a tax base that has increased 1,000 percent.

The bankers also said that preservationists must know that lenders' do not appreciate enthusiastic expressions on such subjects as history, romance and human scale in business undertakings. If they are going to loan money, they have to see the dollars and cents—and they have to see the borrowers' commitment.

John Sower cautioned that preservation projects are sophisticated real estate endeavors requiring commitment and good management on the parts of both developer and lender. Richard Crissman revealed the performance necessary for a professional approach to the mortgage banker, warning that bankers prefer the easiest solutions. They may be a lazy lot, Crissman said, but suggested they can be awakened by a reminder that the majority of their real estate portfolios hold aging properties in the center cities. The financial stability of the central business district is a subject of primary interest to the financial community.

Publication of information from the conference will assist the preservationist's missionary zeal for changing existing attitudes. Still, this is not enough. The Urban Land Institute, one of the conference endorsers, is currently writing case studies of five recycled properties, also for publication by the National Trust. The book resulting from discussions in Seattle plus these studies will provide a beginning.

I am hopeful that the National Trust will react to the continuing need for hard statistical data. For example, a preliminary review of square-foot costs reported in Seattle indicates an average investment of approximately $30 per square foot, but there also was mention of a Boston piano factory project at $10 a square foot and office building conversions in excess of $30. The indications are favorable, but the developers may not be using the same criteria in their financial summaries. The results of the pioneering developments in recycled space need further analysis and translation.

During the past few years, those who talk a lot about preservation have emphasized the techniques for extracting more money from various government bodies. The rhetoric in Seattle represents a refreshing direction into the mainstream of American business philosophy. It would be a mistake, however, to turn too far from the public sector, as successful developments of any kind have three requirements: a developer with staying power, a lender or lenders with staying power and an enlightened, receptive local government.

Local city governments, fighting for solvency, frequently have no funds for street maintenance, let alone preservation of existing amenities. It is to be hoped that a portion of this gap will be filled by the Housing and Community Development Act of 1974 through community development block grants designed to lure private investment back into the cities. This is the newest game in town—one that every preservationist and banker should learn to play. On a formula basis HUD will disperse $2.95 billion in 1976 and the same amount in 1977 to eligible cities of more than 50,000 persons.

Because broad citizen imput is required, block grants promote awareness among voters. One of the primary goals of community development action is neighborhood preservation through consolidated public investment. Forceful citizens groups in tandem with financial leadership can effectively change the prospects for commercial as well as neighborhood districts through investment in highly visible improvements, such as new street lighting.

Positive action and continuous vigilance are also necessary, as local, state and federal governments are constantly changing codes and laws, often impeding preservation progress and sometimes making it impossible. Particular notice is directed to proposed changes in the real estate tax structure that may adversely affect the limited partnership investment vehicle used in Denver in Larimer Square and in Trolley Square in Salt Lake City, among countless other urban revitalizers.

In addition, developers, bankers and all people involved in the preservation movement must assist in changing federal tax laws, which still encourage the demolition of a landmark rather than its renovation.

In closing, it is important for the National Trust and all preservationists to salute the handsome city of Seattle and its great joint venture in Pioneer Square. The economic benefits are evident on every corner, but the inside story of early pitfalls and emerging pitfalls from the venturers who made it all happen are also revealed here. The original motivating factor of civil pride which Mayor Wes Uhlman discussed is the most memorable message from this conference. Development involving the use of solid old buildings engenders this sense of pride, and people want to be part of a city's pride. They want to live with it, have offices and shop with it. It is part of them, the individual spirit of each city. It is apparent then that pride *and* profits are the ultimate joint venturers in this business of urban conservation.

Other Books from the Preservation Press

America's Forgotten Architecture. National Trust for Historic Preservation, Tony P. Wrenn, Elizabeth D. Mulloy. The best overview of preservation today. Surveys in 475 photos what is worth saving and how to do it. 312 pages, illustrated, bibliography, appendixes. Published by Pantheon Books. $20 hardbound, $12.95 paperbound.

Built to Last: A Handbook on Recycling Old Buildings. Gene Bunnell, Massachusetts Department of Community Affairs. Facts and figures on several dozen adaptive use projects, detailing how and why these buildings were saved. 126 pages, illustrated, bibliography. $6.95 paperbound.

A Courthouse Conservation Handbook. Provides step-by-step procedures for reusing courthouses—and many other public buildings — with solutions to space, structural and funding problems. 80 pages, illustrated, bibliography, appendixes. $4.95 paperbound.

Directory of American Preservation Commissions. Stephen N. Dennis, ed. A guide to the more than 800 local historic district and landmark commissions. 132 pages. $6.95 paperbound.

Information: A Preservation Sourcebook. A compendium of two dozen publications from the National Trust "Information" series. Topics range from basic preservation procedures and rehabilitating old houses to public and private financing, revolving funds, economic benefits of preservation, neighborhoods and special building types. Annually updated for permanent reference. 400 pages, illustrated, bibliography. $20 binder. Supplements, $5 each.

Monumentum. Terry B. Morton, ed. International Council of Monuments and Sites. Leading preservationists view the past, present and future of preservation in the United States, providing a concise introduction to preservation and its current concerns. 128 pages, illustrated. $10 paperbound.

New Energy from Old Buildings. National Trust for Historic Preservation. Details the energy conservation benefits of recycling old buildings and describes how to safeguard them during retrofitting for conservation and solar applications. 208 pages, illustrated, glossary, bibliography, index. $9.95 paperbound.

Old and New Architecture: Design Relationship. A provocative exploration by 18 prominent architects and preservationists of how to design new buildings and additions next to old ones. Topics include design theory, historic district protection, architectural controls, design guidelines, review boards and adaptive use. 280 pages, illustrated, bibliography, index. $25 hardbound, $15.95 paperbound.

Preservation: Toward an Ethic in the 1980s. Goals and recommendations for what is being called the "decade of preservation" — a thought-provoking agenda for the 1980s that addresses organizational objectives, funding, standards and practices, communications, education, legislation and more. 248 pages. $8.95 paperbound.

Preservation and Conservation: Principles and Practices. An in-depth examination of the technical aspects of restoration and object conservation, from preservation philosophy and education to restoration materials, techniques and maintenance, with case studies. 547 pages, illustrated, bibliography. $17.95 paperbound.

Tax Incentives for Historic Preservation. Gregory E. Andrews, ed. Rev. ed. Examines tax policies affecting preservation, with surveys of state and local benefits. 240 pages, illustrated. $12.95 paperbound.

What Style Is It? John Poppeliers, S. Allen Chambers, Nancy B. Schwartz. One of the most popular concise guides to American architectural styles, prepared by staff of the Historic American Buildings Survey. 48 pages, illustrated, glossary, bibliography. $4.95 paperbound.

To order Preservation Press books, send total of book prices (less 10 percent discount for National Trust members), plus $2.50 postage and handling, to: Preservation Bookshop, 1600 H Street, N.W., Washington, D.C. 20006. Residents of California, the District of Columbia, Massachusetts, New York and South Carolina please add applicable sales tax. Make checks payable to the National Trust and allow at least three weeks for delivery. A complete list of publications is available by writing: The Preservation Press, National Trust for Historic Preservation, 1785 Massachusetts Avenue, N.W., Washington, D.C. 20036.

8869

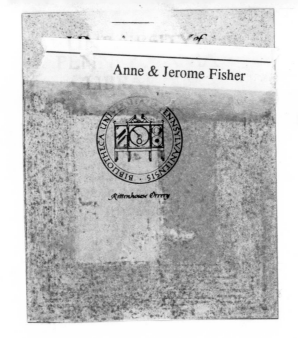